Prevent-Teach-Reinforce
for Families

Prevent-Teach-Reinforce for Families

A Model of Individualized Positive Behavior Support for Home and Community

by

Glen Dunlap, Ph.D.
University of Nevada, Reno

Phillip S. Strain, Ph.D.
University of Colorado, Denver

Janice K. Lee, M.Ed., BCBA
University of Nevada, Reno

Jaclyn D. Joseph, Ph.D., BCBA
University of Colorado, Denver

Christopher Vatland, Ph.D.
University of South Florida, Tampa

and

Lise Fox, Ph.D.
University of South Florida, Tampa

·P A U L·H·
BROOKES
PUBLISHING CO.®

Baltimore • London • Sydney

Paul H. Brookes Publishing Co.
Post Office Box 10624
Baltimore, Maryland 21285-0624
USA

www.brookespublishing.com

Typeset by Absolute Service, Inc., Towson, Maryland.
Manufactured in the United States of America by Sheridan Books, Inc., Chelsea, Michigan.

Individuals in this book are composites based on the authors' experiences. In all instances, identifying details have been changed to protect confidentiality.

Library of Congress Cataloging-in-Publication Data

The Library of Congress has cataloged the print edition as follows:

Names: Dunlap, Glen, author.
Title: Prevent-teach-reinforce for families: a model of individualized
positive behavior support for home and community / by Glen Dunlap, Ph.D.
Description: Baltimore: Paul H. Brookes Publishing Co., [2017] | Includes
    bibliographical references and index.
Identifiers: LCCN 2016040547 (print) | LCCN 2016051350 (ebook) | ISBN
    9781598579789 (pbk.) | ISBN 9781681250687 (pdf) | ISBN 9781681250670 (epub)
Subjects: LCSH: Problem children—Counseling of. | Problem children—Family
    relationships. | Problem children—Behavior modification. | Behavior
    disorders in children—Prevention. | Child development.
Classification: LCC HQ773 .D86 2017 (print) | LCC HQ773 (ebook) | DDC
    649/.64—dc23
LC record available at https://lccn.loc.gov/2016040547

British Library Cataloguing in Publication data are available from the British Library.

2025   2024   2023   2022   2021

10   9   8   7   6   5   4   3   2

Contents

About the Forms

Purchasers of *Prevent-Teach-Reinforce for Families* are granted permission to download, print, and photocopy the following forms included in this book. These materials are included with the print and e-book and are also available for download at brookespublishing.com/downloads with (case sensitive) keycode: 38nlGlP89.

Form 1 (Figure 3.1)   PTR-F Goal Sheet
Form 2 (Figure 3.2)   PTR-F Behavior Rating Scale
Form 3 (Figure 3.3)   Self-Evaluation Checklist: Initiating the PTR-F Process
Form 4 (Figure 4.1)   PTR-F Assessment Checklist: Prevent
Form 5 (Figure 4.2)   PTR-F Assessment Checklist: Teach
Form 6 (Figure 4.3)   PTR-F Assessment Checklist: Reinforce
Form 7 (Figure 4.4)   PTR-F Assessment Summary Table
Form 8 (Figure 4.5)   Self-Evaluation Checklist: PTR-F Assessment
Form 9 (Figure 5.1)   PTR-F Behavior Support Plan Summary
Form 10 (Figure 5.2)   Self-Evaluation Checklist: PTR-F Intervention
Form 11 (Figure 6.1)   PTR-F Fidelity of Strategy Implementation Form
Form 12 (Figure 6.2)   PTR-F Family Coaching Information Sheet
Form 13 (Figure 6.3)   PTR-F Coach Planning and Reflection Log
Form 14 (Figure 7.7)   PTR-F Plan Implementation Guide

About the Authors

Glen Dunlap, Ph.D., is a research professor at the University of Nevada, Reno. Glen has worked for many decades as a researcher and teacher in the areas of positive behavior support, early intervention, autism and related disabilities, child protection, families, and family support. He was involved in establishing the West Virginia Autism Training Center and the Florida Center for Autism and Related Disabilities and was a leading investigator for several federally funded research centers. He has authored more than 240 articles, books, and book chapters and served on 15 editorial boards. He was a founding editor of the *Journal of Positive Behavior Interventions* and served as editor of *Topics in Early Childhood Special Education* for approximately 10 years.

Phillip S. Strain, Ph.D., is Professor of Educational Psychology and Director of the Positive Early Learning Experiences Center in the School of Education and Human Development at the University of Colorado, Denver. Dr. Strain is the author of more than 300 professional papers that have focused on young children with autism, prevention of challenging behavior, and inclusion practices. Over more than four decades in the field, he has been a teacher, early intervention program administrator, and university professor. Dr. Strain's research on challenging behavior and autism has received more than $50 million in grant support, and this work has garnered multiple career achievement awards.

Janice K. Lee, M.Ed., BCBA, is a member of the research faculty at the University of Nevada, Reno. She is a co-author of *Prevent-Teach-Reinforce for Young Children: The Early Childhood Model of Individualized Positive Behavior Support* (Paul H. Brookes Publishing Co., 2013) and coordinated the randomized controlled trial of Prevent-Teach-Reinforce for Young Children in northern Nevada. She also coordinates Nevada's early childhood initiative on promoting social-emotional competence and Pyramid Model implementation across early care and education settings. Janice's experiences and interests include early intervention, early childhood, challenging behavior, positive behavior support, social and emotional competence, autism and developmental disabilities, inclusion, and working with families. For more than 20 years, she has worked with children, families, practitioners, and professionals at the local, state, and national levels as a practitioner, consultant, coach, trainer, and technical assistance provider. Janice has a master's degree in early childhood special education and is a Board-Certified Behavior Analyst.

Jaclyn (Jackie) D. Joseph, Ph.D., BCBA, is project coordinator for the randomized, controlled trial of Prevent-Teach-Reinforce for Young Children (PTR-YC) at the Positive Early Learning Experiences (PELE) Center of the University of Colorado, Denver. She has co-authored articles and book chapters and conducted dozens of training sessions and workshops on PTR-YC. Prior to working at the PELE Center, Jackie was primarily involved with supporting families of young children with disabilities. Jackie's professional and research interests include evidence-based interventions for reducing the challenging behaviors and improving the social-emotional competence of young children in home settings and in early education and care classrooms.

Christopher Vatland, Ph.D., is a research assistant professor in the Department of Child and Family Studies at the University of South Florida in Tampa, Florida, where he collaborates on a number of research and technical assistance projects in the areas of positive behavior support and family and community engagement. Dr. Vatland has extensive experience with coordination of family support services as well as the development and implementation of behavior interventions in home and community settings.

Lise Fox, Ph.D., is a professor in the Department of Child and Family Studies at the University of South Florida in Tampa, Florida, and the Co-Director of the Florida Center for Inclusive Communities: A University Center for Excellence in Developmental Disabilities. Dr. Fox was one of the developers of the Pyramid Model for Promoting Social-Emotional Competence in Infants and Young Children and is engaged in research, training, and technical assistance efforts related to the use of evidence-based practices in early education and care classrooms, professional development and coaching of early educators, family support, positive behavior support, and the implementation of the Pyramid Model within early care and education programs.

Foreword

In 1999, Carr and colleagues reported on their synthesis of positive behavior support (PBS) research focusing on individuals with developmental disabilities and published between 1985 and 1996. Highlights of their findings include the following:

▲ No functional assessment occurred in 41% of the interventions.

▲ Slightly more than half of the research studies were carried out by an atypical intervention agent (i.e., someone who did not provide primary support to the target individual).

▲ Approximately two thirds of the interventions occurred in an atypical setting (i.e., settings not considered to be normative for the individual's age, such as segregated schools, clinics, and sheltered workshops).

▲ Approximately one third of the studies combined PBS interventions with non-PBS interventions (e.g., forced compliance, time out, and brief restraint).

▲ Only 3.5% of the sample had an intervention directly aimed at producing lifestyle change.

At the turn of the 21st century, PBS had made great strides since its inception in the early 1980s, but there was still substantial room for enhancement. Upon careful consideration of the data trends, Carr et al. (1999, p. 86) strongly recommended that future PBS focus on

▲ "Repeated functional assessments that identify, on an ongoing basis, the environmental and behavioral deficiencies that are the root cause of problem behavior

▲ Direct linkage between assessment information and the design of interventions

▲ Intervention in all relevant contexts. . .

▲ Ecologically valid relevant contexts (i.e., typical agents carry out intervention in typical settings)

▲ The long-term perspectives of consumers—by designing and redesigning interventions as changes in life circumstances warrant; that is, intervention plans must have a life span orientation rather than a crisis management orientation

▲ Consumers being an integral part of the system by constructing interventions that respond to the personal needs and concerns of consumers (goodness-of-fit) thereby ensuring practicality and relevance

▲ Social validity issues, defining outcome goals in terms of comprehensive lifestyle change and support and not just reduction in problem behavior"

Now, what does the Carr et al. (1999) analysis have to do with *Prevent-Teach-Reinforce for Families*? In paraphrasing Mahatma Gandhi,

You must be the change you wish to see in the world.

Glen Dunlap and his colleagues were close associates of Ted Carr. Although Ted was killed in a tragic car accident in 2009, Glen and his colleagues have carried on the legacy of Ted's work and the legacy of their own work. *Prevent-Teach-Reinforce for Families* is the result of this author team embracing the opportunity to "be the change they wished to see in the world." They have addressed every one of the recommendations above by fully incorporating the essence of each into the seven chapters of this book:

- ▲ Repeated functional assessments

- ▲ Direct linkage between assessment and interventions

- ▲ Interventions in all relevant contexts

- ▲ Ecologically valid relevant contexts

- ▲ Long-term perspective of consumers

- ▲ Consumers being an integral part of the intervention

- ▲ Social validity of comprehensive lifestyle

The authors recognize and honor families as the first and most enduring unit across the life span to which individuals with disabilities relate. They do this by empowering and supporting families to develop the capacity to carry out successful PBS interventions within the least restrictive environment of their own homes, neighborhoods, and communities.

The PTR-F model is based on a team concept that is both person-centered and family-centered. The team follows core principles and strategies in initiating, assessing, intervening, coaching, and monitoring the process. Their goal is not solely the reduction of problem behavior but also is the enhancement of inclusion and community participation leading to lifestyle change.

The authors include an Intervention Guide with detailed procedures for implementing PTR-F interventions. Furthermore, there are 14 practical, useful forms that are included with the book and available for download free of charge. It is rare for the publisher and authors of a book to allow free access to the tools that are illustrated; therefore, a major bonus of investing in this book is not only having the relevant content of the narrative but also having a toolbox that will aid you in ready implementation.

Undoubtedly, Ted's spirit in the universe is celebrating this new book. All of us who knew Ted want him to be proud of our work, and we are confident that he is proud of these authors and their new PTR-F contribution.

I am unable to end this Foreword without commenting on the senior members of the author team who I am happy to say are longtime friends and colleagues—Glen Dunlap, Phil Strain, and Lise Fox. Although I have not yet had the privilege of personally knowing Janice, Jaclyn, and Christopher, I look forward to meeting them. Glen, Phil, and Lise are the "best of the best" when it comes to combining their heads and their hearts in crafting individualized PBS. I have the utmost respect and affection for them, and it gives me such fervent optimism that they are moving individualized PBS for families in exactly the right direction. It is my great expectation that Janice, Jaclyn, and Christopher, now junior colleagues, will keep honing and improving interventions to enhance individual and family quality of life through individualized PBS for many decades to come.

In closing, let's reflect on another principle of Mahatma Gandhi:

> ### *A small body of determined spirits fired by an unquenchable faith in their mission can alter the course of history.*

Thank you, Glen, Phil, Janice, Jaclyn, Christopher, and Lise, for being those determined spirits who, through this book, are altering the course of PBS history for children who experience challenging behavior and for their parents and siblings who all yearn for a safe, secure home and happy family life.

Ann Turnbull, Ph.D.
Co-Founder, Beach Center on Disability
Beach Distinguished Professor Emerita
University of Kansas, Lawrence

REFERENCE

Carr, E.G., Horner, R.H., Turnbull, A.P., Marquis, J.G., Magito-McLaughlin, D., McAtee, M.L., . . . Braddock, D. (1999). *Positive behavior support as an approach for dealing with problem behavior in people with developmental disabilities: A research synthesis.* Washington, DC: American Association on Mental Retardation.

Acknowledgments

This book would not have been possible without the foundational work of researchers and practitioners in applied behavior analysis (ABA) and positive behavior support (PBS). For more than 50 years, behavior analysts have taught us how to understand the ways in which behaviors are influenced by events in the environment and how to use that understanding to craft logical strategies for changing behavior for the better. Contributors to PBS have taught us how to develop and arrange these behavior-change strategies in ways that can provide optimal benefits for individuals and families affected by challenging behaviors. The content of this book draws fully from the seminal efforts of pioneers in both ABA and PBS, and the model of *Prevent-Teach-Reinforce for Families* (PTR-F) could not have been imagined in the absence of their groundbreaking research.

The prevent-teach-reinforce framework, exemplified in this book, is an application of the basic process of PBS. The sequence of teaming, goal setting, data collection, functional assessment, and assessment-based, multi-component intervention has been well-established in the PBS arena. Indeed, the predecessors of this book—*Prevent-Teach-Reinforce* (PTR) and *Prevent-Teach-Reinforce for Young Children* (PTR-YC)—used the PBS process as the basic structure for their intervention models, and PTR-F does as well. We gratefully acknowledge the PBS researchers and authors who have demonstrated and disseminated the process of PBS, and we are particularly grateful to the many educators, behavior specialists, and early interventionists who have provided generous feedback and suggestions regarding the PTR approach.

Finally, and most significantly, we are indebted to the families we have learned from as we have sought to find effective and feasible strategies to help address their children's challenging behaviors. Over the course of four decades, we have worked closely with hundreds of families whose lives have been affected deleteriously by the presence of severe and persistent destructive, disturbing, and dangerous behaviors. These families, in their own ways, have shown extraordinary commitment, tenacity, and devotion as they have cared for their children and they, incidentally, taught us much about the individuality, interactive functioning, and creativity that is at the core of family life. We learned to avoid support strategies that are not helpful, and we learned ways to offer genuine, respectful assistance that in many cases helped families lead richer, less aggravating, and more satisfying lives, while enabling their children to develop along healthier social-emotional trajectories without the interference of challenging behaviors. We extend our deep appreciation and admiration to these families, and we realize that this book would not exist without their contributions.

Prevent-Teach-Reinforce for Families

Introduction to Prevent-Teach-Reinforce for Families (PTR-F)

Prevent-Teach-Reinforce for Families (PTR-F) is a detailed model and research-based strategy for helping families to resolve their children's serious challenging behaviors in home and community settings. This model is an extension of the Prevent-Teach-Reinforce (PTR) model for use in elementary and middle schools and the Prevent-Teach-Reinforce for Young Children (PTR-YC) model that is designed for preschool and childcare settings. However, the PTR-F model is different from its predecessors in two fundamental ways: 1) PTR-F was developed to be effective in typical family circumstances that do not include professional educators or behavior specialists, and 2) PTR-F has goals that include reducing the child's challenging behaviors and enhancing the overall quality of life for the entire family. We appreciate that the whole family is affected by a child's challenging behaviors, and even though only one or two family members (usually parents) will be responsible for implementing a behavior support plan, all family members are affected by interventions intended to decrease challenging behaviors. The child is inseparable from the child's family, and behavior supports and interventions must be developed with the whole family in mind.

This model is intended to help young children whose behaviors are serious enough that they interfere with the child's ability to engage in positive relationships, participate with family members in regular routines, play with others, and learn expected skills. The model is also intended to improve the child's interactions with parents and siblings so that challenging behaviors no longer disrupt and interfere with the ongoing pleasures and requirements of family life. In this way, it is expected that implementation of the model will help transform patterns of parent–child conflict into more positive and mutually enjoyable relationships.

When we use the term "challenging behaviors," we are referring to any kinds of actions or behavior patterns that interfere with necessary and desired routines, including mealtime, morning preparation, bedtime, playtime, and going out. The most common kinds of behaviors that are referred to as challenging are excessive and inappropriate crying, violent tantrums, throwing objects, kicking, hitting, pushing, spitting, yelling, running, and repetitive or perseverative actions that occur for extended and unreasonable periods of time. Challenging behavior patterns can also be defined as an excessive lack of cooperation (or noncompliance), resistance, and a marked failure to respond or interact with others. Sometimes, challenging behaviors are referred to as "problem behaviors" or "behavior problems." We consider these terms interchangeable, but we will use the term "challenging behaviors" throughout this book. (See "Key Terms Throughout This Book" at the end of this chapter for a list of other terms you will encounter as you read.)

UNDERSTANDING CHALLENGING BEHAVIORS

Effective interventions for persistent and extreme challenging behaviors are possible because there are certain natural laws that determine when and where behaviors occur. These laws, or principles, explain how the environment influences behavior. Effective interventions are based on these principles, and knowledge of how the principles operate can be extremely useful in designing and implementing behavior support strategies. Indeed, PTR-F, like all effective interventions, has its foundation in these natural laws. In this section, we briefly describe the key principles that help us to understand how, when, and why challenging behaviors occur. As we understand the how, when, and why of challenging behaviors, we gain insight into how these behaviors can be resolved.

Principle 1: Challenging Behaviors Are Communicative

This basic principle means that most challenging behaviors serve the same purpose as other forms of communication, such as speech, nonverbal gestures, and many facial expressions. In this sense, challenging behaviors may often be the same as requests or demands. For instance, the loud tantrum of a 4-year-old boy may be communicating a request for food. Or, the crying of a 3-year-old girl may be communicating a request to stay longer in front of a video instead of moving to the dinner table. The hitting and kicking of a boy in a community playground may be indicating that he wants to possess a peer's toy truck and play with it by himself. Sometimes, challenging behavior is used to communicate a desire for attention, a desire to get out of an activity, or a request for a food item or toy. The point is that challenging behaviors are often used because they "work" and act on the social environment in much the same way that other forms of communication act on the environment. For this reason, we usually see more challenging behaviors exhibited by young children whose speech (or other means of communication) is not well developed or by young children whose speech has not been as effective as their challenging behaviors.

A few things are important to note about this principle. First, even though the challenging behavior may be communicative in nature, this does not mean that the behavior represents a conscious or deliberate act. To understand a challenging behavior in terms of its communicative properties does not mean that the behavior is cognitively determined or premeditated. Second, the form of the behavior (what it looks or sounds like) does not represent a specific communicative intent. For example, if a child spits at a parent when she is being escorted to the bathtub, the form of the behavior may be spitting, but the intent (or function) of the behavior may be to escape or postpone the bathing activity. Understanding the particular meaning of the communication involves an assessment that is different from identifying the form. In fact, the process for understanding the communicative purpose (or function) of the child's challenging behavior is an important element of PTR-F and is described in Chapter 4. It is important to appreciate that a child's challenging behavior may look (or sound) the same in different situations, but the communicative purpose might be different. With some young children, for example, a tantrum may have one meaning in the context of one routine but a different meaning in a different routine or circumstance.

Principle 2: Challenging Behaviors Are Maintained by Their Consequences

This principle is perhaps the most basic law of behavioral science. It is the law of reinforcement. It states that a behavior will be maintained if it is followed by a positive reinforcer. For our purposes, a positive reinforcer can be considered a reward. For challenging behavior that is communicative in nature, the reward would likely be the object or action that is being requested. If a child is using tantrums to communicate a desire for attention, the reward would be when the parent attends to the child. If a child is hitting a sibling in order to obtain the sibling's toy truck, the reward would occur when the child actually obtains the truck. If a child is crying to extend her time watching TV, the reward would be the removal or postponement of the parent's request to move to the dinner table. There are many kinds of consequences. Put simply, consequences involve either getting something (such as attention, food, or a toy) or getting rid of something (such as a demand, an unpleasant activity, or a disliked peer). The main point here is that consequences are important. Challenging behaviors will not continue if they are not somehow followed by consequences that serve as rewards. And by the same principle, desirable behaviors will not develop or occur if they are not followed by consequences that work as rewards.

Principle 3: Challenging Behaviors Occur in Context

Challenging behaviors occur at different rates or intensities in different contextual or environmental circumstances. For example, a child's screaming may occur frequently when he is being asked to participate in fine motor activities, but the same child might never scream during snack time or outdoor play. A different child might never throw a tantrum during fine motor activities but might cry and fuss a great deal during snack time. A third child might run around and appear out of control when she is expected to stay close to her father, but she might always be calm and productively engaged when she is with her older sister. The observation that behaviors are not random and that they tend to occur predictably in particular situations or routines is a principle that can be extremely useful in efforts to resolve children's challenging behavior.

The three basic principles we have just described help to understand how a child's challenging behavior is influenced by events that occur in his or her environment. As we will describe in the coming chapters of this book, this understanding is essential to developing an intervention strategy that will be effective, efficient, and respectful of each child's individuality. The way that we go about understanding each child's challenging behaviors is through a straightforward process known as *functional assessment*, described in Chapter 4.

Once we gain insight through the functional assessment, we are then able to *prevent* challenging behaviors, *teach* more desirable behaviors, and *reinforce* these positive behavioral alternatives. Understanding how a child's behavior occurs in context is helpful in developing strategies for arranging the environment and manipulating antecedents that precipitate a behavior. These are categorized as "prevent" strategies because they promote desirable behaviors and discourage challenging behaviors before they occur. When we understand how a child's challenging behaviors serve as communication, we can devise strategies that teach the child to communicate in more desirable ways. These strategies fall under the category of "teach." Finally, an understanding of how consequences maintain challenging behaviors leads to strategies involving modifications of consequences, especially positive reinforcers. These are the "reinforce" strategies. These strategies compose the name of our model: Prevent-Teach-Reinforce.

WHY IS THIS BOOK NEEDED?

This book is intended as a helpful resource and guide for resolving the most persistent and intractable challenging behaviors of children in family contexts. In particular, the process of PTR-F and this book were developed because there is a need for an effective, research-based model that is

1. Geared toward all children and families whose lives are disrupted due to the child's serious challenging behaviors, regardless of the child's characteristics. The process and procedures can be effective if the child has severe intellectual disabilities, autism, developmental delays, emotional and behavioral disorders, learning disabilities, or mild disabilities, or even if the child has no diagnosed disability or disorder.

2. Described in precise, operational detail and designed so that the overall process and assessment and intervention strategies will be implemented with integrity. A high level of integrity, or fidelity, helps increase the likelihood that intervention procedures will be effective. The PTR-F model is very specific and precise in describing the steps of the intervention to enhance fidelity and integrity of implementation and ensure that the process is clear at all times. PTR-F includes self-evaluation questionnaires at the end of each step to ensure readiness to proceed to the next step.

3. Family friendly, in the sense that families should be comfortable with all steps of the process. Although the process is scripted in order to make it as clear and precise as possible, key elements of the intervention are conducted with family choice in mind. PTR-F incorporates family choice to ensure that families have full ownership of the interventions and support strategies. For instance, the book provides a menu of specific intervention strategies that the family can select from so that the strategies will fit well within the individual family's preferences, routines, customs, and values.

We appreciate that there are many books and manuals that describe effective procedures for addressing challenging behaviors in family situations, and many of these are based on solid research. We mention as a partial listing books on positive parenting (Durand, 2011; Latham, 2000); positive behavior support for parents (Hieneman, Childs, & Sergay, 2006); practical applications of professional programs for encouraging appropriate social behavior and reducing problems, such as the Incredible Years series (e.g., Webster-Stratton, 1992); as well as programs by leading researchers such as Alan Kazdin (2009) and Rex Forehand and Nicholas Long (2011). There are many other valuable resources and programs, and we acknowledge that the guidance in these resources can be effective in resolving many difficult behaviors. We believe that PTR-F will supplement these existing resources and perhaps prove to be a preferable alternative, especially for situations in which the behaviors and the circumstances are most challenging and in instances when it is particularly important to implement behavioral interventions with procedural integrity.

WHOM IS PTR-F FOR?

This book is written as a guide for professionals who provide support for families that include children whose lives are compromised by challenging behaviors. Individuals who might use this book include early interventionists, educators, social workers, clinicians and therapists, behavior specialists and behavior analysts, psychologists, and any other professional whose role includes helping families to address challenging behavior in home and community settings. We refer to these professionals as "facilitators" because these professionals guide and facilitate the family in following the steps of the process and implementing the interventions with fidelity. To use the model effectively, the professional must be present in the relevant home and community settings in which challenging behaviors occur often enough to observe and understand the circumstances that influence the challenging behaviors and family interactions. This means that the professional must be able to visit the home and community settings several times before and during the family's implementation of the behavior support plan. The PTR-F model is not ideal for professionals who spend all of their time in their offices and clinics.

As for qualifications, it is expected that professionals using the model will have completed higher education studies in a human service discipline such as education, psychology, applied behavior analysis, social work, or counseling, and they will typically have earned a master's degree, although this is not a strict requirement. More important is that the manual's users have knowledge and experience in supporting families in home and community environments and that they have acquired an understanding of family systems and the social and cultural influences that can affect family functioning. Users should also be knowledgeable about the principles of learning and how functional behavioral assessments are used to develop respectful and effective interventions. Finally, facilitators need a deep understanding of instructional strategies, including how teaching procedures can be implemented effectively in the context of typical home and family routines.

Some families might also use the manual without direct professional assistance and guidance; however, this would not be a common occurrence. For a family to use the model effectively without professional coaching and facilitation, at least one member of the family (usually a parent) would need to have had some kind of successful experience with assessment and intervention on challenging behavior. Even then, the family should have reliable access to professional consultation as they proceed through the steps of the model.

We should be clear about the children for whom this book is intended. The PTR-F model is intended to address the needs of children who exhibit patterns of challenging behaviors, as described previously. The children might be diagnosed with developmental or intellectual disabilities, autism, learning disabilities, social and emotional disorders, developmental delay, or any other disability or disorder. Or the children might not have any diagnosis or classification of a disability or disorder. Some children are considered to be typically developing but happen to have serious and persistent challenging behaviors. PTR-F can be appropriate for all of these children. However, we emphasize that the PTR-F model was designed for especially persistent behaviors that have not been corrected with less intensive procedures. To be effective, PTR-F must be implemented as described in this manual, including all of the steps in the sequence, and this requires an investment of time and diligence that might exceed professionals' or families' expectations. Before starting, it is important for all parties to be aware of the commitment that is needed to implement each step of the process. The initial PTR-F process as described in this manual often takes 2–3 months (sometimes more), and some kind of support for monitoring and transitions is typically needed to ensure maintenance of behavior change well beyond the initial period of implementation.

GUIDING BELIEFS AND PRINCIPLES OF THE PTR-F MODEL

PTR-F is based on extensive research, established models of behavior support, and the authors' lengthy experience in helping children and families resolve challenging behaviors. Altogether, we have well over 100 years of experience in supporting families in home and community settings. This experience has convinced us that certain assumptions are crucial for effectiveness in family support and in implementing strategies for resolving challenging behaviors. We describe these principles and beliefs in the sections that follow.

Family-Centeredness

The most crucial and durable resources available to children come from the family, and the family is the most influential context for child development and the formation of the child's behaviors and patterns of interaction. Of course, many factors play a role in child development, including physiological and genetic predispositions, but the family is overwhelmingly the most significant shaper of learning and behavior from birth through childhood and beyond. Furthermore, hundreds of studies have demonstrated conclusively that family members can assume the role of interventionist in resolving challenging behaviors and helping children acquire healthy trajectories of social-emotional development (Fettig & Barton, 2014; Lucyshyn, Dunlap, & Albin, 2002). Therefore, the family should be at the center of all recommendations and assistance efforts, and individual support efforts must be driven by the family's input and the family's goals. Family-centeredness and sensitivity to and respect for individual family perspectives also involve being responsive to the cultural and linguistic characteristics that each family and child brings to the program; respect for diversity among families is necessary. Appreciation of the family's central role and respect for diversity mean that family choice should be a major consideration in developing behavior support plans and that every effort should be taken to ensure that the support plans are congruent with a family's routines, values, and preferences.

Inclusion and Community Participation

Social behaviors are learned in social contexts, so it is important for all children, including children with serious challenging behaviors, to have rich opportunities to interact regularly in the home and participate in community activities just as if challenging behaviors were not an issue. It is understandable that families might tend to avoid community outings, and even home-based activities, if they are associated with disruptive, challenging behaviors, and we would not expect that these activities be undertaken unless there are strategies in place to ensure safety and control. However, it is important that a full range of preferred and necessary activities and settings be considered in the implementation of the PTR-F model. Otherwise, the child's social and behavioral development would be compromised, as would the lifestyle of the entire family.

Comprehensiveness

All aspects of child and family functioning need to be appreciated and incorporated into the design and implementation of services. This book focuses on procedures for resolving challenging behavior in family contexts and in home and community settings, but those procedures constitute only one aspect of the full array and continuum of services. Individual families might benefit from a diversity of supports, including respite care, counseling, economic planning, and medical intervention. Such services and supports are beyond the scope of this manual, but it is encouraged that families receive access to appropriate assistance based on individual needs.

Preventing Challenging Behaviors Using a Multi-Tiered Framework

Efforts to improve behavior are much more beneficial and cost-efficient if they serve to promote desirable social skills and *prevent*, rather than repair, social and emotional distress and challenging behaviors. There is much that can be to done to promote resilience and prevent the emergence of social and emotional difficulties. A child's social and emotional competence requires providing a nurturing and responsive parenting relationship, ensuring the child's physical health and nutrition, fostering the child's development of skills, and engaging in reciprocal interactions for learning social and emotional skills. These are universal parenting practices that, if implemented consistently, can possibly prevent the emergence of challenging behaviors to the point that individualized strategies, such as PTR-F, are not necessary. Even if challenging behaviors do occur and individualized intervention strategies are required, the use of universal parenting practices can make these interventions more effective and easier to implement. Therefore, we strongly recommend that universal practices be used prior to or in addition to the PTR-F model described in this book. In this way, PRT-F is based on a multi-tiered framework of behavior support.

Multi-tiered frameworks of behavior support have become common in elementary and secondary schools and in preschool and early intervention programs and have proven effective in addressing behavior problems. The basic logic of multi-tiered frameworks is that evidence-based strategies are organized along a continuum, with low-cost, low-intensity strategies used at the foundational, or universal, level, and more expensive and more intensive strategies deployed as needed at higher levels of the continuum. Multi-tiered frameworks addressing challenging behaviors often have the following three levels: 1) universal strategies designed to promote desirable behaviors for all members of a designated population (such as students on a school campus), 2) secondary strategies intended for a smaller proportion of the population that might be at higher risk, and 3) tertiary strategies, which are the most intensive and individualized practices, intended only for students who already exhibit serious levels of challenging behavior.

Schoolwide positive behavior support (SWPBS) is a multi-tiered system that has been adopted by over 25,000 elementary and secondary schools as of January 2016. In SWPBS, the universal level of support involves the establishment of clear behavioral expectations, instruction for all students on how to comply with these expectations, and systems for acknowledging compliance and for correcting failures to comply. Additional strategies with higher levels of complexity and intensity are provided for secondary prevention and tertiary intervention purposes. SWPBS has been supported by extensive research on its implementation process and social, behavioral, and academic outcomes (Sailor, Dunlap, Sugai, & Horner, 2009; Sugai & Horner, 2006; see www.pbis.org). The Pyramid Model is another multi-tiered framework addressing challenging behaviors, but this framework addresses social-emotional competence in young children in childcare, preschool, and home and community settings (Dunlap & Fox, 2011; Fox, Dunlap, Hemmeter, Joseph, & Strain, 2003; Johnson & Monn, 2015). Like SWPBS, the Pyramid Model has been implemented in many programs nationwide and has been supported by a growing base of research data (e.g., Branson & Demchak, 2011; Fox & Hemmeter, 2014; Snyder, Crowe, Miller, Hemmeter, & Fox, 2011). The Pyramid Model includes specifications for implementing evidence-based practices at the universal, secondary, and tertiary levels, with PTR-YC being the recommended approach for young children with challenging behavior in group settings.

We have emphasized consideration of multi-tiered systems because the use of low-intensity and low-cost strategies can be extremely useful for children not only in group settings, such as schools and childcare, but also in home and community settings. We strongly encourage the implementation of universal parenting strategies before, or at least during, implementation of the PTR-F approach. These universal parenting strategies are described more thoroughly in Chapter 2. They include providing high rates of positive adult attention, being very clear about behavioral expectations, and having family routines that are carried out regularly and predictably. In addition, there are other family strategies that can be used to promote desirable interactions and prevent challenging behaviors. We cited some resources earlier in this chapter, and many other books and Internet sites offer suggestions for parenting practices that can be used in home and community settings. We encourage readers to explore low-intensity options as long as the practices are supported by empirical research and are congruent with the family's values, routines, and preferences.

CONCEPTUAL AND EMPIRICAL FOUNDATIONS OF PTR-F

The PTR-F model is based on a well-established conceptual foundation as well as extensive research on the procedures and process of positive behavior support. In this section, we describe the scientific logic underlying the model and summarize the applied research that pertains directly to the PTR approach and its application with families in home and community settings.

Conceptual Foundations

First, it is important to recognize that the procedures of PTR-F are derived from fundamental principles of behavior, as explained in the earlier section titled "Understanding Challenging Behavior," as well as extensive practical research on strategies of intervention for challenging behavior. The intervention strategies of PTR-F primarily originate from two closely related approaches: applied behavior analysis and positive behavior support.

Applied behavior analysis (ABA) is a broad discipline in which principles of learning are applied to produce socially meaningful changes in a person's behavior. ABA has influenced and contributed to a great number of fields, including education, social work, psychology, child development, and business. Research conducted over approximately 50 years has clearly demonstrated the validity and widespread contributions of ABA. It is important to understand that the principles of ABA can be implemented in many ways that can appear on the surface to be quite dissimilar. As a result, the term "ABA" can be misunderstood. For example, some people refer to ABA as a single, highly structured curriculum for treating children with autism. However, ABA is a much broader approach than could ever be captured in a particular program, and it is relevant for virtually all populations in virtually all contexts. Programs that are strongly rooted in ABA may appear to be very different when they are, in fact, based on the same conceptual and philosophical foundations (Cooper, Heron, & Heward, 2007).

Positive behavior support (PBS) is also a broad approach that is, in large part, derived from ABA (Dunlap, 2006). PBS emerged in the mid-1980s and has become an increasingly popular strategy for addressing difficult behaviors and promoting quality of life (Bambara & Kern, 2005; Carr et al., 2002; Dunlap, Carr, Horner, Zarcone, & Schwartz, 2008; Sailor et al., 2009). PBS is an approach for improving behavior that includes an ongoing process of research-based assessment, intervention, and data-based decision making focused on building social and other functional competencies and preventing the occurrence of problem behaviors (Kincaid et al., 2016). PBS seeks to reduce the occurrence of behavior problems because they interfere with learning and with the ability to pursue preferred lifestyles and positive relationships with adults and peers. PBS is a "positive" approach in that it avoids harsh and stigmatizing punishments and, instead, emphasizes shifts in instruction and adjustments to the environment that support the child in learning and adopting more desirable behaviors. Although this book and the PTR-F model are concerned with applications of PBS at the individual level, readers will recognize that PBS is also applied in larger contexts, such as classrooms, preschool programs, and entire schools. Such applications of PBS are usually referred to using additional labels, such as positive behavior interventions and supports (PBIS), schoolwide positive behavior support (SWPBS), and program-wide positive behavior support (PWPBS) (see Dunlap, Kincaid, Horner, Knoster, & Bradshaw, 2014).

Research on Assessment-Based Behavioral Interventions

Over the past five decades, researchers relying on behavior analytic concepts and methods have produced an immense scientific literature documenting the efficacy of behavioral procedures for reducing problem behaviors. Specific strategies have been evaluated using careful research designs, with results published in numerous journals, including, most prominently, the *Journal of Applied Behavior Analysis*.

An important development occurred in the early 1980s with the advent of the assessment technologies, functional analysis, and functional assessment (Iwata, Dorsey, Slifer, Bauman, & Richman, 1994; O'Neill et al., 1997; Repp & Horner, 1999). These assessment strategies allowed interventionists to identify how environmental events influenced the occurrence of challenging behaviors. Functional assessment (or functional behavioral assessment [FBA]) is the larger term referring to a variety of strategies for determining these environmental influences on behavior, whereas functional analysis refers only to the strategy in which environmental events are systematically manipulated in order to observe environmental influences empirically. The significance of these assessment methods is that they can document conditions under which problem behaviors are more or less frequent and, thus, can reveal the "functions" of the challenging behavior or, in other words, the communicative purpose of the behavior. For example, some challenging behaviors might be more frequent if they are followed by attention, whereas other challenging behaviors might be more frequent if they are followed by an opportunity to escape from a less desired activity such as a nonpreferred household chore. Functional assessment procedures are also useful in revealing the antecedent conditions under which challenging behaviors are more or less prevalent (Dunlap, Kern-Dunlap, Clarke, & Robbins, 1991; Touchette, MacDonald, & Langer, 1985). Ultimately, functional assessment and functional analysis procedures are important because they lead to interventions that are more effective, efficient, and individualized.

One way to summarize the empirical foundations for the PTR-F process is to note that hundreds of individual studies reveal four important messages. First, FBAs can provide information that leads to effective and efficient (assessment-based) interventions for challenging behavior. Second, numerous assessment-based antecedent manipulations have been shown to reduce levels of challenging behaviors rapidly and substantially (*prevent*). Third, assessment-based instructional interventions targeting functionally equivalent communication skills have been demonstrated to produce sustainable reductions in challenging behaviors and important increases in appropriate communication (*teach*). And fourth, the use of positive reinforcement for desired responses results in increases in positive behaviors and concomitant reductions in challenging behaviors (*reinforce*).

Research on Prevent-Teach-Reinforce

PTR-F is based on the earlier versions of Prevent-Teach-Reinforce for school-age children and PTR-YC for toddlers and preschoolers. All three versions have in common the basic process of individualized PBS consisting of planning; goal setting; data collection; functional assessment; and intervention development, implementation, and evaluation. They also share similarities in their approach to functional assessment and use individualized interventions that always include prevent, teach, and reinforce strategies.

Research has demonstrated that the PTR model is effective in reducing challenging behaviors and increasing desirable alternatives. For example, the PTR model for school-aged students was evaluated in a randomized controlled trial with 245 participants and was found to produce statistically significant benefits in favor of the PTR group compared with a group that received the schools' "business as usual" in terms of challenging behavior, social skills, and academic engagement (Iovannone et al., 2009). In another study, using a single-case experimental design, Strain, Wilson, and Dunlap (2011) found consistent benefits in three students with autism spectrum disorders when they were presented with the PTR model.

In a more recent study, researchers in Nevada and Colorado have been conducting a group comparison experiment designed to investigate differences in outcomes between PTR-YC and typical services provided for preschoolers with persistent challenging behavior. Although the 4-year study had not been completed at the time of this writing, preliminary results have revealed statistically significant differences in levels of challenging behavior, engagement, and social skills (Dunlap, Lee, Strain, & Joseph, 2016). These findings mirror those from the previous investigation with school-age participants described by Iovannone and colleagues (2009).

Finally, important research has been conducted on using individualized and assessment-based interventions in family contexts. The research demonstrates that parents and other family members can implement assessment-based strategies with their children effectively and with fidelity in home and community settings (Dunlap & Fox, 1999; Fettig & Barton, 2014; Fettig, Schultz, & Sreckovic, 2015; Lucyshyn et al., 2002). In addition, preliminary studies have shown positive effects of using the PTR model in family contexts (Bailey, 2013; Sears, Blair, Iovannone, & Crosland, 2013).

THE PROCESS OF PTR-F

PTR-F is implemented similarly to the well-established, research-based process of individualized PBS that has been described in hundreds of articles, books, and web sites (e.g., www.apbs.org; Bambara & Kern, 2005; Brown, Anderson, & DePry, 2015). The PTR-F process is also similar to its predecessors, PTR (Dunlap et al., 2010) and PTR-YC (Dunlap, Wilson, Strain, & Lee, 2013). The PTR approach is distinguished by the precision with which it is presented, the step-by-step guidelines for implementing the model, and its strategies for enhancing the fidelity of implementation. PTR-F is distinguished further by its focus on implementation by parents and other family members in homes, communities, and other natural environments. The primary purpose of this book is to describe in detail each of the steps in the PTR-F process. This is accomplished in Chapters 3–7. In preparation, the basic steps are described briefly in the sections that follow.

Step 1: Initiating the PTR-F Process

Implementing PTR-F begins with the formation of a team that will be involved in the PTR-F process. The team may consist of just the professional facilitator and the key family members, or it may involve additional people who are invested in the process, implementation, and outcomes. Such additional team participants may include extended family members, close friends, or other professionals involved with the child and family. Forming a team involves a review of the purpose and steps of PTR-F, discussion about the importance of family-centeredness and working as a team, and agreement on the roles of different team members throughout the process.

It is important to establish a unified vision for improved child and family functioning so that every participant understands the overall outcomes that are desired and realistic. This includes discussing long-term goals and also specifying short-term objectives regarding parent–child interactions, social-emotional development of the child, and the settings prioritized for intervention. The team should also carefully define the specific challenging behaviors that will be targeted initially for reduction and should list desirable behaviors that will be taught or strengthened. Finally, the team needs to formulate feasible strategies for measuring the target behaviors, beginning with challenging behaviors, so that every member of the team will be able to monitor the progress that is occurring.

Step 2: PTR-F Assessment

The next step (see Chapter 4) involves the assessment of behavior in the routines that have been described as troublesome. The purpose of the assessment is to obtain an understanding of the way that the environment influences behavior. This kind of assessment is referred to as a functional assessment or an FBA. It is accomplished by completing simple questionnaires (primarily by parents) and then summarizing the responses to arrive at a consensual understanding of the relationship between events in the environment and the occurrence of challenging behavior and desirable behavior. Questionnaires and forms are included to aid in the summary and synthesis of the assessment information.

Step 3: PTR-F Intervention

This step of the process (see Chapter 5) moves from assessment to developing the intervention plan and then actually implementing the intervention. Each intervention plan includes at least three strategies, including at least one prevent strategy, at least one teach strategy, and one reinforce strategy. These available, research-based strategies are described in detail in this book. Intervention strategies are selected by the team, with the family being the essential decision makers. In addition to the process for developing the intervention plan, the intervention step of PTR-F includes detailed recommendations for helping family members implement the strategies. Steps are recommended for implementing each intervention component to maximize the probability of success and ensure individualization of the strategies so that they best fit the child and family context.

Step 4: Coaching

The coaching step is actually part of Step 3, but its importance in the PTR-F process warrants a separate chapter (see Chapter 6). Chapter 6 discusses the role of the facilitator as coach in helping families and other caregivers to implement the intervention strategies with fidelity. Attention is paid to the importance of the coaching relationship, the significance of cultural differences, and the process of fading support so that implementers of the intervention (family members or other caregivers) are competent and confident in using the selected intervention strategies.

Step 5: Monitoring Plan Implementation and Child Progress

Step 5 (see Chapter 7) focuses on practical and family-friendly strategies for monitoring progress and for assessing the effective use of the PTR-F model. Emphasis is placed on embedding progress-monitoring strategies within a home setting. In addition, Chapter 7 discusses how to use data to improve implementation and how to share data within the family and with relevant professionals and agencies.

FACTORS THAT ARE VITAL FOR PTR-F EFFECTIVENESS

Several factors contribute to the effectiveness of PTR-F, and the presence of these factors will vary across families and across the professionals who provide support. Some of these variables can greatly impact whether or not the PTR-F process is successful.

Commitment to Successful Outcomes

The family's level of commitment to working together to reduce challenging behavior and to improve patterns of adult–child interactions will be a major factor in determining outcomes. It is important for family members who are involved with PTR-F to understand that improvements are both possible and likely if the team works with the same goals in mind and with a commitment to following the PTR-F process as it is intended. This commitment must be sustained over time through an ongoing, unified dedication to improving the child's behavior and increasing quality of life for both the child and his or her family.

We understand that a willingness to change responses to the child's challenging behavior and interactions during family routines may be contradictory to some families' preferences and abilities. Some families might prefer to have outside professionals attempt to "fix" their child's behavior without engaging the family system in a collaborative effort. However, the family's willingness and commitment are essential ingredients in effectively implementing the PTR-F model.

Fidelity of Implementation

The following point has been made already, but it bears repeating. PTR-F is designed to be effective if it is implemented as described in this manual. It is crucial that the basic steps be followed in the prescribed sequence. It may be tempting to jump ahead and, for example, begin designing and implementing an intervention before the functional assessments have been completed. This is almost always a bad idea. The effectiveness of the model will be compromised if the steps are not implemented as described and in the order that is emphasized throughout this book.

Most families have busy lives, multiple responsibilities, and complex schedules that can contribute to making fidelity a difficult ambition. Arranging meetings with the facilitator can be a challenge, particularly because some of the meetings and coaching sessions need to occur during specific problematic routines, which may occur at times of the day that are not especially convenient. Arranging such sessions requires commitment to coordinate on the part of both the family and the facilitator, and on occasion, it might be useful (although not optimal) to use video-communication technology to conduct a session when a face-to-face meeting is impossible.

Relationship Between the Family and the Supporting Professional

In addition to positive relationships within the family, positive and constructive relationships between key family members and the professionals who provide support in the

PTR-F model are important. The professionals are those who are involved in facilitating the process, helping the family to design the intervention plan, and providing coaching during the intervention process. A desirable relationship means that communication is open and that trust has been established. The better the rapport that exists between the professional and family members, the more effective will be the support and, therefore, the entire process of PTR-F implementation. Sometimes, the establishment of a trusting and constructive relationship requires time, but it is time well spent.

LIMITATIONS AND ACCOMMODATIONS TO CONSIDER WHEN IMPLEMENTING PTR-F

We are confident that PTR-F will be effective most of the time if the model is followed with care, if the family has the time and the capacity to implement the assessment and intervention strategies, and if professionals are available to provide individualized facilitation and support.

However, the model cannot be effective in every situation. First, there are some factors that may contribute to behavior problems that are beyond the capacity of PTR-F to address. For instance, some children experience medical or neurological conditions that require interventions other than the educational and behavioral strategies that make up PTR-F. When children have chronic illness, uncontrolled seizures, or other physiological disorders, it would be inappropriate to attempt to resolve such problems with educational–behavioral procedures alone. When neurological or medical issues are involved, it is necessary to arrange for multidisciplinary input that could include PTR-F as well as appropriate medical, neurological, or psychiatric services.

It must also be acknowledged that some children's challenging behaviors are influenced by severe problems in the family system produced by mental illness, alcohol and substance abuse, marital discord, economic stress resulting from unemployment, and any number of precipitating circumstances leading to a home atmosphere characterized by traumatic and dysfunctional interactions and neglect. The PTR-F approach is not designed to address this level of serious problems in the family system. In such circumstances, the family should have access to assistance and resources provided by systems such as social services, social work, and mental health counseling.

There are also times when, despite the best efforts of the family and supporting professionals, the PTR-F approach does not produce fully adequate behavior change. For example, the child's behavior may be so difficult to observe (e.g., hurting animals, setting fires, injuring others) or so infrequent or unobservable that it is impossible to complete an adequate FBA based on family members' observations. In this situation, team members may be at a loss to determine the function of the challenging behavior and therefore cannot implement an individualized intervention. For serious challenging behaviors that rarely occur and/or occur when adults may not typically be present, it may be necessary to call in outside help to monitor the child on something close to a 24/7 basis. Such monitoring should have completion of a reliable FBA as its end point. Additionally, it may be necessary to solicit a diagnostic evaluation by a licensed child psychologist or psychiatrist for behaviors that have a covert quality to them; that is, the child seems to purposely engage in challenging behavior when adults are absent. The goal of this assistance should be to determine whether other supports and/or professionals need to be involved in this child's life.

In other circumstances, the team may have designed an individualized intervention plan and implemented the plan with fidelity, but the child's behavior has not improved over a period of several weeks. In this kind of situation, we first recommend checking to see if the reinforcers are sufficiently powerful and then repeating the PTR-F assessment to confirm the "communicative message" of the problem behavior. It is not uncommon to find that a behavior originally served one function, and then subsequently to find that this behavior now serves different and/or multiple functions. If the step of repeating the PTR-F assessment does not yield satisfactory results, then it may be appropriate to call on a consultant who is more experienced in FBA. This individual may decide to use alternative observation procedures to analyze behavior, more thoroughly explore the possible role of events that are external to the setting where the behavior occurs, or ask the team to briefly try interventions that are consistent with several different functions. When using this type of consultative help, it is vital that team members become trained to implement the methods used by the consultant. We address circumstances such as these more thoroughly in Chapter 7.

SUMMARY

PTR-F is a specific model of intervention planning and implementation for young children with serious challenging behavior in home and community settings in which families provide supervision and guidance. It is applicable for children from about age 30 months through elementary school and for children with a broad range of developmental and intellectual characteristics. An extensive research base supports the effectiveness of PTR-F's steps and components, as well as the process as a whole.

This book is intended to be used primarily as a manual by professionals who are actively supporting families that include a child with severe, persistent challenging behaviors. The purpose of this book is to describe the PTR-F model in sufficient detail so that it can be used by home visiting professionals to support families in their efforts to effectively resolve their children's challenging behaviors. This introductory chapter has described the background and the rationale for the model. Chapter 2 discusses important issues having to do with families and, in particular, understanding and resolving challenging behaviors in the context of the family system. Subsequent chapters provide detailed guidelines and instructions for implementing each step of the model. We include descriptions of assessment and intervention strategies and examples of the use of PTR-F with a variety of families, children, and challenging behaviors.

Two detailed case examples accompany each chapter. The case examples are intended to illustrate each step as the process unfolds across the entire period of implementation. The examples include completed forms in the assessment and intervention phases, and the text describes various circumstances that can expedite or hinder the process. The content of the chapters is designed to be specific enough for teams to follow the PTR-F process without difficulty. If the steps are followed carefully and with precision, evidence indicates that there is a good chance that the child's behavior will improve in meaningful ways.

KEY TERMS THROUGHOUT THIS BOOK

The following list describes some terms that may not be familiar to all readers. These terms are defined as they are used in this book and in relation to the PTR-F model.

Antecedents or **antecedent variables** are events, actions, items, and circumstances that are present in the environment and have an influence on the occurrence of a child's behavior. Antecedents can serve as "triggers" for challenging behavior or desirable behavior, or they can act to make a behavior more likely to occur. Almost anything can potentially serve as an antecedent variable. However, common antecedents for challenging behavior are requests for a child to do something that the child does not want to do.

Applied behavior analysis (ABA) is a scientific discipline that includes practical approaches for assessing and modifying behavior. ABA uses principles of learning theory to develop intervention strategies. ABA is a broad approach that has been demonstrated to be useful for helping many populations of children and adults to develop improved behavior.

Baseline is the period of time before the PTR-F intervention is implemented. It is the period during which data are collected (described in Chapter 3) and during which families are using their regular procedures for dealing with challenging behaviors.

Challenging behavior is a term used to describe any repeated pattern of behavior that interferes with optimal learning or engagement in prosocial interactions with peers and adults. In this book, we refer to challenging behavior as persistent behaviors that appear to be unresponsive to normative guidance strategies, with common topographies being prolonged tantrums, physical and verbal aggression, disruptive vocal and motor responding (e.g., screaming, stereotypy), property destruction, self-injury, noncompliance, and withdrawal (Smith & Fox, 2003).

Contextual fit is a term that refers to the congruence between a behavior support plan and a family's preferences, culture, habits, capabilities, and values. The greater the contextual fit, the more likely it will be that the behavior support plan will be implemented with fidelity.

Coaching refers to building others' capacity to implement specified practices, strategies, or actions. In PTR-F, coaching refers to providing the family member with instruction and support for the implementation of PTR-F strategies. Coaching involves using specified strategies while conducting observations, guiding reflection, and providing feedback to the family member who implements the PTR-F strategies.

Data encompass facts or information. In PTR-F, data usually refer to observations made about a child's behavior. Data obtained for purposes of conducting a functional assessment (see Chapter 4), monitoring progress (see Chapter 7), and assessing fidelity of implementation (see Chapters 6 and 7) are especially important in the PTR-F model.

Desirable behavior is a broad term used in PTR-F and refers to a child's behaviors that the team would like to establish or increase. Desirable behaviors include positive social and communicative behaviors and can also include cooperative or parallel play, attending, independent responding, self-care, and self-regulation.

Fidelity in PTR-F refers to the extent that an intervention strategy is implemented accurately and as intended. The term is often stated as "fidelity of implementation" or "integrity of implementation."

Function is the purpose of or motivation for the child's challenging behavior. There are many possible functions, but they usually can be categorized as "to get something" (such as a toy or someone's attention) or "to get rid of something" (such as a demand or the presence of an irritating peer). As discussed in Chapter 1, the function of challenging behavior can almost always be understood as an attempt to communicate.

Functional assessment (or functional behavioral assessment [FBA]) is a process that involves collecting information (data) to develop an understanding of how a challenging behavior is influenced, or controlled, by events in the environment. There are many methods for conducting an FBA. In PTR-F, the FBA is conducted by having team members independently complete three checklists (for prevent, teach, and reinforce) and then synthesize the information on an FBA summary form (described in Chapter 4).

A **hypothesis (hypothesis statement)** is a simple statement that summarizes the team's understanding of how a challenging behavior is influenced by the environment. The hypothesis has three elements: the antecedent conditions, a description of the behavior, and the consequences that appear to be maintaining the behavior. With some children, there may be more than one hypothesis statement.

An **operational definition** is a definition, or description, of a behavior that is presented in terms that are fully observable and measurable. A good operational definition allows all team members to be able to agree at any moment in time on whether or not the behavior is occurring.

Positive behavior support (PBS) is an approach for helping people (including children) to develop improved desirable behaviors and reduce challenging behaviors. It is an individualized approach that is based on data (information), results of an FBA, and a multi-element behavior support plan. PTR-F is a PBS model that is designed for optimal practicality. It is worth noting that PBS can also be applied to larger units such as classrooms, entire programs, and schools. However, PTR-F is a model of *individualized* PBS, and this book is focused on the needs of individual children with persistent challenging behaviors.

Prevent is the first intervention component of the PTR-F approach. It refers to intervention strategies involving antecedent variables.

Reinforce is the third component of the PTR-F approach. It refers to intervention strategies involving changes in the delivery of consequences, especially positive reinforcers.

Reinforcer (or positive reinforcer) is a consequence provided to a child following a behavior that results in the behavior being increased or strengthened. Part of the PTR-F approach involves using reinforcers to help increase desirable behaviors, as well as removing reinforcers that may be inadvertently maintaining the child's challenging behaviors.

Target behavior is a term that is used to refer to a behavior that is identified by the team as being in need of change. Target behaviors can be challenging behaviors as well as desirable behaviors.

Teach is the second component of the PTR-F approach. It refers to intervention strategies involving the delivery of instruction on desirable behaviors.

How to Work with Families

2

In Prevent-Teach-Reinforce for Families (PTR-F), the family should play a role in all aspects of the model for effective implementation. PTR-F is more than just a focus on home and family routines. Family-centeredness (see Chapter 1) is a guiding principle of the PTR-F process, in which the family unit is the primary implementer of the support plan. The goals, input, and unique characteristics of the individual family inform the PTR-F process and help determine the interventions and supports that are provided for a child's challenging behaviors. An understanding of families is therefore crucial to all steps of the PTR-F process, from assessment to planning to implementation. In this chapter, we describe how challenging behaviors affect the family system, and we discuss issues related to supporting families in addressing challenging behavior. This chapter also discusses principles that should guide the PTR-F process with families and provides strategies for ensuring that families are collaborative partners in implementing the PTR-F model.

Before discussing ways to support families, we should begin by defining the concept of "family" and who a family entails. For the purposes of this book, we define family broadly. As described by Poston and colleagues (2003, p. 319), family is inclusive of "people who think of themselves as part of the family, whether related by blood or marriage or not, and who support and care for each other on a regular basis." In many cases, the family may be headed by a set of parents or a single parent; however, depending on cultural, interpersonal, historical, and other factors, parenting duties are often shared with other individuals in the child's life. Based on this broad definition, family members may include foster parents; nonparent caregivers, including individuals related (e.g., a grandparent, uncle, aunt, cousin) or unrelated (e.g., neighbor, friends, in-home staff) to the child; or a combination of parents and other caregivers. The planning and intervention processes must be able to support any and all potential configurations of caregivers. (See the case example of Lucy in the Appendix at the end of this chapter for an example of a situation in which multiple individuals might be invited to participate in the PTR-F process, including grandparents and teachers.)

GUIDELINES FOR SUPPORTING FAMILIES THROUGH THE PTR-F PROCESS

A number of key principles are pivotal to successful family engagement in PTR-F. These foundational principles are presented as guidelines for how facilitators can be most effective in supporting families. These guidelines describe how to develop rapport with families throughout PTR-F assessment, behavior support planning, and ongoing implementation. They are in line with an approach that celebrates family strengths and acknowledges the family voice as necessary in development and implementation of behavior intervention.

Establish and Maintain Collaborative Partnerships

Families are central to the PTR-F process and ultimately have ownership of the behavior support plan. Although a professional facilitator plays a crucial role in actual PTR-F implementation, the facilitator should also serve as a guide, coach, supporter, and cheerleader in the family's efforts to address challenging behavior. From the initial steps of involvement with families, the facilitator should convey to the family and all other caregivers that they are central members of the team, that they have valuable information to contribute, and that their perspectives are valid and appreciated. Research indicates that families can provide valid and reliable information for functional behavioral assessments, can develop accurate hypotheses for challenging behaviors, and can implement effective interventions in reducing challenging behaviors (Arndorfer, Miltenburger, Woster, Rortvedt, & Gaffaney, 1994; Frea & Hepburn, 1999; Lucyshyn et al., 2007; Vaughn & Fox, 2015). When we treat parents and family members as equals in the process, and when we empower families by giving them strategies to reduce challenging behaviors and effectively teach their child useful and desirable skills, we increase the likelihood of pronounced and sustainable change that will positively affect both the child and the family.

The case example of Timmy, introduced in the Appendix at the end of this chapter, provides a good example of a successful initial meeting in which one facilitator, Kaci, builds early rapport with a family implementing PTR-F with their child.

Remain Family Centered in All Aspects of the PTR-F Process

Family-centeredness will be a primary focus in implementing PTR-F. When planning for an individual with support needs, a family-centered approach uses systematic procedures for bringing people together who are important to the family (e.g., relatives, friends, support providers) to work as a team. Together, the team sets a vision and goals for the family based on the family's values (Epley, Summers, & Turnbull, 2010; Keen, 2007; O'Brien & O'Brien, 2002). Although initially developed to support families of children with developmental disabilities, family-centered processes can lead to valuable outcomes for families with typically developing children and can be a useful tool for all families. Family-centered planning approaches provide a broader view of the family that takes into account the larger contexts and factors (e.g., family and agency values, funding, any disability, community supports) that substantially impact quality of life (Fleisher, Ballard-Krishnan, & Benito, 2015; Kincaid, Knab, & Clark, 2005).

The PTR-F model emphasizes the use of family-centered practices to provide all families with access to supports that are relevant to their values and needs. It is not a "one-size-fits-all" model but a dynamic model that allows support providers to modify practices to ensure that family supports are efficacious and sustained over time. The PTR-F approach to family support mirrors Turnbull and Ruef's (1996) recommendations that families need an alliance with those who can provide dependable, trusted, and nonjudgmental assistance that is adaptable to their needs.

Ensure Contextual Fit of Behavior Support Plans

Contextual fit refers to the match between the elements of the intervention and the values, needs, skills, and resources of those who are implementing the intervention (Albin, Lucyshyn, Horner, & Flannery, 1996; Singer & Wang, 2009). In the case of PTR-F, the context is family and includes all members of the family's household. If the family is implementing an intervention that is not a good match with the workings of the home or with their vision and values, there is little chance that it will be implemented for any extended period of time. When contextual factors are accounted for, with an awareness of culture, personal and group ambitions, and attitudes and preferences, a plan can be created that is not only more likely to be implemented with fidelity but also is more likely to be embraced and owned by the family.

Any behavior support that occurs within the home should also be tailored so that it is minimally intrusive to the family and to the family's functioning. When designing behavioral interventions, remember that their level of intrusiveness may vary from family to family and may depend on numerous factors, including the prevalence of challenging behavior, cultural norms for the family, and level of intervention required. Families can provide a great deal of input on how interventions might work in their home and how coaching and other supports might be best provided in an unobtrusive manner. Parents may also have specific ideas about the scripting, modeling, and role-playing aspects of the intervention. These family perspectives can be invaluable in creating interventions that fit the child, the implementer, and the environment in which they are applied.

Use a Strength-Based Approach

While the PTR-F assessment and behavior support plan attend to a child's behavioral challenges, they must also capture the strengths of the child, which help inform strategies and provide a foundation for future successes. In efforts to support families with children who have challenging behavior, too often conversations focus on challenging behavior and what else is going on when this behavior occurs, with little acknowledgment of the successes, strengths, and skills of the child and family. Increased focus on these strengths and successes not only builds morale, but allows the team to learn important lessons from what went right as well as what went wrong. Thus, data should always reflect not only decreases in challenging behaviors but also increases in prosocial behaviors. Equipped with this information, effective facilitators help to direct conversation to these positive trends in desired or prosocial skills and behaviors.

Families that make positive behavior happen need to be supported. Research emphasizes that parents' optimism and confidence in their ability to alter their child's challenging behaviors have an important impact (Durand, 2001; Hastings & Brown, 2002; Jones & Prinz, 2005). We also know that we, as practitioners, can positively affect parents' outlook on their own abilities and belief in their potential to impact their child's behavior (Durand, Hieneman, Clarke, Wang, & Rinaldi, 2012). In PTR-F, the family is foundational to both planning and implementation of behavioral interventions. The facilitator in this process plays the role of cheerleader, reminding families of their strengths, helping families to feel both prepared and empowered, and setting expectations for success.

Recognize the Importance of Coaching and Support

Coaching and support have long been seen as vital aspects of effective, sustained behavior intervention in early childhood programs (Conroy, Sutherland, Vo, Carr, & Ogston, 2014; Fox, Hemmeter, Snyder, Binder, & Clarke, 2011). Similarly, coaching has been shown to be effective in family contexts (Fettig & Barton, 2014; Sandall, Hemmeter, Smith, & McLean, 2005). Thus, it is no wonder that coaching is a core element of the PTR-F process.

Behavior support plans change child behavior by also altering adult behavior in the context of the routine. Coaching provides scaffolding to help families learn new skills outlined in a plan and gain comfort and proficiency with using these skills with their child in a natural setting. It is this support following plan development that sustains parents' continued optimism in the plan, ensures fit of the intervention with the child's and family's needs, and allows for adaptations or changes to the plan if warranted. If we are to develop a plan that is the best fit for both the child and the family, this initial support is necessary. The goal in PTR-F is eventual independent implementation by family members, but providing a plan with little scaffolding will not ensure success over time.

Provide Support that Is Tailored to Both Family Needs and Preferences

Family-centered positive behavior support acknowledges that parents can be and are experts regarding their child's behavior (Turnbull & Turnbull, 2001; Vaughn & Fox, 2015).

We recognize that with education in positive approaches to intervention and support, parents can be empowered to use this knowledge and insight to develop positive plans of support that work within their home. A collaborative planning process also helps families to identify and find resonance with the developed plan of support.

When supporting families in their home, it is vital that the language used is accessible to all. This goes beyond translating for the family—the facilitator should ensure that all communication welcomes dialogue and is free of jargon that might alienate anyone from the conversation. Listening is crucial in these initial meetings so that families are heard and can express their views. The facilitator can also help keep conversations positive and productive by actively shaping and reinforcing communication that describes desired behaviors and notes the strengths of the child and other individuals in the family (Lucyshyn, Dunlap, & Albin, 2002).

UNIVERSAL PARENTING PRACTICES

In the past two decades, emphasis has been placed on promoting desirable social-emotional behaviors as a way to prevent the emergence of serious challenging behaviors. In the previous chapter, we referred to the Pyramid Model (Fox et al., 2003) as a framework for organizing effective strategies for promoting desirable behavior, preventing behavior problems, and, when necessary, implementing individualized intervention procedures. We briefly mentioned some general parenting strategies that are used by many families and that can be effective in averting challenging behaviors. These are also known as *universal practices* and are similar to strategies used in preschool, kindergarten, and elementary school classrooms to establish a positive approach to social behavior. When implemented consistently, these practices can reduce the occurrence of problems and help children acquire useful patterns of interaction. There are many universal strategies that families can adopt. We recommend four strategies: 1) provide high rates of positive attention and acknowledge occasions in which the child is behaving appropriately; 2) establish and maintain regular and predictable daily routines; 3) include consistent patterns of activities within those routines; and 4) clearly define behavioral expectations within daily routines and be clear about the difference between desirable behavior and undesirable behavior.

Provide High Rates of Positive Attention and Acknowledge Occasions in Which the Child Is Behaving Appropriately

It is easy for parents to fall into a pattern of giving time and attention to a child when he or she is exhibiting challenging behavior and to largely ignore that child when he or she is behaving appropriately. This conveys to the child that a good way to attract attention is to engage in problem behaviors. Likewise, when little attention is given to desired behavior, the child does not learn that his or her actions have merit and value beyond the intrinsic reinforcement for engaging in the behavior. Therefore, it is critical that families spend the vast majority of time interacting with their child when he or she is behaving well and provide positive feedback with great frequency and sincerity. We recommend that families provide attention for their child's positive behaviors at a rate of at least five times the amount of attention provided as corrective feedback for challenging behavior.

Although positive interactions are important throughout the day, parents have an especially valuable influence when they sincerely acknowledge their child's desirable social interactions. Examples of particular opportunities for special attention are when the child is responsive to a parent's request, shares toys with a sibling, or participates happily in a daily routine (such as dinner, bathing, or getting ready in the morning) that has been associated previously with challenging behaviors. The universal practice of "catching them being good" is a time-tested and helpful strategy for children of all ages.

Establish and Maintain a Predictable Daily Schedule

As a general rule, children do better and have fewer challenging behaviors when the family has regular routines that the child can learn to anticipate on a daily basis. Predictable daily schedules can be useful in preventing problems. Almost every household has a schedule of activities in place (e.g., getting dressed, mealtime, bathing, bedtime); however, sometimes the schedule does not have the level of predictability or certainty necessary for children to fully understand and be comfortable with upcoming activities. When schedules are interrupted or altered in some way, it is important for parents to do everything possible to inform their children and to be sure that they can adapt successfully. It is helpful to teach children to understand and follow schedules and to review schedules and routines on a regular basis.

Develop Consistent Routines within the Elements of the Daily Schedule

Along the same lines as having a predictable daily schedule, it is also important to have regularly occurring activities within the daily routines. For example, having a family breakfast after the early morning routines (getting up, using the bathroom, and getting dressed) is a common activity that occurs on a regular basis. However, simply having breakfast as a routine may not offer sufficient predictability to help prevent challenging behavior. It can be even more helpful if the family has a regular sequence in which, for example, members decide what they want for the breakfast meal, one member helps set the table, one member pours the juice, and so on. As much as possible, it is useful for children to have active roles in the sequence of activities that compose the daily routines.

Clearly Define Behavioral Expectations and the Difference Between Desired Behavior and Undesired Behavior

A vitally important step for helping children learn how to behave appropriately is for the family to explicitly teach the behavioral expectations for each family routine. Many families have at least a basic set of rules in place (e.g., use walking feet, share toys and materials, use inside voice, keep toys and friends safe), and these guidelines can be very worthwhile. But in many cases, these general rules are not translated into how they are applied to specific routines. In some cases, parents make the mistake of assuming that children know how to behave appropriately and that their doing otherwise is simply noncompliance. For example, when considering the expectation of respecting others, a rule of "hands to self" can look very different at the dinner table than it might when playing games outside. Noncompliance should not be assumed unless the difference between good behavior and challenging behavior is taught directly and until the child has demonstrated that she or he knows the difference and can behave accordingly.

It is critical for children to be taught the boundaries of desired behavior in all routines, including playtime, mealtime, bathing, and bedtime, and to appreciate that those boundaries will differ from routine to routine. Children must also learn that challenging behaviors will be followed by corrective feedback. Such feedback should include a clear message that the behavior is not acceptable along with instructional guidance so that the child knows what she or he should do instead. And, of course, the child's desirable behavior should be enthusiastically acknowledged. It is important to remember that a child's positive social behavior is the result of learning, and learning valuable life lessons (like how to get along in a family context) is something well worth acknowledgment and celebration.

DESIGNING INDIVIDUALIZED INTERVENTION FOR CHALLENGING BEHAVIOR WITHIN THE FAMILY CONTEXT

Challenging behavior affects all functioning in the home and can dramatically change the dynamics of the living environment. At a point of crisis, a family is often identified as requiring supports when they state that they are unable to support the child or effectively address the severity of the behaviors within the current functioning of the family system. When a child exhibits this degree of challenging behaviors, the quality of life for the child and anyone else he or she interacts with is affected in profound ways. For example, challenging behaviors can affect a family's ability to go shopping, eat out, attend family and community activities, or find and keep a babysitter. Understanding that a child's challenging behavior impacts the family as a whole is important to consider when including families as essential and valued team members for the PTR-F process. When children have social and emotional needs, this may reflect the family's needs as well, and a family's needs should always be considered when designing individualized behavior support.

When a child's challenging behavior is significant enough to require the need for individualized interventions, families need to feel supported and empowered to play a key role in helping the child learn more socially appropriate skills. Families are typically the one constant in a child's life, providing the most essential roles in their child's development, and thus are an invaluable resource. They often know many of the situations that contribute to a child's challenging behaviors, and thus, involving families in meaningful ways can help improve the effectiveness of any behavior intervention process. Families also often develop strategies to cope with or avoid the challenging behavior, and these intervention or preventative strategies can be informative when designing an effective intervention plan because they provide some insight into the function (or purpose) of the behavior, the outcomes that are valued by the parent, and a history of approaches that have been implemented, including those that have shown some promise and those that have failed. For example, when a child engages in challenging behaviors in a store, a family might prevent these challenging behaviors by not walking down certain aisles in the store to avoid items (like candy) that may cause a tantrum. Or, when a child demands something, a family might bargain with the child for the amount of time that he or she can engage in the desired activity. The parent may state that the child can spend 1 minute engaged in the activity and then respond to pleadings from the child with increased time. These are only two examples, but the key is that families often have identified interventions and preventative strategies to manage challenging behavior throughout the day and across settings. We recommend getting information about the way in which current and past interventions were applied, including the frequency and consistency of their application.

SUMMARY

Families are the cornerstone of the PTR-F process. They are experts on their child, their culture, their environment, and themselves, and have invaluable information to contribute. When families are valued and appreciated, it becomes easy and natural to include them in all steps of the PTR-F process. It is up to us, the facilitators, to ensure that the families are fully invested and that everyone has the same goals and vision for the future. This leads to lasting behavioral change that not only affects the child but also overall family functioning and quality of life.

APPENDIX

Case Examples

To illustrate how to implement the Prevent-Teach-Reinforce for Families (PTR-F) process, two case examples are provided—Timmy and Lucy. These cases describe two young children with challenging behaviors and detail how the PTR-F process is facilitated with family members to develop and implement strategies for improving their child's social-emotional competence and reducing challenging behaviors. These cases are fictitious, but they are based on real experiences.

The case examples are introduced here and include background information about the child and family. At the end of each chapter, both case examples are continued, demonstrating how the step of the PTR-F process described in the chapter is implemented with and by the family. The case examples include details of facilitating the process, as well as completed PTR-F forms and checklists.

The extent of home-based services varies widely, and these examples attempt to describe how the PTR-F process *may* be facilitated. Delivering services in home and community settings typically requires more flexibility and specificity in individualizing supports, making contextual fit vitally important for successful outcomes. Refer to the case examples as needed, and we hope they help you understand how to facilitate the PTR-F process most effectively.

INTRODUCING TIMMY AND HIS FAMILY

Family Background

Timmy is a 27-month-old boy who lives with his mother and father, Jodie and Phil, and his 1-year-old brother, Dakota. The family lives in the city in a three-bedroom apartment near some extended family. Both Jodie's mother and Phil's mother live nearby, and each grandmother visits the family about once a month. Jodie and Phil both work full time during the week; Jodie is a third-grade teacher at a local school, and Phil is a truck driver for a local construction company. Timmy and Dakota attend a community-based childcare center 5 days a week, where Timmy has been attending since he was an infant. Jodie and Phil have a strong relationship and share parenting responsibilities, but Timmy's behavior is starting to add stress to the family.

Description of Child

Timmy is a playful and busy little boy who does not have any identified developmental delays and does not receive any supplementary services outside of childcare. Timmy has about 20 words in his verbal vocabulary that are difficult to understand, even to his parents and teacher who know him the best. Other than being difficult to understand, Timmy seems to demonstrate age-appropriate skills across the developmental domains. When in new situations or environments or in the presence of strangers, Timmy appears shy and may hide behind a familiar adult or physically turn his body away from the situation. Sometimes, he does not respond to adult requests and/or may pull on the familiar adult, attempting to pull him or her from the situation.

Description of Behavior

At the childcare center, Timmy exhibits challenging behaviors on a fairly consistent basis, but he has not been identified for additional supports at the center. The teacher and director recognize that Timmy has some behavioral concerns, but they are not unlike those exhibited by some of the other children currently in Timmy's classroom. At school, Timmy has tantrums, throws toys, takes toys from peers, screams "at the top of his lungs," and sometimes runs and hides in a small space (e.g., under a small table, in one of the cubbies). There are a few other children who exhibit similar behaviors, some of whom only attend the center part time. At the center, the classroom can get chaotic when there are several 2-year-old children who are struggling with getting along and when there are several crying children at one time. When these situations occur at school, the teachers try to keep the children who are having problems apart from each other, but the distraction is usually temporary.

At home, Timmy demonstrates significant challenging behaviors during various daily routines, consisting of extreme tantrums and physical aggression toward his parents. These behaviors have been occurring for the past several months and recently seem to be getting more intense. Jodie and Phil talked with Timmy's teacher and the director about how they were dealing with Timmy's behaviors at the center, and they shared that they try to keep certain kids apart as much as possible. For issues that occur with some of the routines, like diapering, they just do their best to finish diapering as quickly as possible, even when Timmy is squirming around on the changing table. Jodie and Phil were looking for help with Timmy's behaviors at home because his tantrums were creating problems with their immediate neighbors due to the screaming and other loud noises. Jodie asked the center's director if she knew of any help that she could get for addressing Timmy's behaviors at home. The director referred her to a program that she knew about in the community that works with parents to manage behavioral issues in the home. Jodie called the program and scheduled an initial appointment.

The Initial Meeting

At the first meeting, required paperwork needed to be completed, including consent forms and agreements. Once the program's paperwork requirements were completed, the facilitator began the process of developing a behavior support plan with Jodie and Phil. The facilitator, Kaci, began the first meeting by introducing herself, briefly describing her experiences and background in supporting children with challenging behavior, and detailing the process of ways in which her agency provides support to families. Kaci described how she would facilitate the behavior support plan process but indicated that Jodie and Phil would ultimately be the ones who decide how the process will develop, which intervention strategies to implement, and how they will implement the strategies. The five steps of the PTR-F process were briefly reviewed, including a description of the coaching process.

This initial meeting ended with scheduling the next three meetings and planning what would be accomplished at the first meeting. Because Jodie and Phil both work full time, they agreed that it would be easier to schedule the meetings on Thursday evenings for the next 3 weeks, and they would plan to get home a little earlier than usual in order to have time to meet and then have a quick dinner before getting the boys ready for bedtime. Kaci asked Jodie and Phil to think about including anyone else in these meetings who might also struggle with these same behaviors with Timmy. Timmy's parents could not think of anyone else at the time but stated they would discuss it. Kaci reminded Jodie and Phil that they would be identifying specific goals during the next meeting and creating an easy data collection plan. In preparation for the next meeting, Kaci encouraged Jodie and Phil to think about appropriate behaviors that they would like to see Timmy either learn or display more often.

Jodie and Phil were thankful for Kaci's time and were anxious to get a behavior support plan in place. They stated that they would do whatever Kaci recommended, and she reminded them that they are the experts on Timmy and their family and that they would be identifying what strategies were appropriate and the most helpful. Kaci further reassured Timmy's parents that they would have a behavior support plan in place in a short amount of time and that their daily routines would be calmer. Kaci joked that, in a few months, they might look back at this time of their lives in amusement or awe, wondering how they survived. Phil responded that he could only hope to look back on these days and laugh about them and that he could not wait to be in that position.

INTRODUCING LUCIA (LUCY) AND HER FAMILY

Family Background

Gabriella (Gabby) is a single mother to her 5-year-old daughter Lucia (Lucy), who has Down syndrome. Gabby and Lucy have recently moved into Gabby's parents' home because Gabby separated from her husband (who is Lucy's father) about 1 month ago. Gabby's parents, Marguerite and Hector, primarily speak Spanish in the home but are both fairly fluent in English. Gabby is bilingual and uses both English and Spanish with Lucy. Lucy only receives instruction in English from school and seems to equally understand English and Spanish, according to Gabby. Gabby has two sisters and one brother who live in the area, all with families of their own.

Gabby is currently a stay-at-home mom but wants to get back to work once life settles down so that she can save money and find a place to live on their own. She does not want to live with her parents, but she does not have any other options at this moment. Gabby and her parents currently live in a modest home in an urban city, and Gabby and Lucy are sharing a room while they live with Marguerite and Hector. Hector is in poor health and was diagnosed with cancer several months ago; he is currently undergoing chemotherapy. Marguerite was working but recently quit her job to help care for Hector. Because of Hector's illness, he often sleeps during parts of the day, and the noise level when Lucy is home is causing problems between Gabby and her parents. When Lucy is at home, she is often running around the house and loves to jump on the couch as well as jump from the couch to the floor; these antics are usually followed by squeals of laughter and other loud sounds of glee. Gabby tries to get Lucy out of the house, but that can lead to other problems when Lucy resists going back home. In those circumstances, Gabby has to carry her into the house while she is having a tantrum. Gabby currently describes life as being "in chaos" and recognizes that this is affecting Lucy, but she does not know where to start as far as moving forward, taking control, and getting their lives back into a new routine.

Description of Child

Lucy is a rambunctious and charming little girl who is "very busy" most of the time. She receives special education services through the local school district where she attends kindergarten in the morning 5 days per week. Gabby loves to be around others and is typically very affectionate to anyone with whom she interacts. She has an infectious smile and laugh, and adults typically respond to her with kindness and affection. Lucy has emerging verbal language skills with a few intelligible words, but most of her verbalizations are difficult to understand. Lucy seems to understand most of what is being said to her and can follow some simple two-step directions. Lucy has many emerging skills across the developmental domains.

Description of Behavior

Although Lucy is not physically very big, she is very strong and sometimes hits and kicks others when she does not get her way. Lucy will also yell, scream, take her clothes off, throw things, break things (seemingly on purpose), and sometimes run away and hide. Gabby is also concerned that Lucy does not regularly sit to eat for meals, resists getting dressed, resists getting ready for bed, and resists most activities if they are not of interest to her. Lucy seems to understand what is being said to her "when she wants to," but Gabby thinks that Lucy ignores her most of the time unless she wants something from her. Lucy does exhibit some of these behaviors at school, but according to Gabby, the teacher is able to handle Lucy's behaviors and has given suggestions for Lucy's behaviors at home. Gabby has tried some of the things that the teacher told her, like using a picture schedule to let Lucy know what is happening during the day, but Lucy would destroy or throw the pictures, so Gabby stopped using the schedule because it was not working and seemed to make things harder.

The Initial Meeting

Lucy receives services from the local regional center, and Gabby reached out to her case manager to get help with Lucy's behaviors at home, especially because they have been getting more intense and Lucy is getting bigger and stronger. It took several weeks, but Gabby was able to access services to address Lucy's challenging behaviors at home. Gabby scheduled an appointment at the house with the facilitator, Roberta, who is also bilingual.

When Roberta first arrived at the house, the door opened and Lucy, partially dressed, ran out the door with Gabby right behind her. Gabby scooped Lucy up and invited Roberta inside. Gabby apologized, struggled with Lucy to get her back into her clothes, and gave Lucy her cell phone so she could "take pictures" with it. Lucy loves to take Gabby's phone to take pictures of anything and everything, and Gabby was hoping her phone would distract Lucy long enough for her and Roberta to meet.

Roberta introduced herself and told Gabby that she has worked with children with challenging behavior for almost 20 years in a variety of contexts, including working with several children with Down syndrome over the years. Roberta asked Gabby to tell her a little bit about Lucy and her concerns, as a way for Roberta to start to get to know their family. Roberta explained that she would be working with Gabby (and whoever else she identified) to create a plan that she would be able to implement to address Lucy's challenging behaviors at home. Given all the details that Gabby provided, Roberta wanted to be able to observe Lucy at school. Gabby signed a consent form for Roberta to contact Lucy's teacher to schedule an observation and talk with her teacher about successful strategies that could be used at home.

Roberta reviewed the PTR-F steps they would follow for creating and implementing a behavior support plan and the coaching process. Roberta asked Gabby if either of her parents would be interested in participating. Gabby really did not want them involved at this point but said she would talk with her mom. Roberta encouraged Gabby to consider having them participate if they were going to be involved in the interventions. Gabby said she would consider it and wanted time to think about it. Roberta also asked about Lucy's teachers, and Gabby said that she would ask them as well but felt bad about it because they already have such a hard job. Roberta said she would talk with the teachers when she visits the school to see if they would like to participate in some way. Roberta asked if there was anyone else to include in this process, including Lucy's dad, but Gabby stated that she does not want that kind of contact with her ex-husband. Also, because she is the one who is raising Lucy, she is the one who needs the help. Roberta assured Gabby that if there were others to include, they could participate at any time in whatever way worked for her.

Roberta reviewed that the next meeting's purpose was to identify goals and develop an easy data collection system, and they scheduled a meeting the following week after school. Roberta asked Gabby to think about specific goals she would like to focus on with Lucy's behavior, because Gabby's initial response was "everything." Roberta provided some examples, including follow directions, sit for a meal, keep her clothes on, and so forth, and suggested that Gabby think about what would be helpful to make the day go more smoothly. Roberta assured Gabby that they would work together to develop a plan to create new routines.

Initiating the PTR-F Process

3

This chapter describes the steps involved in getting ready to implement the assessment and intervention steps of the Prevent-Teach-Reinforce for Families (PTR-F) process. We begin by describing the first connections between the family and the facilitator, the importance of this relationship, and the establishment of a constructive rapport. From there, we discuss the possibility and advantages of adding people to this team and how such a team can function to help the family through the behavior support process. A next step is describing and agreeing upon long- and short-term goals and then carefully defining the challenging behavior that must be reduced. In addition to a challenging behavior, a desirable behavior will also be defined and targeted; however, the desirable target behavior is not selected until after the PTR-F assessment is completed (see Chapter 4), because the assessment information will be important in determining the most efficient desirable behavior to include in the behavior support plan. The final step in this initial phase is figuring out a way to collect data that can be a reliable gauge of progress.

ESTABLISHING RAPPORT AND BUILDING A TEAM

The PTR-F process begins when a family that includes a child with serious challenging behaviors becomes connected with a professional (whom we refer to as a *facilitator*), and the two entities (family and facilitator) agree to use the PTR-F model as a means for resolving the child's challenging behavior and improving the child's overall behavior in the context of family interactions. This connection can be made in many ways, but it almost always begins when a parent (or parents) comes to realize that outside support is needed to help the family deal with a child's challenges. Such a realization may arise when parents are unable to control a child's disruptions; when violent tantrums present risks of injury to the child, siblings, peers, or even parents; or when a child displays a profound resistance to engagement and participation in family routines. Sometimes, a comment from a friend or a teacher might spark a parent's concern. At some point (hopefully before the problem escalates too far in intensity), a parent might actively seek information that can lead to a recommendation or referral for professional assistance.

As we noted in Chapter 1, help can come from a variety of sources, depending on the community and the ways in which child and family services and funding streams are provided. Early intervention services and early care and education offer one alternative. Children's and family mental health agencies are another possibility. Some social workers provide relevant kinds of assistance. Behavior specialists, psychologists, and, in particular, applied behavior analysts are often the professionals with the most relevant training and experience for the PTR-F facilitator role. These professionals may work in publicly funded agencies or in private agencies or practices. As noted previously, an important consideration in selecting a professional (facilitator) is the ability of that professional to provide in-home consultation and facilitation services.

The role of the facilitator can be filled by professionals from a variety of disciplines, but it is important for the facilitator to have certain important skills, experiences, and competencies. The facilitator should be knowledgeable about learning principles, the process of developing and implementing behavior support plans, and the prompting and shaping procedures that are useful in activity-based instruction. It is also vital that the facilitator have experience in working with families and be sensitive to the stress that challenging behavior can produce as well as the difficulties that families can face when attempting to implement behavioral interventions (Dunlap, Newton, Fox, Benito, & Vaughn, 2001; Fox, Vaughn, Dunlap, & Bucy, 1997; Turnbull & Turnbull, 2001). The success of the PTR-F model requires that the family is the focus of the assessment and intervention process and that the family acquires the ability and the confidence needed to implement the PTR-F procedures. The facilitator's role is to facilitate—to guide, encourage, and coach the key family members throughout the process. To facilitate effectively, the facilitator must recognize and respect the family's individuality, help create a context for family-centered participation, and approach the behavior support process from a comprehensive perspective that appreciates the effects that the assessment and intervention strategies can have on the entire family system (Dunlap et al., 2001).

A first meeting between the family and the facilitator should include the following objectives: 1) getting to know one another by sharing information about the facilitator's background and perspectives and the family's situation, structure, and priorities; 2) discussing the priority concerns regarding the child's behavior and the contexts and routines in which the behaviors occur; 3) sharing information about the target child's strengths and interests, as well as information about any siblings and the manner in which the siblings interact; and 4) discussing the important goals, in general, that the family has for the intervention process. An essential part of the first meeting is to review the PTR-F model by going over this manual together and discussing each step so that there is a mutual understanding of what the process entails. There should be a clear agreement by all parties that the process will be followed with every effort to implement each step with fidelity.

 Be sure to establish clear methods of communication during the first meeting and to maintain communication between all team members throughout the PTR-F process.

The PTR-F Team

The PTR-F team consists of the people who are available to support the family in implementing the assessment and intervention process. Support can be provided in multiple forms. First, there are those who actually participate in conducting the assessments and implementing the intervention. In PTR-F, these processes are within the family purview, because the model is designed to address challenging behaviors in the context of family routines in the home and community. Often, both parents are the principal individuals who must implement the PTR-F plan; however, sometimes it may only be one parent. In some cases, other members of the household may be available to participate in implementing the plan. For instance, extended family members, such as grandparents, may be present and actively engaged on a regular basis with family routines. A nanny or other childcare provider may also be centrally involved in the child's daily life. If so, these individuals should be engaged as part of the team.

Others can fill important support roles in the team. For instance, friends can be instrumental in providing social and emotional support for the family. When a child exhibits serious challenging behaviors, it is easy for families to become isolated from a social community, and this isolation can be very difficult when families are attempting to muster the strength and commitment to resolve behavioral challenges. Having people who family members can talk with about the stress and logistical intricacies of dealing with challenging behaviors can be vitally important, and such communication is enhanced greatly when the friend truly understands the particulars of the intervention process. In such cases, close friends can be valuable members of the team.

Finally, teams can be strengthened when other service providers are available to contribute information about the child's behavior and about strategies that might be helpful in developing the PTR-F support plan. The child's teachers or therapists can provide valuable input, and it can be useful for these providers to be aware of the development and progress of the PTR-F process. In addition, service providers can be extremely useful in making sure that the PTR-F process and the PTR-F behavior support plan are consistent with other plans (e.g., individualized education programs [IEPs] and individualized family service plans [IFSPs] and procedures.)

Still, the absolute core of the team is the family and the facilitator. Even if there are no other team members, the partnership of the family and facilitator is fundamental to the PTR-F model. Other potential team members can be extremely valuable throughout the process, but the family–facilitator connection is essential.

 TIP *A crucial element in the PTR-F process is a respectful and responsive relationship between the facilitator and the family.*

Team Processes and Meetings

After the family and facilitator decide who should be on the team, invitations are issued and roles specified. The roles of the family and facilitator are clear from the beginning—the family is responsible for implementing all aspects of the assessment and intervention process, and the facilitator is responsible for doing what is necessary to help the family members fulfill their role. Other team members' roles depend on their availability and the preferences of the family.

It is helpful for the family and facilitator to engage in frequent communication throughout all phases of the process. In addition, it is important to hold face-to-face planning meetings:

1. Meeting 1, as described previously, is when the family and facilitator establish a relationship and initiate the process.

2. Meeting 2 occurs shortly after the first meeting and should include the family, facilitator, and any additional team members that will be involved directly in the assessment and intervention activities. Other team members are encouraged to participate. This meeting is for the purpose of finalizing the definition of the initial target behaviors, establishing a system for collecting and sharing data, and beginning the functional behavioral assessment (FBA).

3. Meeting 3 is scheduled 1–2 weeks following the second meeting and is for the purpose of reviewing the FBA information, building hypothesis statements, and developing a behavior support plan (this last element might require a separate meeting). Data that have been obtained since the previous meeting are reviewed. All team members who will be involved in implementing the intervention should be at this meeting.

4. Meeting 4 is for the purpose of finalizing the behavior support plan and ensuring that all aspects of the intervention have been considered, including needed materials, training, and coaching. Implementation of the plan is expected to be initiated immediately following this meeting. Again, all team members who have an active role in plan implementation must be at this meeting, and other team members are encouraged to participate.

5. Coaching sessions and progress monitoring reviews begin as soon as possible following Meeting 4. These sessions focus on reviewing the ongoing data, determining whether progress is satisfactory or adjustments are needed, and providing coaching for plan implementation (see Chapter 6). The scheduling of these meetings is at

the discretion of the family and facilitator, but it is recommended that they occur frequently enough so that the key team members are always up to date with the details of how the child and family are responding to the plan.

GOAL SETTING

Another extremely important step in initiating the PTR-F process involves discussion and agreement on the family's goals for the child. This includes long- and short-term goals and involves prioritizing specific behaviors to be targeted in the intervention. It can be useful to have multiple team members involved in these discussions, but ultimately it is the family's decisions that must be understood and embraced. The facilitator should guide the discussion and help families articulate their hopes and dreams for their child and for their family as a whole. Other team members can contribute, although such participation should be at the family's discretion.

A first order of business in setting goals is to discuss goals for the child that the family would like to see over the course of 2–5 years into the future. These goals can be quite broad and include domains such as school placements, academic achievement, social and communicative competencies, friendships, independent functioning, and the nature of family dynamics. The facilitator can encourage these discussions with questions such as, "What would you like to see Brad doing in school in 3 years?" "What skills would you like to have Charlie learn before he enters first grade?" or "In an ideal world, what would you expect Larry to be able to do for himself when he is 9 years old?" The idea here is to formulate a vision for the child's development so that the family, facilitator, and other team members have a unified understanding of big-picture goals for the child over a period of several years. It is not necessary to be specific about these goals, but it is valuable to create an optimistic view of the child's developmental trajectory if the child is provided with effective supports.

Goal setting in PTR-F does not linger on this broad and long-term vision, however. Instead, the focus moves quickly to goals and specific target behaviors that can be reasonably achieved in a period of 2–3 months. These short-term goals will focus on the child's challenging behaviors that the family and team would like to decrease and the desirable behaviors that the team would like to increase. Goals can include, but are not limited to, positive sibling relationships, cooperation, participating in family routines, communication, expressing and regulating emotions, and playing agreeably with others. The PTR-F Goal Sheet (see Figure 3.1) described in the following paragraph will help teams identify target behaviors with which to begin the process. The goal sheet considers challenging behaviors to decrease and desirable behaviors to increase. The facilitator guides the family to consider the following questions: 1) What are the most serious challenging behaviors, and in what contexts or routines are the behaviors displayed?; 2) What kinds of desirable behaviors would team members like to see the child exhibit?; and 3) What challenging and desirable behaviors are the highest priorities to target and focus on when creating an intervention plan? These targets must then be defined in operational terms so that the behaviors described are observable (can be seen or heard), measurable (can be counted or timed), and understood completely by everyone involved in the process.

Figure 3.1 presents the PTR-F Goal Sheet, to be completed by the family and facilitator with input from available team members, especially from team members who are part of the household or who are otherwise actively engaged in family activities in the home or community. This form provides space to identify and list challenging behaviors as well as the routines and contexts where these behaviors occur. The team then begins by prioritizing one target behavior to focus on within important family routines or activities and then writes an operational definition for that behavior being targeted (i.e., the behavior is

FORM 1 **PTR-F Goal Sheet**

Instructions:
1. Identify and write out the child's challenging behaviors to decrease and the contexts or routines where these behaviors need to improve.
2. Select ONE challenging behavior to target within family contexts or routines.
3. Operationally define this target behavior—observable (seen or heard) and measurable (counted or timed).
4. Identify and write out the child's desirable behaviors to increase.
5. Select target desirable behavior (to be completed following PTR-F assessment).
6. Operationally define the desirable behavior (to be completed following PTR-F assessment).

Child: _____   Date: _____

Goals: Challenging behaviors		
	Behaviors	*Context/routines*
Challenging behaviors to decrease		
Target behavior		
Operational definition		

Goals: Desirable behaviors		
Desirable behaviors to increase		
Target behavior	(to be completed following PTR-F assessment)	
Operational definition	(to be completed following PTR-F assessment)	

Figure 3.1. PTR-F Goal Sheet.

described in observable or measurable terms). The same steps apply for identifying and prioritizing desirable behaviors on the form, except the target behavior and operational definition are not determined until after the assessment process. The reason for this is that in order to decide what skill or desirable behavior to teach in place of the challenging behavior, it is first important to determine the function of the child's challenging behavior through an FBA. When we understand the function of (reason for) a behavior, we should be able to identify other, more desirable behaviors that could replace the challenging behavior and serve the same function (see Chapter 4). For filled-out examples of initial PTR-F Goal Sheets for Timmy and Lucy, our case example students, see Figures 3.1a and 3.3a in the Appendix to this chapter. The following sections provide an overview of the steps to setting the goals outlined on the goal sheet.

Step 1: Identify Challenging Behaviors to Decrease

To begin, the family describes any and all challenging behaviors that the child exhibits in home and community contexts. Other team members can contribute; however, it is expected that the family knows best about the behaviors that occur and that create problems for the functioning of the family and the completion of regular routines. An effort is made to prioritize the challenging behaviors in terms of their intensity and the impact on family members' lives. Behaviors that are violent or that present physical risks to the child or to others are usually viewed as priorities. In addition to describing the behaviors, the context or routine in which the behaviors occur should be noted. For example, a challenging behavior might be "hitting siblings or parents" and the context might be "when asked to turn off a video game." There might well be several contexts that accompany a challenging behavior. At this point, it is not critical to describe the behavior with any particular terminology, and it is not necessary to identify all of the challenging behaviors that might occur. The idea is to list the most important and most troublesome behaviors along with the situations in which they are most likely to be seen.

Step 2: Select One Challenging Behavior to Target

This step is when the team (primarily the family and facilitator) decides which challenging behavior will be selected as the initial target for the PTR-F process. In some circumstances, there might be several behaviors that the family would want to decrease right away, and that is understandable. In our experience, however, it is much easier to target one behavior at a time in order to increase the likelihood of success for the child as well as the adults who will be implementing the behavior support plan. If the plan is too complicated and has too many behaviors to address, it is likely that difficulties will arise and the effort will be unsuccessful. If there are any behaviors that are a threat to the child's safety or to another's safety (e.g., physical aggression toward self, physical aggression toward others, throwing items, running away), it is vital to begin with these types of behaviors, and in general, these types of behaviors are what the family and others will typically identify as the most important. By targeting one challenging behavior to start with, the team has an opportunity to focus all of its efforts around effectively decreasing or eliminating the target challenging behavior and teaching the child more desirable behaviors. As success is evident with the initial target behavior, then efforts can be directed at additional problems. Chapter 7 provides information about next steps when challenging behaviors have been decreased to a manageable level or have been eliminated.

When we emphasize the importance of selecting one challenging behavior, we should point out that the *one* behavior may actually be a cluster of behaviors that may appear to be different in terms of their form but that actually tend to occur together and tend to serve the same purpose for the child. Some aggressive behaviors may cluster together, and these behaviors may be functionally the same. For example, Erin is a 6-year-old girl who reacts violently when she is asked to do something that she does not like to do. She may scream and hit, kick, or pull hair, but these behaviors are essentially the same because they occur under the same circumstances and appear to serve the same purpose. We can consider this cluster of violent disruption to be one behavior. The different forms (e.g., hitting, kicking) in Erin's case are interchangeable and will be treated the same in the assessment and intervention process.

TIP *Sometimes a group of challenging behaviors has a sequence of escalation. For example, first Mario engages in violent rocking, then he screams, and then he hits. When behaviors have a consistent pattern of escalation or co-occurrence, a team may choose to target the first behavior in the sequence, such as Mario's rocking.*

Step 3: Operationally Define the Target Behavior

The next step is to describe the target behavior in terms that are observable (can be seen and/or heard) and measurable (can be counted or timed). It is important to create these definitions so that whoever observes the behavior can agree that the target behavior is, in fact, occurring; so that interventions are used in the appropriate situations and contexts; and so that the data that will be collected are valid (measure what they are supposed to measure) and reliable (everyone agrees). As a general rule, if a behavior is defined so that it can be observed by more than one person in the same way, then that behavior can also be measured reliably. One way to make sure that definitions are clear is to say them out loud and pretend you are describing the actual behaviors over the phone to someone who cannot see what is happening. If a person who has never seen the child's challenging behavior before can create a mental picture of what you observe, then it is likely that you have a sufficient operational definition. See Table 3.1 for good and poor examples of operational definitions for challenging behaviors.

Step 4: Identify Desirable Behaviors to Increase

Now that a challenging behavior has been identified as an initial target, it is time to turn to desirable behaviors. At this point, in a manner similar to Step 1, the family, facilitator, and other team members identify any and all desirable behaviors that the team would like the child to exhibit to improve his or her ability to adapt to situations, learn, and interact with family members. Some common examples of desirable behaviors include communicating wants and needs verbally or nonverbally, tolerating delays in gratification, taking turns,

Table 3.1. Operational definitions of challenging behavior

Challenging behavior	Poor example of operational definition	Good example of operational definition
Aggression toward others	Hurting others	Kicking, biting peers/adults, pinching, scratching, falling to the floor, and/or picking up and throwing items at peers/adults
Noncompliance/ not following directions	Wants control (manipulates the situation)	When asked or told to do something that she doesn't want to do, she will walk away from the adult or continue to engage in the activity that she was engaged in when the direction was given.
Tantrum and destroying property	Throws a fit when he doesn't get his way	Falls to the floor, kicking his legs and flailing his arms while screaming, "I hate you!" or "That's not fair!" or runs around the room (may scream with or without words), pushes people, throws items, and may tear things off the walls

completing self-care activities independently, and accepting being told "no." It is important to identify behaviors that will help the child be an active participant in daily routines and activities. The facilitator can help the family identify the kinds of desirable behaviors that will be pivotal in improving the child's overall functioning within the social context of family activities.

It is likely that one of the desirable behaviors listed by the team will be selected as the target desirable behavior for the behavior support plan. However, as stated previously, this designation will occur following the completion of the PTR-F assessment, described in Chapter 4.

DATA COLLECTION

After goal setting, a final important step in initiating PTR-F is designing and implementing a clear, simple, and valid system for collecting data. If PTR-F is going to be used, then data must be collected. Obviously, because we are concerned with behaviors that occur in family contexts in home and community settings, the responsibility for collecting data on the child's behavior will belong to the family members who are accompanying the child. We realize that it is not easy for family members to collect data while they are attending to their many other important responsibilities. At the same time, however, it is necessary in the PTR-F model to have some dependable information on an ongoing basis in order to evaluate whether or not progress is occurring and whether some kind of adjustment is necessary. Data collection and the use of data to make decisions are critical elements of the process, as they are with any intervention that is being implemented in an effort to solve a serious concern. PTR-F deals with behaviors that interfere with a child's healthy development, and these behaviors, if left untreated, can have serious and negative consequences for the child's future. Thus, if a challenging behavior is persistent enough or severe enough, then we have to do the best we can to resolve the problem as effectively and efficiently as possible, which requires data collection. The good news is that data collection does not need to be difficult, and in the PTR-F model, it is reasonably simple.

We appreciate that people are often asked to collect data that are effortful, cumbersome, and essentially useless. Data collection in PTR-F is different for two main reasons: 1) the data are easy to collect, and 2) the data are useful as one proceeds through the process. In the remainder of this chapter, we will simplify the process of data collection and describe the specifics of how data collection is implemented in PTR-F.

Important Properties of Data

Before we describe the method of data collection that we recommend, it may be useful to discuss considerations of data collection that are essential if the data are to have value. First, the data must be reasonably *accurate*. That is, the data that are collected should conform closely to what actually happened. For instance, if the data we collect indicate that Billy burst into a violent tantrum on six separate occasions in the afternoon between arriving home from school and bedtime, we must assume that, in fact, that was exactly or at least close to the number of times that Billy actually displayed tantrums. The data would not be helpful if Billy actually engaged in tantrum behavior on 15 or more occasions because the magnitude of such an error would mean that we would not be able to trust the data. Reliability is a second quality that we want to see in our data. What reliability means is that two or more people using the same data collection procedures to observe the same behavior over the same time period would end up with the same result, or at least a very similar result. If Billy's mother recorded six instances of tantrums and Billy's grandfather (who was also home during this time) also recorded six instances, then those data would be considered reliable. If the grandfather recorded seven instances, then the comparison would still be reasonably reliable. But if the grandfather recorded only two instances, then the reliability would be poor, and we would be unable to trust the data. Reasons for such poor reliability could be an inadequate definition of tantrums (perhaps Billy's mother was counting low-magnitude instances that Billy's grandfather ignored as insignificant), or it could be that the grandfather failed to pay attention during some crucial periods when Billy was most volatile. Either way, the problem would have to be identified and corrected before the data could be trusted. This is very important because data that are not trustworthy are not worth collecting.

A third important quality of data is *face validity*, and this simply means that the data being collected actually represent the behavior of greatest interest to the team. In Billy's case, it would be important to make sure that low-magnitude instances of a behavior actually constituted a tantrum, were concerning enough that they warranted intervention, and were a genuine priority. Face validity means that the definition of a behavior used by the team captures exactly what the family and other team members are most interested in improving and measuring.

Behavior Rating Scale

The Behavior Rating Scale (BRS) is the data collection procedure that we recommend for PTR-F. The BRS was described first in the initial PTR textbook (Dunlap et al., 2010). The BRS is a perceptual scale, which means that it relies on observers' perceptions, or estimates, of the magnitude of a behavior during the specified observation period. The BRS has a number of advantages. The chief advantage is that it is completed only once at the end of every observation period, and therefore, it is much less demanding than other data collection strategies that require ongoing data recording. Also, studies have shown that the BRS can be sufficiently accurate and reliable for typical purposes of progress monitoring. Most important, we recommend the BRS for use because it is feasible for typical families.

TIP *If used correctly, the BRS can provide all of the data that are needed to track progress and make informed decisions during PTR-F intervention.*

The BRS can be used to collect data on a child's challenging behavior and on a child's desirable behavior (the use of the BRS for desirable behavior is described in Chapter 4). A separate scale is used for each behavior. The key issue in using the BRS effectively is to spend a little time at the front end to create the individualized scale and to be sure that the data collectors can use it in a manner that is valid and reliable. The steps for developing a BRS for a particular child are as follows:

▲ Step 1: Define target behavior in terms that are observable and that correspond to the goals established by the family and team. The first target behavior to be defined is the challenging behavior. You should use the definition already developed by your team. The second target behavior to be defined is your selected desirable behavior (see Chapter 4). For simplicity, the following description of steps focuses on challenging behavior. The same process should be used to develop a BRS data system for desirable behaviors.

▲ Step 2: Determine the most important dimension of the behavior that should be measured. Dimensions include:

  ▲ *Frequency*, which is the number of times a behavior occurs during the period of observation. For instance, frequency is a good dimension for measuring the number of times during a morning session that Alberto screams (or engages in an episode of screaming).

▲ *Duration*, which is the overall amount of time that the behavior lasts. Duration is a reasonable dimension for behaviors that occur for long periods of time and may include some tantrums or crying episodes.

▲ *Intensity*, which refers to how forceful or loud the behavior is. For example, a highly intense instance of hitting might produce pain or result in injury, but a mildly intense instance of hitting might barely be noticed. Similarly, an ear-piercing scream that breaks windows would be scored as highly intense, but a gentle scream might be more like a squeak and be scored as having low intensity.

▲ *Percentage of time*, which is the percentage of actual time in which the behavior is present over a total observation period. A good example of this dimension is *engagement*, where the behavior of interest is the child's active involvement with appropriate activities.

▲ *Percentage of opportunities*, which refers to how often the behavior occurs in relation to the available opportunities. For instance, if the team is concerned with a child's responsiveness to spoken requests, the measure of interest might be the percentage of verbal requests or questions to which the child makes a response.

Each dimension represents a different way of assessing magnitude, or how much of the behavior is exhibited, but different behaviors are measured best with different dimensions. The dimension is important because it determines how the scale on the BRS will be constructed, so the team must decide which dimension is most important.

▲ Step 3: Determine when the behavior will be observed. In this step, the team decides the time period during which the behavior will be measured. The time could be all day, all morning, or only during specifically targeted routines. This time period should be the one that is most important and is often the time when the problem is most conspicuous.

▲ Step 4: Develop anchors for the rating scale. The BRS is based on a rating scale of 1 to 5. Each number in this rating scale is considered an anchor. These numbers are used to measure behavior. For challenging behavior, the day with the highest magnitude of the behavior would be rated a 5, and the best day would be a 1. For example, consider a 3½-year-old boy named Larry who had a serious problem with hitting family members. The team agreed that Larry's most difficult days were those with 10 or more episodes of hitting. Therefore, a score of 5 on the BRS was recorded if there were 10 or more episodes during the day. An ideal day would be no instances of hitting, so such a day would be scored as a 1. The team then needs to specify anchors for the intermediate instances of hitting. For Larry, the team decided that a score of 4 would mean six to nine instances of hitting, a score of 3 would mean three to five instances, and a score of 2 would mean one or two instances. These anchors are then written on the BRS data sheet.

Anchors are also developed for desirable behaviors (following the PTR-F assessment). For Larry, the team had decided that he should learn how to get family members' attention by tapping them on the shoulder and saying their name. The dimension for measurement was decided to be the percentage of times when it was clear that Larry wanted to interact. Although this is a dimension that might be difficult to determine with great precision, it was agreed that family members could make good enough estimates and that they could agree on general percentages. Therefore, it was decided that a great day would be when Larry used the tapping and naming on 80% or more of opportunities. This level became the anchor point for a score of 5. A day without any instances of Larry using the desired strategy was scored as a 1. Intermediate anchors were defined as follows: 4 = about 51%–79%; 3 = about 21%–50%; and 2 = about 20% or less. Again, it was not expected that observers would calculate precise percentages. The scores represented observers' perceptions of the percentage of opportunities that

Larry used the desired strategy for obtaining others' attention. It is worthwhile to note here that high scores for desirable behavior (e.g., 5) are positive, and the team will wish for a child's behavior to move toward these high scores, whereas high scores for challenging behavior represent difficult days, and the team will wish for challenging behavior ratings to descend in the direction of 1.

▲ Step 5: Determine who will be responsible for recording the BRS score at the end of the observation period each day. This person can be any member of the team who is in a position to make accurate judgments. That is, it is a person who will be in a good position to observe Larry's behavior. The person might be Larry's mother, but it also might be a paid caregiver or an extended family member. From time to time, it is a good idea to have more than one person complete the BRS independently so that the scores can be compared for agreement. This is a good and important strategy for making sure that the BRS is well calibrated. If there are large differences in the scores, then the team should figure out the reasons and provide some correction. It might be that the definition of the behavior needs to be reviewed, or it might be that one of the observers missed some crucial part of the observation. It is important for the team to be alert to possible problems with the accuracy of the data.

▲ Step 6: Determine where the permanent records will be maintained, and establish a system for graphing the data on the PTR-F Behavior Rating Scale (see Figure 3.2). The location where data will be maintained should be in a convenient and central area, such as a kitchen drawer. As soon as the observational period is concluded, the BRS score should be entered directly on the PTR-F Behavior Rating Scale. This form provides a simple template for producing a graph of the scores, showing trends of progress over time. The graph is created by simply connecting the points on the BRS and creating a simple line graph (see Chapter 7).

Once the BRS is developed, the team is ready to begin the process of data collection.

SUMMARY

Initiating PTR-F involves first building a collaborative team, establishing rapport, and forging a connection with families so that the family develops the confidence and skills needed to implement PTR-F procedures independently. The core team in the PTR-F process is the facilitator and the family, but the team can also include other household members, relatives and extended family, friends, teachers, and other service providers who may fulfill a variety of supportive roles for the family, including emotional support, input and advice, and sometimes assistance in implementing the assessment and intervention activities, particularly when these individuals directly participate in the child's care. Once the team is formulated, initial steps entail developing a long-term vision for the child's future and also short-term goals for improvement. These goals involve defining and prioritizing challenging behaviors to decrease and brainstorming positive behaviors to increase. Finally, in the initial stages of the PTR-F process, the team must establish a system of data collection that will be used to monitor the child's progress over time, because collecting data is a necessary and required component of the PTR-F process. The BRS is recommended for PTR-F.

Figure 3.3 provides a self-evaluation checklist for each of the steps involved in initiating PTR-F. It is important that all these initial steps are scored as *yes* before moving to the next phase of the PTR-F process.

Once all of the items on this checklist have been accomplished, the team is ready to develop and implement a behavior support plan that is based on careful assessment. The following chapter, Chapter 4, is a step-by-step guide to completing the FBA, the process of gathering information needed to individualize the behavior support plan for the child and family.

FORM 2 PTR-F Behavior Rating Scale

Child: _____ Rater: _____ Routine: _____ Date/time: _____ Month: _____

Desirable behavior	☐5 ☐4 ☐3 ☐2 ☐1	☐5 ☐4 ☐3 ☐2 ☐1	☐5 ☐4 ☐3 ☐2 ☐1	☐5 ☐4 ☐3 ☐2 ☐1	☐5 ☐4 ☐3 ☐2 ☐1	☐5 ☐4 ☐3 ☐2 ☐1	☐5 ☐4 ☐3 ☐2 ☐1	☐5 ☐4 ☐3 ☐2 ☐1	☐5 ☐4 ☐3 ☐2 ☐1	☐5 ☐4 ☐3 ☐2 ☐1	☐5 ☐4 ☐3 ☐2 ☐1	☐5 ☐4 ☐3 ☐2 ☐1	☐5 ☐4 ☐3 ☐2 ☐1	☐5 ☐4 ☐3 ☐2 ☐1	☐5 ☐4 ☐3 ☐2 ☐1	☐5 ☐4 ☐3 ☐2 ☐1	☐5 ☐4 ☐3 ☐2 ☐1	☐5 ☐4 ☐3 ☐2 ☐1	☐5 ☐4 ☐3 ☐2 ☐1
Challenging behavior	☐5 ☐4 ☐3 ☐2 ☐1	☐5 ☐4 ☐3 ☐2 ☐1	☐5 ☐4 ☐3 ☐2 ☐1	☐5 ☐4 ☐3 ☐2 ☐1	☐5 ☐4 ☐3 ☐2 ☐1	☐5 ☐4 ☐3 ☐2 ☐1	☐5 ☐4 ☐3 ☐2 ☐1	☐5 ☐4 ☐3 ☐2 ☐1	☐5 ☐4 ☐3 ☐2 ☐1	☐5 ☐4 ☐3 ☐2 ☐1	☐5 ☐4 ☐3 ☐2 ☐1	☐5 ☐4 ☐3 ☐2 ☐1	☐5 ☐4 ☐3 ☐2 ☐1	☐5 ☐4 ☐3 ☐2 ☐1	☐5 ☐4 ☐3 ☐2 ☐1	☐5 ☐4 ☐3 ☐2 ☐1	☐5 ☐4 ☐3 ☐2 ☐1	☐5 ☐4 ☐3 ☐2 ☐1	☐5 ☐4 ☐3 ☐2 ☐1

Desirable behavior: _____

5 = _____
4 = _____
3 = _____
2 = _____
1 = _____

Challenging behavior: _____

5 = _____
4 = _____
3 = _____
2 = _____
1 = _____

Figure 3.2. PTR-F Behavior Rating Scale.

FORM 3

Self-Evaluation Checklist:
Initiating the PTR-F Process

		YES	NO
1.	Have the family and facilitator established good communication and agreed to adopt the PTR-F model?	❏	❏
2.	Have the family and facilitator agreed on additional team members and invited them to participate?	❏	❏
3.	Have long-term goals been discussed as a vision for the child and family?	❏	❏
4.	Have short-term goals for challenging behaviors and desirable behaviors been listed on the PTR-F Goal Sheet?	❏	❏
5.	Has a specific challenging behavior been identified as a target, and has it been operationally defined?	❏	❏
6.	Have anchors for challenging behavior on the Behavior Rating Scale (BRS) been carefully specified so that data collection will be reliable and sensitive to behavior change?	❏	❏
7.	Have the procedures of BRS data collection (e.g., who, when) and data summary been agreed upon?	❏	❏
8.	Have the data collection procedures been implemented so that all are comfortable with their roles and how data will be shared?	❏	❏

Figure 3.3.   Self-Evaluation Checklist: Initiating the PTR-F Process.

APPENDIX
Case Examples

TEAM MEETING 1: TIMMY

Initiating The Process

Kaci, the Prevent-Teach-Reinforce for Families (PTR-F) facilitator, arrived for the scheduled meeting at Jodie and Phil's home. She asked how their last week went, which was exhausting. They shared that at first, they thought Timmy's tantrums seemed to be getting better, but then the last few days had been the worst days they have had. They were anxious to get strategies put into place as soon as possible, especially because they received another noise complaint from one of the neighbors and they are afraid that they might get kicked out of the complex if they don't get a handle on Timmy's tantrums right away.

Kaci asked if they could think of a reason for why Timmy's tantrums were worse over the last few days, and they couldn't really identify any specific reasons for this increase in the intensity of the tantrums. Phil was really at his wit's end and was dreading getting Timmy ready for bed that night. Kaci listened to Phil's exasperation and validated his feelings of frustration and anger about Timmy's tantrums; she expressed that she completely understood their concern, that they would be beginning the process of developing a behavior support plan, and that she wished that she could make things easier for tonight.

Kaci talked with Jodie and Phil to identify a plan for managing Timmy's tantrums for tonight, and possibly the next week, if his tantrums continued to be as intense as they had been over the past few nights. Jodie suggested that, instead of both her and Phil putting both the kids to bed, she would get Timmy ready for bed until a plan was developed and ready to implement. She felt that she would be able to tolerate the tantrums a little better and could calm Timmy down more easily than Phil could. Phil would take care of Dakota for those nights, and they agreed to do bedtime separately for now. Once this problem-solving process occurred and Phil and Jodie had a plan for the current concerns, Kaci started the PTR-F process. She asked if they had identified anyone else to participate in this process.

Jodie shared that she talked with Timmy's teacher, Ms. Ronda, who is willing to participate or share information if that is helpful to the process. After some discussion, Kaci recommended that they include Ms. Ronda by asking for her input about Timmy's behaviors at school and that they should share with her the plan they developed to implement at home. Kaci asked if they thought anyone else should be involved in this process, and although both of the grandmothers watch the boys somewhat regularly, Timmy did not have tantrums that often with either of the grandmothers. Jodie and Phil agreed that if the grandmothers had concerns, they would be able to share any of the strategies that they implemented through this process. The grandmothers also offered to help watch the kids during the parents' meetings with Kaci, if that was needed.

PTR-F Goal Sheet

To start the process, Kaci provided Jodie and Phil with a copy of the PTR-F Goal Sheet to look at while they identified goals. Kaci had taken notes about Jodie and Phil's concerns at the initial meeting and reminded them that one of the goals for that day would be to identify a challenging behavior to target for the PTR-F process. Kaci briefly reviewed the steps again and explained that identifying a target challenging behavior would be the first step toward getting a behavior support plan in place.

As Jodie and Phil began talking about Timmy's challenging behaviors, Kaci recorded them on the PTR-F Goal Sheet. Once the most problematic behaviors were recorded, Jodie and Phil began discussing other challenging behaviors. Kaci reminded them that they did not need to list *every* challenging behavior, just the ones that were the most problematic. Kaci clarified that they would like a behavior support plan to target Timmy's tantrum behavior, especially at bedtime. When this was clarified, Kaci asked Jodie and Phil to describe Timmy's tantrums in order to develop an operational definition. Kaci recorded the operational definition on the PTR-F Goal Sheet.

Since Jodie and Phil already identified bedtime as the most problematic routine, Kaci asked if there were other times of the day or other daily routines that were problematic. Timmy's parents indicated that diapering and bath time are consistently a problem but that those tantrums are not as significant or intense as the ones that occur at bedtime. The tantrums that occur in the later evening seem to be the most related to the noise complaints they have been receiving from their neighbors. Jodie and Phil shared that they have been discussing the bedtime issue and that they think it might be related to moving Timmy into the toddler bed a couple of months ago. They didn't realize it at first, because for over a month he did just fine moving into the toddler bed, but the tantrums at bedtime might be related to Timmy being able to get out of bed on his own. Kaci noted that being able to get out of bed on his own might be a factor contributing to his tantrums, and they would be addressing that possibility at the next meeting. (See Figure 3.1a for Timmy's completed PTR-F Goal Sheet.)

Kaci talked with Jodie and Phil about what longer term goals they had for Timmy, looking at the next several years. They said that their primary concern is to make sure Timmy's behaviors do not get worse, especially at childcare. They want him to be ready to go to school (specifically kindergarten) and for him to be able to get through the day without a major tantrum. They also want to make sure that Dakota does not end up copying his brother and start exhibiting tantrums as well. Kaci asked additional questions to specify what skills Jodie and Phil would like to see Timmy exhibit in the next few years.

After some clarifying questions, Jodie and Phil stated that they would like to see Timmy be able to go to sleep on his own (at least stay in his room), complete daily routines calmly, speak more clearly, be able to express himself appropriately and calmly, learn how to handle or accept when he can't have something that he wants, be able to get along with his brother and/or friends, listen to directions from mom and dad, and overall, meet developmental milestones. Although the PTR-F process would not be addressing all these skills directly, Kaci shared that it is important to recognize long-term goals and use those to guide the short-term goals for this process. The goals developed for the PTR-F behavior support plan would be one small step toward reaching the longer term goals Jodie and Phil identified.

PTR-F Behavior Rating Scale

Kaci then introduced the Behavior Rating Scale (BRS) and explained that this is the form that they will be using to collect data. After describing the different dimensions of measuring behaviors, Kaci talked with Jodie and Phil about what dimension of behavior they wanted to keep track of with Timmy. They contemplated rating the intensity of the tantrums, but that could vary quite a bit during the day or across days. They ultimately decided on keeping track of an approximate number of minutes per day that Timmy was having a tantrum. Jodie and Phil thought this might be the most helpful for them in terms of gauging how much tantrum behavior was occurring every day.

Kaci asked about how many minutes, on average, tantrums currently occur on a daily basis. After talking about it, Jodie and Phil agreed that tantrums could occur for a total of anywhere from 20 to 30 minutes in a typical day. Sometimes, tantrums could be close to an hour in total, but most days, the behavior did not exceed 30 minutes. The team agreed that a score of 5 on the BRS would be for tantrum behaviors lasting 30 minutes or longer, and they scaled the rest of the anchors to correspond to how a typical day goes (see Figure 3.2a). Jodie and Phil agreed that they would keep the BRS on the refrigerator, and they would both agree on a rating after they put the boys to bed and were getting lunches ready for the next day.

FORM 1 **PTR-F Goal Sheet**

Instructions:
1. Identify and write out the child's challenging behaviors to decrease and the contexts or routines where these behaviors need to improve.
2. Select ONE challenging behavior to target within family contexts or routines.
3. Operationally define this target behavior—observable (seen or heard) and measurable (counted or timed).
4. Identify and write out the child's desirable behaviors to increase.
5. Select target desirable behavior (to be completed following PTR-F assessment).
6. Operationally define the desirable behavior (to be completed following PTR-F assessment).

Child: Timmy _____   Date: 6/25/15 _____

Goals: Challenging behaviors		
	Behaviors	*Context/routines*
Challenging behaviors to decrease	"Fits" (tantrums)—especially high-pitched screaming, rolling around on the floor, kicking his legs Hitting mom and dad Throwing toys Saying/yelling "no" Running away/hiding	Diapering Bath time Bedtime
Target behavior	Fits/tantrums	Bedtime
Operational definition	Timmy emits a high-pitched scream (often for several seconds) and usually rolls around on the floor and kicks his legs; if someone is near, he may hit or kick whoever is close. He sometimes screams "NO!" during these episodes.	

Goals: Desirable behaviors		
Desirable behaviors to increase	Go to sleep on his own (at least stay in room) Complete routines—calm, agreeable Speak more clearly Express himself appropriately and calmly Accept when he can't have something Get along/play with brother, friends Listen to Mom and Dad Do what other boys his age do—age-appropriate development	
Target behavior	(to be completed following PTR-F assessment)	
Operational definition	(to be completed following PTR-F assessment)	

Figure 3.1a. Timmy's PTR-F Goal Sheet.

FORM 2

PTR-F Behavior Rating Scale

Child: Timmy   Rater: Mom and Dad   Routine: Bedtime   Month: July

Date/time:

Desirable behavior	☐5 ☐4 ☐3 ☐2 ☐1 (repeated across columns)
Challenging behavior / Tantrums	☐5 ☐4 ☐3 ☐2 ☐1 (repeated across columns)

Challenging behavior: Tantrums - number of minutes

5 = 30 minutes or more

4 = 20-30 minutes

3 = 10-20 minutes

2 = 5-10 minutes

1 = less than 5 minutes

Desirable behavior:

5 = _____

4 = _____

3 = _____

2 = _____

1 = _____

Figure 3.2a. Timmy's PTR-F Behavior Rating Scale.

The team then briefly discussed some general parenting practices that could be implemented with Timmy, specifically establishing routines and the 5:1 ratio of positive to negative or neutral statements. After briefly discussing the bedtime routine, it was clear that a routine was developed and had been in place up until very recently Jodie and Phil agreed that the bedtime routine had been disrupted because of Timmy's tantrums but felt that they would most likely continue to follow the same routine they have been using since shortly after Dakota was born.

When it came to the 5:1 ratio discussion, Jodie and Phil readily admitted that they could provide more positive feedback to their boys, especially during diapering and bedtime, but that it is difficult to do that when they are concerned about getting through those routines without a struggle. Kaci acknowledged their feelings and validated that implementing this practice can be difficult, especially at first. However, she assured them that the more they provide positive praise, the easier it will be, and that they could support each other in this practice by reminding each other and stepping in to provide positive feedback when possible without being judgmental or condescending to each other about it. They both agreed that they would try to implement this in the next week and would work on supporting each other in this new way of interacting with the boys. Kaci had Jodie and Phil identify a few daily scenarios where they could practice providing positive feedback to the boys.

Self-Evaluation Checklist

As Kaci wrapped up the meeting, she talked about the next steps and introduced the following three checklists that would be essential in completing the PTR-F assessment process, or functional behavioral assessment: the PTR-F Assessment Checklist: Prevent, the PTR-F Assessment Checklist: Teach, and the PTR-F Assessment Checklist: Reinforce (see Chapter 4). Kaci asked Jodie and Phil to each fill out a checklist separately in preparation for their meeting next week, where they would identify the function and purpose of Timmy's tantrums at bedtime. Kaci explained that, if possible, it would be best for them to each fill out the checklists individually to compare their perceptions about Timmy's tantrums. She reminded them to fill out the checklists only based on Timmy's tantrums during bedtime. Kaci then reviewed the Self-Evaluation Checklist: Initiating the PTR-F Process with Jodie and Phil to ensure that they completed all the steps for their initial meeting.

Kaci ended the meeting by encouraging Jodie and Phil to continue with the PTR-F process, assuring them that these steps are important to developing a plan that can address Timmy's tantrums as quickly and effectively as possible. Kaci again acknowledged Phil's frustration with Timmy's tantrums and said that next week they would begin identifying strategies to implement. Phil was somewhat relieved but still anxious about bedtime for this next week.

TEAM MEETING 1: LUCY

Initiating the Process

Roberta arrived at the house for their scheduled visit to identify goals and develop the BRS. Gabby told Roberta that she had not really spent much time thinking of specific goals for Lucy, as the past week was pretty hectic. Roberta let Gabby know that she was able to contact Lucy's teacher, Mrs. Williams, and was scheduled to observe Lucy at school later in the week. Mrs. Williams also said that she would be more than willing to participate in this process and provide any information if needed. Because this participation was up to Gabby, Roberta told Mrs. Williams that she would let Gabby know and then she could decide how she wants to proceed from there.

Roberta asked how the past week had gone with Lucy, especially given that this past week was "hectic." Gabby shared that the week had been full of personal issues with her ex-husband and that she had been distracted by trying to get things taken care of while Lucy was in school, which wasn't for very long during the day. Gabby described things with Lucy as "pretty much the same" and was not sure where to even begin. Gabby shared that Lucy seemed to be more demanding of her time this past week, as Lucy has been wanting Gabby to be with her or to watch almost everything that she has been doing, and that makes it hard for Gabby to get anything done around the house when Lucy is home.

Roberta asked Gabby to think about what she envisions for Lucy in the next 3–5 years and what goals she has for Lucy in the near future. Gabby said she wasn't sure; she told Roberta that it was hard to think that far ahead into the future amid all the current turmoil, but that she wants Lucy to continue to make progress. Roberta asked her about what kind of progress she wants Lucy to make, and after some additional clarifying questions, Gabby replied that she wants Lucy to grow up to be happy, to have friends, to do well in school, to be able to express herself, to obey adults, to be able to learn and not get in trouble, and to get along with her cousins and family. Roberta noted these future goals that Gabby identified and explained that being aware of this long-term vision would help with identifying short-term goals to support the future goals. Roberta told Gabby that they would start talking about more immediate goals for Lucy, thinking about the next few months.

PTR-F Goal Sheet

Roberta gave a blank copy of the PTR-F Goal Sheet to Gabby to refer to, and asked Gabby what her concerns were with Lucy's behaviors, even though she had mentioned several during their previous meeting. Roberta had noted the list of behaviors that Gabby identified the previous week and had them to refer to, but wanted Gabby to identify which of Lucy's behaviors were the most problematic. Gabby listed behaviors that were troublesome, and Roberta recorded Gabby's answers on the goal sheet. Roberta asked Gabby which behavior would be the most important or the most helpful to decrease or eliminate. Although she felt that they were all important to address, Gabby stated that she wants the most help with hitting because Lucy will often hit Gabby in the face, which she said really pushes her buttons. Roberta asked more clarifying questions, and it seemed that more often than not, when Lucy was upset, she got physically aggressive, and that was when Gabby became the most frustrated with Lucy. It was clear to Roberta that Lucy's aggressive behaviors seemed to typically occur in similar circumstances, so Roberta talked with Gabby about thinking about those aggressive behaviors as a group or cluster of behaviors that they could target for this process. Gabby felt much more comfortable being able to address all of the aggressive behaviors together, because decreasing all of them was important to her.

Roberta then asked Gabby to identify the times of day or routines when the aggression was most likely to occur. Gabby essentially listed every daily routine as potentially problematic depending on the day, with some days being harder than others. Roberta asked if there were one or two particular routines that were more difficult than others, or if there were one or two routines that would be the most helpful to focus on. Gabby could not really identify any routines that were more important than others, except for getting ready for school because they were often late or in a hurry to get there. Roberta talked with Gabby about establishing some clearly identified routines for the day and then teaching Lucy the expectations for those routines. This began the discussion about desired behaviors to increase.

Gabby shared that they had had pretty good daily routines before, even though Lucy wasn't that happy with following them, but at least she wasn't resisting as much as she does now. Gabby admitted that, in the last year, there hasn't been much consistency and that the daily routines were rushed and forced on Lucy inconsistently because of all of the other chaotic things happening between Gabby and Lucy's dad.

Roberta then turned to brainstorming desirable behaviors that were goals for Lucy, asking Gabby what other things she would like to see Lucy do in the next few months. Gabby identified some short-term positive behaviors that she would like Lucy to learn, which Roberta recorded on the goal sheet. Roberta wanted to clarify whether there was a particular routine that would be the most helpful to focus on initially, which was difficult to pinpoint. Gabby stated that getting ready in the morning would be the most helpful on school days, but that every routine was difficult in some way. Also, meals were identified as particularly challenging because they occur multiple times during the day. Gabby stated that she really would like strategies to help with multiple routines throughout the whole day. Roberta assured Gabby that they would develop a plan that would meet her needs and moved on to the BRS. (See Figure 3.3a for Lucy's completed PTR-F Goal Sheet.)

PTR-F Behavior Rating Scale

Roberta gave a copy of a blank BRS to Gabby and explained how the form is used and that they would be setting the anchors for the rating scale in order to collect easy but relevant data. After explaining the different ways behavior could be measured, Roberta asked Gabby what kind of data would be easy and meaningful to collect for Lucy's aggressive behaviors. After some consideration and discussion about how to measure Lucy's behaviors, Gabby decided that measuring frequency would probably be the easiest and most helpful at this time.

Next, Roberta asked Gabby to estimate how often Lucy currently engages in physically aggressive behaviors, on average, throughout a typical day. Gabby was having a hard time trying to estimate, so Roberta talked Gabby through the routines of a typical day to help her count and estimate the number of incidents of physically aggressive behavior that tend to occur. It was easy to identify at least eight incidents in a day, so they agreed that a score of 5 on the BRS would be eight or more incidents in a day, and then they set the rest of the anchors accordingly (see Figure 3.4a for the completed scale). Once the anchors were set, Roberta talked with Gabby about the rest of the details of data collection, including how she would be able to keep track of the incidents throughout the day and when she would record Lucy's rating. Gabby stated that she would be able to record the data once Lucy fell asleep and was trying to think of a good place to keep the data sheet. After some consideration, Gabby decided to keep the data sheet by her bed so she could fill it out once her day was complete. Gabby was certain that she would be able to remember, at least close enough, how many times Lucy was physically aggressive throughout the day.

Self-Evaluation Checklist

When the plan for data collection was solidified, Roberta explained that they would be completing the PTR-F assessment checklists at the next meeting to identify the function or purpose of Lucy's physically aggressive behavior. The meeting was scheduled for the following week when Lucy was in school so that Gabby could devote her full attention and perhaps they wouldn't be interrupted as much. As they were wrapping up, Marguerite entered the room. Gabby showed Marguerite the data collection form, explained how it would be used, and described how it would track Lucy's progress. Marguerite seemed interested and wanted to be able to sit with Gabby to look at it in more detail at a later time, as she was currently getting Hector something to eat.

Roberta reviewed the Self-Evaluation Checklist: Initiating the PTR-F Process with Gabby to ensure that they completed all the steps for their meeting and could continue with the process. Roberta reminded Gabby that she would be observing Lucy at school and would be talking with Lucy's teacher, Mrs. Williams, to get her input and perspective about Lucy's physically aggressive behavior. As Roberta was leaving, she reminded Gabby to collect data every day, and Gabby said that she would set an alarm on her phone to help her remember.

FORM 1 PTR-F Goal Sheet

Instructions:
1. Identify and write out the child's challenging behaviors to decrease and the contexts or routines where these behaviors need to improve.
2. Select ONE challenging behavior to target within family contexts or routines.
3. Operationally define this target behavior—observable (seen or heard) and measurable (counted or timed).
4. Identify and write out the child's desirable behaviors to increase.
5. Select target desirable behavior (to be completed following PTR-F assessment).
6. Operationally define the desirable behavior (to be completed following PTR-F assessment).

Child: Lucy   **Date:** 7/29/15

Goals: Challenging behaviors		
	Behaviors	*Context/routines*
Challenging behaviors to decrease	Hitting Kicking Biting Scratching Taking her clothes off Running away/hiding Screaming/yelling	Getting dressed Meals—grazes, likes snacking Toileting Going to school Ending preferred activities Bedtime
Target behavior	Physically aggressive behaviors	Getting ready for the day Meals
Operational definition	When Lucy is physically aggressive, she may hit, slap, kick, bite, scratch, pull on clothes/hair, scream/yell, or try to take her clothes off.	

Goals: Desirable behaviors	
Desirable behaviors to increase	Follow daily routines calmly (without resisting) Follow directions—listen to mom Eat at the table Eat a more complete meal Say more words—communicate better Play more independently Play with toys appropriately (vs. throwing, breaking)
Target behavior	(to be completed following PTR-F assessment)
Operational definition	(to be completed following PTR-F assessment)

Figure 3.3a. Lucy's PTR-F Goal Sheet.

FORM 2

PTR-F Behavior Rating Scale

Child: Lucy   Rater: Mom   Routine: Throughout the day   Month: August

Date/time:

Desirable behavior	5 4 3 2 1	5 4 3 2 1	5 4 3 2 1	5 4 3 2 1	5 4 3 2 1	5 4 3 2 1	5 4 3 2 1	5 4 3 2 1	5 4 3 2 1	5 4 3 2 1	5 4 3 2 1	5 4 3 2 1	5 4 3 2 1	5 4 3 2 1	5 4 3 2 1	5 4 3 2 1	5 4 3 2 1	5 4 3 2 1	5 4 3 2 1
Challenging behavior / Aggressive behaviors	5 4 3 2 1	5 4 3 2 1	5 4 3 2 1	5 4 3 2 1	5 4 3 2 1	5 4 3 2 1	5 4 3 2 1	5 4 3 2 1	5 4 3 2 1	5 4 3 2 1	5 4 3 2 1	5 4 3 2 1	5 4 3 2 1	5 4 3 2 1	5 4 3 2 1	5 4 3 2 1	5 4 3 2 1	5 4 3 2 1	5 4 3 2 1

Challenging behavior: _Aggressive behaviors_

5 = 8 or more times
4 = 6-7 times
3 = 3-5 times
2 = 1-2 times
1 = 0

Desirable behavior: _____

5 =
4 =
3 =
2 =
1 =

Figure 3.4a. Lucy's PTR-F Behavior Rating Scale.

PTR-F Assessment (Functional Behavioral Assessment)

Chapters 4 and 5 describe the preparation for developing an individualized, assessment-based intervention, the Prevent-Teach-Reinforce for Families (PTR-F) behavior support plan. This chapter focuses on assessment. The general purpose of assessment is to understand a child's challenging behaviors in order to develop and implement an intervention that will be optimally effective; sensitive to the individual child's characteristics, parents, and home contexts; and as efficient as possible. The majority of this chapter addresses specific steps for conducting a functional behavioral assessment (FBA), or a PTR-F assessment. The information gathered through the PTR-F assessment process will help your team to understand the purpose or function of the child's challenging behavior. The PTR-F assessment will also help teams identify and understand the antecedent and environmental conditions that precede challenging and desirable behavior, as well as the consequences that may be maintaining these behaviors. This understanding is summarized in what we call *hypothesis statements*, which are simple ways of describing how the behavior is influenced by the environment. These statements then lead directly to the child's individualized behavior support plan. The information and guidance on assessment and intervention provided in this chapter are grounded strongly in scientific knowledge, as is the PTR-F model as a whole (see Chapter 1 for more on the conceptual and empirical foundations of PTR-F). For readers who are interested in learning more about research-based learning and behavioral principles underlying the steps of FBA and intervention, we recommend texts in the areas of learning theory, applied behavior analysis, and positive behavior support (e.g., Bambara & Kern, 2005; Cooper et al., 2007).

PTR-F ASSESSMENT

This section of the chapter provides the background and describes the steps for completing the PTR-F assessment process. In many ways, the PTR-F assessment is the heart of the PTR-F process because it results in an understanding of how the challenging behavior is influenced by the environment and then provides guidance for the development of the behavior support plan.

The field is replete with manuals, articles, and books that spell out procedures and offer forms for completing an FBA (e.g., Iwata, DeLeon, & Roscoe, 2013; O'Neill et al., 1997; Umbreit, Ferro, Liaupsin, & Lane, 2007). Many of these are excellent resources, offering strategies that we readily endorse. However, many of them are also complicated and require dedicated observations that can involve more resources than what are available to home visitors and families. Our strategy is different in that it depends solely on familiarity with the child's behavior that team members have accumulated over weeks or months of observing the child's behavior in many contexts. Although our process may be somewhat less precise than more effortful procedures, we believe (and our experience indicates) that the strategies we present are more practical and quite sufficient for the vast majority of young children with challenging behaviors.

The PTR-F assessment process involves three checklists that are completed by all team members, including any outside professionals who may be involved with the child. The checklists pertain to the three components of the model: prevent, teach, and reinforce. The questions on the checklists are designed to help complete the following major objectives: 1) identify the antecedents and environmental influences that are associated with (and trigger) challenging behavior (prevent); 2) identify skills that can be taught to the child to replace the challenging behavior and make it unlikely to occur (teach); and 3) determine the function or purpose of the challenging behavior and identify the events, items, people, and activities that serve as reinforcers for the child's challenging behavior (and desirable behavior) (reinforce).

To begin, we will describe the three components of the PTR-F assessment process (i.e., prevent, teach, reinforce) and the three checklists that correspond to these components. We will then describe how the checklists are completed, how they are summarized, and how the summarized information is presented in hypothesis statements. Be sure to refer to the case examples at the end of this chapter for completed examples of the PTR checklists and a thorough walkthrough of the PTR-F assessment process for Timmy and Lucy.

Prevent

The first component of the PTR-F assessment is *prevent*. Prevent refers to antecedent events and circumstances that precede challenging behaviors. Once these have been identified, it should be possible to make changes in those events and circumstances so that challenging behavior will no longer occur (e.g., Dunlap et al., 1991; Ervin et al., 2000; Luiselli, 2006). Antecedents are firmly entrenched in the science of learning and behavior and have documented, practical implications for improving behavior. Two categories of antecedent events are of concern: 1) those that make the challenging behavior more likely to occur and 2) those that make desirable behavior more likely to occur (or, put another way, those that make the challenging behavior least likely to occur). The prevent component involves identifying what those antecedent events are for a particular child's behavior (which is the subject of the current chapter) and then changing those events so that challenging behavior is less likely and desirable behavior is more likely (the intervention step of the PTR-F process involves changing the events and is the subject of Chapter 5).

As mentioned previously, relevant antecedent variables can include a broad array of events that occur in the environment and that somehow affect the child's likelihood of engaging in a particular behavior. For example, some events may serve as triggers. These are usually discrete events or stimuli that occur just before the challenging behavior and may seem to set off the behavior or to cause the behavior to occur. Common triggers are parents' requests to perform a task or to transition from a preferred activity. Other triggers can be when a sibling interferes with a play activity or when somebody says "No." Although there are some events that are common triggers, it is important to appreciate that triggers are idiosyncratic and that every challenging behavior has its own triggers that are individually developed over time. It is also important to remember that triggers do not necessarily always work the same way. If a child is in a good mood, is well rested, and feels happy, then triggers that had previously set off a challenging behavior might be inactive. This brings us to another type of antecedent event.

The second type of antecedent variable is referred to as a setting event. Setting events do not act as immediate triggers but instead tend to make triggers more likely to set off a challenging behavior. Setting events are conditions that are separate from the challenging behavior in time and space but nevertheless have effects on the child. For instance, common setting events are physiological circumstances such as illness, pain, exhaustion, and hunger. If a child experiences any of these conditions, it is understandable that a trigger would be more likely to lead to problems than if the child is in a good place physiologically and emotionally. For instance, if 4-year-old Mia did not sleep well the previous night, she might be more likely to engage in a tantrum when asked to turn off the movie she is watching on a tablet. Similarly, if Roberto is upset because his older brother and mother were arguing during breakfast, his distress could increase the chance that his challenging behaviors will occur. Like triggers, setting events are individualized phenomena, but they do not cause behavior in the same way that triggers do. Nevertheless, they are important circumstances to consider in the assessment and intervention steps of the prevent component.

The PTR-F Assessment Checklist: Prevent (see Figure 4.1) is intended to help identify the antecedent conditions that influence both challenging behavior and desirable behaviors. The Prevent checklist (along with the Teach and Reinforce checklists) should be completed by the team and summarized in a group team meeting. Each of the three checklists (i.e., Prevent, Teach, Reinforce) is filled out, and then the PTR-F Assessment Summary Table is completed to synthesize the information obtained from the three checklists. The specifics of these steps are described later in the chapter.

Teach

One of the core strategies of an intervention plan is teaching a skill (or multiple skills) to the child that will make challenging behavior unnecessary and much less likely to occur. To determine what skills to teach, it is important to consider the function of the behavior. The function of a behavior, or purpose that the behavior serves, relates to the results and effects the behavior has on the immediate environment. Therefore, it is important to teach desirable behaviors that act on the environment in the same way that challenging behaviors do and that can be said to serve the same function. For example, a child can learn desirable behaviors in order to get something, such as attention or a toy. Children can also learn desirable behaviors that can be used to get rid of something, such as a nonpreferred activity.

Recall from Chapter 1 that behaviors usually are communicative. Thus, communication is the primary type of desirable behavior that acts on the environment in the same way as challenging behavior. The best type of behavior for us to teach as a central part of an intervention plan is a specific communicative behavior that will actually serve as a *replacement* for the challenging behavior. In selecting specific replacement behaviors and in preparing to move toward developing the intervention plan, it is important to keep in mind that the desirable behavior must meet two criteria: 1) it must be as efficient at gaining reinforcement as the challenging behavior, and 2) it must be met with the same consistency of reinforcement as the challenging behavior. That is, the desirable behavior cannot take more time or more effort than the challenging behavior, and it must serve the same function and lead to reinforcement as easily and predictably. The desirable behavior must also be reinforced at the same rate and amount as the challenging behavior. For example, if a child is able to avoid an activity for 20 minutes through tantrum behavior, the team cannot, in the beginning, teach a skill that only leads to a 2-minute break from the activity. Later in the behavior support process, the team can teach more complex skills and have less time available for a break, but team members cannot assume that a child will be able to do this when they first start implementing the PTR-F behavior support plan. Along these lines, we also suggest that, initially, skills that are already in the child's skill repertoire be taught. This will help to ensure that the desirable behavior meets the two criteria mentioned previously.

The purpose of the PTR-F Assessment Checklist: Teach (see Figure 4.2) is to help teams identify skills that can be taught to children through the PTR-F behavior support plan that will replace the challenging behaviors and serve the same function. The team can check off those communication, social, and problem-solving skills that might most benefit the child and reduce challenging behavior, with space to brainstorm other skills or options. However, before team members know exactly what they should be teaching, they first need to understand the function of the child's challenging behavior, and the final assessment checklist (i.e., the Reinforce checklist) is instrumental in this process.

FORM 4

PTR-F Assessment Checklist: Prevent

Challenging behavior: _____   Person responding: _____   Child: _____

1. Are there times of the day when challenging behavior is most likely to occur?
   If yes, what are they?

| ____ Waking up | ____ Before meals | ____ During meals | ____ After meals | ____ Preparing meals |
| ____ Morning | ____ Afternoon | ____ Nap time | ____ Evening | ____ Bedtime |

Other: _____

2. Are there specific activities when challenging behavior is very likely to occur?
   If yes, what are they?

____ Leaving home	____ Nap time	____ Interactions with sibling/child	____ Taking medicine
____ Arriving home	____ Toileting/diapering	____ Indoor play	____ Medical procedure
____ Family celebrations	____ Bathing	____ Outdoor play	____ At doctor or therapist
____ Church/religious activities	____ Toothbrushing	____ Meals	____ At dentist
____ Looking at books	____ Play group/classes	____ In the car/bus	____ Children's attractions (e.g., zoo)
____ Watching television/ device	____ Eating out	____ At a store	____ Transitions (specify):
____ Special event (specify): ____	____ Visiting others	____ Park/playground	_____
	____ Snack		

Other: _____

3. Are there other children or adults whose proximity is associated with a high likelihood of challenging behavior? If so, who are they?

____ Siblings	Specify: _____	____ Parent
____ Family member(s)	Specify: _____	____ Other children
____ Care provider(s)	Specify: _____	(specify): _____
____ Other adults	Specify: _____	

Other: _____

(continued)

Figure 4.1. PTR-F Assessment Checklist: Prevent.

Figure 4.1. *(continued)*

FORM 4 **PTR-F Assessment Checklist: Prevent** *(continued)*

---

4. Are there times of the day when challenging behavior is least likely to occur?
    If yes, what are they?

____ Waking up	____ Before meals	____ During meals	____ After meals	____ Preparing meals
____ Morning	____ Afternoon	____ Nap time	____ Evening	____ Bedtime

Other: _____

---

5. Are there specific activities when challenging behavior is least likely to occur?
    What are they?

____ Leaving home	____ Nap time	____ Interactions with sibling/child	____ Taking medicine
____ Arriving home	____ Toileting/diapering	____ Indoor play	____ Medical procedure
____ Family celebrations	____ Bathing	____ Outdoor play	____ At doctor or therapist
____ Church/religious activities	____ Toothbrushing	____ Meals	____ At dentist
____ Looking at books	____ Play group/classes	____ In the car/bus	____ Children's attractions (e.g., zoo)
____ Watching television/device	____ Eating out	____ At a store	____ Transitions (specify): _____
____ Special event (specify): _____	____ Visiting others	____ Park/playground	
	____ Snack		

Other: _____

Additional comments not addressed:

FORM 5

PTR-F Assessment Checklist: Teach

Challenging behavior: _____   Person responding: _____   Child: _____

1. What communication skill(s) (using words, pictures, signs, augmentative systems) could the child learn in order to reduce the likelihood of the challenging behavior occurring in the future?		
___ Asking for a break ___ Asking for help ___ Requesting wants and needs	___ Expressing emotions (e.g., frustration, anger, hurt) ___ Expressing aversions (e.g., "No," "Stop")	___ Expressing preference when given a choice (e.g., "Yes, I like that," "I want the ___ one.")

Other: _____

2. What social skill(s) could the child learn in order to reduce the likelihood of the challenging behavior occurring in the future?		
___ Getting attention appropriately ___ Sharing—giving a toy ___ Sharing—asking for a toy ___ Taking turns ___ Beginning interactions with peers and adults ___ Responding to or answering peers and adults	___ Staying on topic with peers and adults in a back-and-forth exchange ___ Offering a play idea ("You be the mommy") ___ Playing appropriately with toys and materials with peers	___ Accepting positive comments and praise ___ Making positive comments ___ Giving praise to peers ___ Waiting for acknowledgment or reinforcement ___ Skills to develop friendships

Other: _____

3. What problem-solving skill(s) could the child learn in order to reduce the likelihood of the challenging behavior occurring in the future?		
___ Controlling anger ___ Controlling impulsive behavior ___ Strategies for calming down ___ Asking for help ___ Using visuals to support independent play	___ Self-management ___ Playing independently ___ Playing cooperatively ___ Following directions ___ Following schedules and routines ___ Accepting "no" ___ Managing emotions	___ Getting engaged in an activity ___ Staying engaged in activities ___ Choosing appropriate solutions ___ Making choices from appropriate options ___ Following through with choices

Other: _____

Additional comments not addressed:

Figure 4.2. PTR-F Assessment Checklist: Teach.

Reinforce

The third component of PTR-F assessment involves the consequences that occur for challenging behavior and for other behaviors. The PTR-F assessment process is used to understand, as much as possible, why the challenging behavior is occurring and what the *function* or purpose of the challenging behavior is from the child's perspective. In what way does the challenging behavior serve the interests of the child? How does the challenging behavior act on the environment to help the child to get something (such as attention or a toy)? Or, how does the challenging behavior act on the environment to help the child escape something, avoid something, or get rid of something (e.g., a parent's demand, the need to transition to a new activity, a sibling's pestering)?

It is well known that consequences have a great influence over the frequency of behavior. If favorable consequences (reinforcers) follow a behavior, it is likely that the behavior will be strengthened and will occur more often and perhaps with greater magnitude. If reinforcers do not follow a behavior, then that behavior will be weakened and will occur less frequently. This law of positive reinforcement is the most basic and most important principle of behavior. However, just because a principle is well known does not mean that it is simple or that it is effectively applied in practice.

Reinforcement can be complicated for a number of reasons. A first source of complexity is that it is not always easy to identify the reinforcer for challenging behavior. This is because the reinforcer is almost always inadvertent. Nobody intentionally sets out to reinforce a child's challenging behavior, but nevertheless, when challenging behavior has developed to the point that it is persistent and severe, then reinforcement must be occurring in one form or another. Sometimes the reinforcement is in the form of adult, sibling, or peer attention; sometimes it is in the form of obtaining a preferred item (e.g., a toy, food); and sometimes it is in the form of escape or avoidance of nonpreferred activities. In any case, some kind of consequence is reinforcing the behavior.

Another complication is that for reinforcement to be effective, it does not have to occur with every instance of the behavior. This can make the reinforcer more difficult to observe, and in fact, sometimes the reinforcer is more effective if it follows the behavior only some of the time (this is referred to as a partial or intermittent schedule of reinforcement).

A third reason that reinforcement is complicated is that reinforcers are idiosyncratic, meaning that a reinforcer for one child will not necessarily be a reinforcer for another child. Although it is true that most children enjoy positive attention (such as praise or favorable acknowledgment), the form that such attention takes may affect children in different ways. Some children respond very well to a smile and a thumbs-up gesture; others may respond better to a pat on the back or a hug. Although it may seem counterintuitive, in many cases, a child is reinforced by negative attention, such as a scolding or a reprimand. For some children, a concrete reinforcer such as a sticker may be powerful, but for others, a sticker might have little or no meaning. The point is that it is important to know which consequences or events actually are effective as reinforcers for a particular child if they are to be included in a behavior support plan.

A behavior support plan in PTR-F must always include some kind of adjustment to the way that reinforcers are delivered. For some children, this might involve using more reinforcers, and it also might involve ensuring that reinforcers for challenging behavior are withheld. For other children, it will be important to ensure that certain kinds of desirable behavior are reinforced, and for still others, it might mean that the specific kinds of consequences (reinforcers) need to be changed.

At this point, it is probably important for us to explain our position with respect to negative consequences, such as time out or other forms of punishment. First, we do not believe that time out or other forms of punishment are necessary. It is our experience that even the most persistent and severe behavior can be changed effectively without relying on negative consequences. If the procedures described in this book are followed with fidelity, then positive change will occur. If challenging behavior occurs in the course of implementing the PTR-F behavior support plan, and it usually will, then we recommend that such occurrences be viewed as errors or mistakes. Errors are corrected most effectively through instruction, not punishment, so the behavior support plan should be developed to account for these occurrences. This is explained more completely in Chapter 5.

Figure 4.3 presents the PTR-F Assessment Checklist: Reinforce, which helps identify the consequences of the challenging behavior and prompts the team to think about what the function of the behavior might be. It also invites the team to consider preferred items and activities that motivate the child and that can be used as positive reinforcers.

Summarizing the PTR-F Assessment Data

The first responsibility of team members in conducting the PTR-F assessment is to complete the three checklists. As noted in earlier chapters, the team will often comprise one family member and the PTR-F facilitator. If this is the case, it is important to be sure that observations from both team members are included in the assessment. It should be mentioned, though, that other individuals who are not part of the team but who nevertheless are involved with the child in a professional or nonprofessional capacity can provide input for completing the checklists. All observations are potentially valuable. Completing the checklists does not require much time—probably not more than 15–30 minutes.

When the checklists are completed, they should be compiled and summarized. This summary involves reviewing each checklist and entering summary information on the PTR-F Assessment Summary Table (see Figure 4.4). The table includes multiple sections that correspond with each of the three PTR-F components, so the information for prevent, teach, and reinforce is entered in the pertinent box. One person should be responsible for entering the information in brief summary statements on the PTR-F Assessment Summary Table as the data (i.e., the information on the checklists) are reviewed and discussed. The idea is to synthesize the information and seek to identify patterns in the data. Although all observations are valid, and although it is understandable that there will be differences in individuals' observations and perceptions, it is useful to note consistencies in the antecedents and consequences that are recorded on the different checklists. For example, if, when completing the Reinforce checklist, the team notes that many of the consequences that follow the challenging behavior involve the child getting out of a particular activity (e.g., sent to time out, given personal space, activity ended), it is important for the team to note this consistency because a likely function of the challenging behavior is to escape. Or, if the team notices that challenging behavior is likely to occur during times of the day when the child is required to change activities (e.g., leaving home, coming to the dinner table, cleaning up to play outside), it could be that the child is more likely to demonstrate challenging behavior during transitions. Identifying such consistencies in the information recorded on each of the Prevent, Teach, and Reinforce checklists is central to the PTR-F assessment process.

The PTR-F Assessment Summary Table can be completed in a linear fashion (from numbers 1 through 6) that moves the team directly from summarizing the relevant prevent and reinforce data, to developing a hypothesis statement regarding the perceived function of the child's challenging behavior, to using the Teach checklist data to determine skills to teach the child that can replace the challenging behavior and achieve the same purpose (i.e., desirable behaviors). The summary process includes the following tasks that correspond with each numbered section.

1. Challenging Behavior: Prevent

The data that should be summarized in this section are those that pertain to when the challenging behavior is most likely/very likely to occur (numbers 1 through 3 on the Prevent checklist). As noted previously, it is important to note those antecedents that are consistently triggers or settings events for the challenging behavior.

FORM
6

PTR-F Assessment Checklist: Reinforce

Challenging behavior: _____   Person responding: _____   Child: _____

1. What consequence(s) usually follow your child's challenging behavior?

___ Sent to time out	___ Calming/soothing	___ Gets desired item/toy/food
___ Sent to bedroom	___ Talk about what just happened	___ Gets access to desired activity
___ Sent to quiet spot/corner	___ Spanking	
___ Given personal space	___ Assistance given	
___ Delay in activity	___ Verbal warning	Other:
___ Activity changed	___ Verbal redirect	
___ Activity ended	___ Verbal reprimand/scolding	
___ Removed from activity	___ Review house rules	
	___ Physical guidance	
	___ Sibling/peer reaction	
	___ Physical restraint	

2. What is the likelihood that privileges or preferred items/activities are removed from your child following your child's challenging behavior?

_____ Very likely	_____ Sometimes	_____ Seldom	_____ Never

3. What is the likelihood of your child's challenging behavior resulting in acknowledgment (e.g., reprimands, corrections, restating house rules) from adults and children?

_____ Very likely	_____ Sometimes	_____ Seldom	_____ Never

4. Does the challenging behavior seem to occur in order to gain attention from other children (e.g., siblings, peers)?

___ Yes   *List specific children* _____
___ No

5. Does the challenging behavior seem to occur in order to gain attention from adults?

___ Yes   *List specific adults* _____
___ No

6. Does the challenging behavior seem to occur in order to obtain objects (e.g., toys, games, materials, food) from other children or adults?

___ Yes   *List specific objects* _____
___ No

7. Does the challenging behavior seem to occur in order to delay a transition from a preferred activity to a nonpreferred activity?

___ Yes   *List specific transitions* _____
___ No

(continued)

Figure 4.3.   PTR-F Assessment Checklist: Reinforce.

Figure 4.3. *(continued)*

FORM 6   **PTR-F Assessment Checklist: Reinforce** *(continued)*

---

8. Does the challenging behavior seem to occur in order to terminate or delay a nonpreferred (e.g., difficult, boring, repetitive) task or activity?

____ Yes   *List specific tasks or activities* _____
____ No

---

9. Does the challenging behavior seem to occur in order to get away from a nonpreferred child or adult?

____ Yes   *List specific children or adults* _____
____ No

---

10. What is the likelihood of your child's appropriate behavior (e.g., participating appropriately, cooperating, following directions) resulting in acknowledgment or praise from adults or children?

_____ Very likely	_____ Sometimes	_____ Seldom	_____ Never

---

11. Does your child enjoy praise from adults and children? Does your child enjoy praise from some people more than others?

____ Yes   *List specific people* _____
____ No

---

12. What items and activities are most enjoyable to the child? What items or activities could serve as special rewards?

____ Social interaction with adults	____ High fives	____ Small toys, prizes (e.g., stickers, stamps)
____ Physical interaction with adults (rough-housing, tickle, cuddle)	____ Praise from adults	____ Device time (e.g., tablet, electronic game system)
____ Social interaction with siblings/ peers	____ Praise from siblings/ other kids	____ Art activities (e.g., drawing pictures, painting)
____ Playing a game	____ Music	____ Objects/toys:
____ Parent helper	____ Puzzles	(specify) _____
____ Extra time outside	____ Books	____ Food:
____ Extra praise and attention from adults	____ Special activity	(specify) _____
____ Extra time in preferred activity	____ Special helper	
	____ Computer time	
	____ Television time	

Other: _____

Additional comments not addressed:

FORM 7

PTR-F Assessment Summary Table

Child: _____   Date: _____

Challenging behavior:	
1. PREVENT	**2. REINFORCE**

3. Hypothesis statement: When _____
then _____ ;
as a result _____ .

Desirable behavior:	
4. PREVENT	**5. REINFORCE**

6. TEACH

Figure 4.4. PTR-F Assessment Summary Table.

2. Challenging Behavior: Reinforce

This section should include a summary of data from the Reinforce checklist in regard to the consequences that usually follow the child's challenging behavior (numbers 1 through 9 on the Reinforce checklist).

TIP *On the Reinforce checklist, responses to the first question are organized to help teams determine the primary function of the challenging behavior. If most of the items checked are in the left column, it is likely that the function of the challenging behavior is escape (i.e., to get away from something, to get out of doing something). If most of the items checked are in the middle column, it is likely that the function of the behavior is to gain attention (e.g., from adults, siblings). If the items checked are in the right column, the function of the behavior may be to get access to a preferred item (e.g., food, toy, game) and/or a preferred activity.*

3. Hypothesis Statement

The first two sections of the PTR-F Assessment Summary Table and the patterns they reveal set the stage for the team to develop hypothesis statements. Hypothesis statements are simply a concise and useful way to summarize the team's understanding of the challenging behavior and, in particular, the way that the challenging behavior is currently influenced by the environment. Hypothesis statements lead directly to the development of the behavior support plan.

Hypothesis statements take a simple "A-B-C" form. The A-B-C stands for Antecedent–Behavior–Consequence. The information can be taken directly from the PTR-F Assessment Summary Table. Antecedents come from the Prevent section; behavior comes from the team's definition of the child's challenging behavior; and consequence comes from the Reinforce section. Another useful way to look at formulating hypothesis statements is to describe the equation as

> *WHEN* (description of the antecedent or what occurs in the environment), → *THEN* (description of the behavior), → and *AS A RESULT* (description of the typical consequence that reinforces the behavior).

To write a hypothesis statement based on this formula, the team specifies the antecedent events that are observed to lead to the challenging behavior—the **WHEN** statement. The team then describes the child's challenging behavior—the **THEN** statement. Finally, the **AS A RESULT** statement describes what the child often receives as a consequence. Here are a few specific examples:

▲ *WHEN* Jill is asked to engage in a fine motor activity, *THEN* she will scream and/or engage in other disruptive behaviors, and *AS A RESULT*, she will avoid having to perform the fine motor task.

▲ *WHEN* Mahmud is outside playing and his sister gets within 3 feet to attempt to play with toys, *THEN* Mahmud will hit or kick his sister, and *AS A RESULT*, his sister will withdraw and leave Mahmud alone.

▲ *WHEN* Thomas has gone for a period of time (usually at least 10 minutes) without adult attention, *THEN* he may slap his head repeatedly, and *AS A RESULT*, he will usually receive adult attention in the form of holding, soothing, and comforting.

In developing hypothesis statements, it is important to appreciate that it may be necessary to prepare more than one. For example, the PTR-F assessment for Thomas (a boy with severe intellectual disabilities and some sensitivities to certain loud noises) revealed that there were a number of different circumstances associated with his challenging behavior and, in some of those circumstances, the function (maintaining consequence) was different. In the first hypothesis statement written for Thomas his slapping was reinforced by adult attention. In the following hypothesis statement, the head slapping was reinforced by escape from an unpleasant sound.

> **WHEN** Thomas encounters noises, including music or laughter that is excessively (for him) loud or high pitched, **THEN** he may slap his head repeatedly, and **AS A RESULT**, he will be removed by an adult from the offending noise.

Once formulated, the hypothesis statement should be written in the hypothesis statement box (number 3) of the PTR-F Assessment Summary Table. As you can see, the first portion of the PTR-F Assessment Summary Table relates to the development of a hypothesis statement. The second half of the table will help teams to use the information gained about the function of the child's challenging behavior to incorporate and summarize additional information that will be used in the development of the intervention plan.

4. Desirable Behavior: Prevent

This section should summarize the information from the PTR-F Assessment Checklist: Prevent that indicates when the challenging behavior is least likely to occur (numbers 4 and 5). Knowing this information is helpful for teams to better identify the environmental triggers to challenging behavior. For example, if an antecedent is present when challenging behavior occurs but is not present when the challenging behavior does not occur, this section can provide confirmation that the identified antecedent is a trigger for the challenging behavior. The information summarized in this section also reveals those circumstances in which the child is successful. With this understanding, activities and supports can be structured to increase the child's success. For example, if the team notes that Anna is more successful during the times of the day that follow a structured routine (e.g., bath time, bedtime) and that she demonstrates challenging behavior during times that are not as structured (e.g., morning routine), the team can note this information and keep it in mind for behavior support plan development. Perhaps the team will want to consider prevent strategies that will enhance the predictability of the morning routine and increase Anna's explicit understanding of what is expected of her during this time.

5. Desirable Behavior: Reinforce

The information that should be summarized in this section relates to the reinforcers that are identified by the team as the items and activities that are most enjoyable to the child (numbers 11 and 12). When considering reinforcers, it is beneficial for teams to pick the most reinforcing items and activities. Knowing that a child likes stickers sometimes but that he always likes high fives indicates that high fives are more reinforcing than stickers and that they should be used (particularly during the initial implementation of the behavior support plan) as reinforcement.

6. Teach

The purpose of this section is to summarize the data that indicate what desirable behaviors can be taught to children that will replace the challenging behavior and that will also serve the same function as the challenging behavior. The Teach checklist should be used to complete this section. In addition, teams should consider the hypothesis statement that has been developed when deciding what alternative desirable behaviors could serve the same function as the challenging behavior. Children often display challenging behaviors because they have not been systematically taught an alternative desirable behavior to use that leads to the same outcome. Also, it is often the case that if a desirable behavior has been taught, it has not been reinforced the same way that the challenging behavior has, which means that the desirable behavior is unlikely to be used by the child in the future. This section of the PTR-F Assessment Summary Table helps teams to identify a desirable behavior that is a functional replacement for the challenging behavior and that can be incorporated into the Teach section of the behavior support plan.

TIP *When considering what desirable behaviors and skills can be taught to replace the challenging behavior, it is important to look at the Teach checklist and also the hypothesis statement that has been created. By referring to the hypothesis statement in addition to the Teach checklist, teams can consider whether particular desirable behaviors and skills are likely to serve the same function as the challenging behavior.*

RETURN TO GOAL SETTING: DEFINING AND DETERMINING THE DESIRABLE BEHAVIOR

Before intervention planning begins, it is important to revisit goals that were set in the initial steps of the PTR-F process. Recall from Chapter 3 that during the second meeting, teams used the PTR-F Goal Sheet to identify challenging behaviors to decrease, choose one challenging behavior to target, operationally define the challenging behavior, and identify desirable behaviors to increase (Steps 1 through 4 of the PTR-F Goal Sheet). Just as the team used the PTR-F Goal Sheet to identify and operationally define one challenging behavior to reduce, now that the team knows the function of the challenging behavior, they should identify and operationally define a specific desirable behavior to teach or increase that will replace the challenging behavior. The same PTR-F Goal Sheet should be used to operationally define the desirable behavior. To do this, these two additional steps should be followed:

▲ Select *one* desirable behavior to target. It is likely that many teams will have several desirable behaviors that they want to see increase, but as with targeting one challenging behavior, it is easier for those who are implementing strategies to be able to focus on one desirable behavior or skill at a time. As teams discuss which desirable behavior to target, it is important to consider behaviors that improve the child's ability to interact and form relationships with family members, communicate appropriately with others, and participate in the family's daily routines and activities. Again, it is also important for teams to select a desirable behavior to target that is a functional replacement for the challenging behavior. To complete this step, teams should consider the initial desirable behaviors that were identified to increase (from number 4 of the PTR-F Goal Sheet), and they should also refer to the hypothesis statement and the Teach box on the PTR-F Assessment Summary Table to select a desirable behavior to target.

▲ Operationally define this desirable behavior. This step is an opportunity for teams to describe the desirable target behavior in terms that are observable (can be seen and/or heard) and measurable (can be counted or timed). As with challenging behavior, it is important for teams to create this definition so that all team members can agree on whether or not the desirable behavior is occurring. Having an operational definition for desirable behavior will also be important when monitoring progress to see if the child is learning the new skill. It can be difficult for teams to identify and define exactly what they want to see a child do, so some teams may take a while for this step. See Table 4.1 for good and poor examples of operational definitions for desirable behaviors.

After identifying a desirable behavior to target, the team will need to incorporate the desirable behavior into the existing data collection system that was developed for the challenging behavior in Chapter 3. The team can repeat the process of creating a Behavior Rating Scale (BRS) described in Chapter 3 for the desirable behavior. The same steps can be used for creating desirable behavior anchors, and the desirable behavior data can now be tracked on the same BRS form as the challenging behavior.

Table 4.1. Operational definitions of desirable behavior

Desirable behavior	Poor example of definition	Good example of definition
Uses appropriate communication	Uses her words	When she wants something that her brother or a parent has, she will say "please" and put her hand out.
Follows directions	Is obedient	When asked to do something or given a direction (paired with a picture of what she is supposed to do), she does what has been asked.
Engages in positive social interactions with brother	Is nice to Jimmy	Communicates with or responds to Jimmy by smiling and using words that convey cooperation or positive feelings

SUMMARY

This chapter has described each step of conducting the PTR-F assessment, a practical, family-friendly FBA process that is dependent on the family's knowledge of and familiarity with the child as well as frequent observations of the child's behavior in many contexts. The purpose of this assessment process is to understand behavior more comprehensively—from the antecedent conditions in the environment that cause the behaviors (i.e., triggers and setting events), to the function or purpose that the behavior serves, to the consequences that reinforce the behavior. The family compiles its observations of the child's challenging and desirable behaviors into the Prevent, Teach, and Reinforce checklists and then summarizes the information from each checklist into the PTR-F Assessment Summary Table. An important part of synthesizing this information is to craft a hypothesis statement, which is a concise description of how the environment influences the child's behavior. Once team members have hypothesized the function of the child's challenging behavior, they can also select a desirable behavior to increase that serves the same function and that can replace the challenging behavior, taking care to ensure that this desirable behavior does not require more effort than the challenging behavior and is equally reinforcing. The team should be sure to operationally define the desirable behavior as well as establish a system for collecting data on this behavior using the BRS.

To be sure that each crucial step of the PTR-F assessment process has been followed, the team should complete the Self-Evaluation Checklist: PTR-F Assessment (see Figure 4.5). If the answer to each of the questions on the checklists is "yes," then the team is ready to begin intervention planning, discussed in Chapter 5.

FORM 8 — **Self-Evaluation Checklist: PTR-F Assessment**

		Yes	No
1.	Did the team complete the three PTR-F assessment checklists (i.e., Prevent, Teach, Reinforce)?	❏	❏
2.	Were the completed checklists reviewed by the team and summarized on the PTR-F Assessment Summary Table?	❏	❏
3.	Were hypotheses developed to summarize the team's understanding of the function of the child's challenging behavior and the ways that the behavior is influenced by the environment?	❏	❏
4.	Has a specific desirable behavior been identified as a target, and has it been operationally defined on the PTR-F Goal Sheet?	❏	❏
5.	Have anchors for desirable behavior on the Behavior Rating Scale been carefully specified so that data collection will be reliable and sensitive to behavior change?	❏	❏

Figure 4.5. Self-Evaluation Checklist: PTR-F Assessment.

APPENDIX
Case Examples

TEAM MEETING 2: TIMMY

Review the Behavior Rating Scale

Kaci returned the following week to an exhausted family, as Timmy's tantrums continued at a high intensity most of the nights since they had last met. Jodie and Phil were relieved to see Kaci, and she started the meeting by asking how things had been in the past week to fully understand their concerns. Jodie and Phil described that most nights were similar to what had been occurring when they met the previous week, and that it was not making a difference that Phil was not involved with getting Timmy ready for bed because the house is so small that you can hear everything that is happening in the house unless you are outside. It was clear that they were both frustrated and impatient to get some strategies in place. Jodie reported that she was doing the best she could but that she, too, was at a loss for what might work with Timmy. Although they did not directly receive any noise complaints this week, they were afraid that a complaint could still be coming.

Kaci asked whether Phil and Jodie were able to implement the 5:1 practice, and it was clear that they did not. They were so exhausted mentally and physically from dealing with Timmy's tantrums that they were barely able to keep everything together over the past week. Kaci assured them they could incorporate the 5:1 practice in their behavior support plan if they still wanted to implement this practice, and their meeting today would get them one step closer to identifying strategies.

Kaci asked to see their Behavior Rating Scale (BRS), which they reported was easy to fill out because Timmy had tantrums for well over 30 minutes every night over the past week! Kaci congratulated them for filling out the BRS every day, even if it was easy to measure because the behavior was so long each night, and asked whether they thought the anchors needed to be changed or modified. Although Timmy's tantrums exceeded the 30-minute mark every night, they felt that they did not want to change the BRS now because they had gotten familiar with filling it out. Plus, they were hopeful that the tantrums would not continue to be that long after implementing strategies. Kaci said that they would be identifying and adding the desirable behavior tonight and would be collecting data on that as well.

PTR-F Assessment and Summary Forms

Kaci then turned to the Prevent-Teach-Reinforce for Families (PTR-F) assessment and asked whether they were able to fill out the checklists. Jodie and Phil both had filled out their respective checklists, since they took the paperwork to work with them after the last meeting and filled it out during their lunch break. While Kaci recorded the answers on a new checklist, the team quickly went through the questions and came to an agreement on the relevant aspects contributing to Timmy's behaviors. Because Jodie and Phil's answers were very similar, it was evident that they agreed on what contributed to Timmy's tantrums and why the tantrums kept occurring. (Figures 4.1a–4.3a show Timmy's completed PTR-F assessment.)

Their answers were summarized on the PTR-F Assessment Summary Table, and Kaci confirmed that the summary aligned with how Jodie and Phil understood Timmy's tantrums for bedtime from Timmy's perspective. It was obvious to the team that Timmy was throwing tantrums to avoid bedtime, and this knowledge was used to develop the hypothesis statement. (Figure 4.4a shows Timmy's completed PTR-F Assessment Summary Table.) The team also discussed that Timmy's behavior was reinforced by Jodie and/or Phil staying in his room longer, sometimes lying with him in his bed or sitting with him by his bed, singing additional songs, and/or reading another story. On some nights, the additional songs or books lasted

---

FORM
4   **PTR-F Assessment Checklist: Prevent**

Challenging behavior: <u>Tantrums</u>   Person responding: <u>Mom and Dad</u>   Child: <u>Timmy</u>

---

1. Are there times of the day when challenging behavior is most likely to occur?
    If yes, what are they?

___ Waking up	___ Before meals	___ During meals	___ After meals	___ Preparing meals
_X_ Morning	___ Afternoon	___ Nap time	_X_ Evening	_X_ Bedtime

Other: _____

---

2. Are there specific activities when challenging behavior is very likely to occur?
    If yes, what are they?

___ Leaving home	___ Nap time	___ Interactions with sibling/child	___ Taking medicine
___ Arriving home	_X_ Toileting/diapering	___ Indoor play	___ Medical procedure
___ Family celebrations	_X_ Bathing	___ Outdoor play	___ At doctor or therapist
___ Church/religious activities	_X_ Toothbrushing	___ Meals	___ At dentist
___ Looking at books	___ Play group/classes	___ In the car/bus	___ Children's attractions (e.g., zoo)
___ Watching television/ device	_X_ Eating out	___ At a store	___ Transitions (specify): _____
	___ Visiting others	___ Park/playground	
___ Special event (specify): _____	___ Snack		
	_X_ Bedtime		

Other: _____

---

3. Are there other children or adults whose proximity is associated with a high likelihood of challenging behavior? If so, who are they?

___ Siblings	Specify: _____	_X_ Parent
___ Family member(s)	Specify: _____	___ Other children
___ Care provider(s)	Specify: _____	(specify): _____
___ Other adults	Specify: _____	

Other: _____

(page 1 of 2)

(continued)

Figure 4.1a.   Timmy's PTR-F Assessment Checklist: Prevent.

Figure 4.1a. *(continued)*

FORM 4 **PTR-F Assessment Checklist: Prevent** *(continued)*

---

4. Are there times of the day when challenging behavior is least likely to occur?
If yes, what are they?

____ Waking up	____ Before meals	_X_ During meals	____ After meals	____ Preparing meals
____ Morning	____ Afternoon	____ Nap time	____ Evening	____ Bedtime

Other: _____

---

5. Are there specific activities when challenging behavior is least likely to occur? What are they?

____ Leaving home	____ Nap time	____ Interactions with sibling/child	____ Taking medicine
____ Arriving home	____ Toileting/diapering	____ Indoor play	____ Medical procedure
____ Family celebrations	____ Bathing	_X_ Outdoor play	____ At doctor or therapist
____ Church/religious activities	____ Toothbrushing	____ Meals	____ At dentist
____ Looking at books	____ Play group/classes	____ In the car/bus	____ Children's attractions (e.g., zoo)
_X_ Watching television/ device	____ Eating out	____ At a store	____ Transitions (specify):
____ Special event (specify): _____	____ Visiting others	____ Park/playground	_____
	____ Snack		

Other: _____

Additional comments not addressed:

FORM
5

PTR-F Assessment Checklist: Teach

Challenging behavior: <u>Tantrums</u>   Person responding: <u>Mom and Dad</u>   Child: <u>Timmy</u>

| 1. What communication skill(s) (using words, pictures, signs, augmentative systems) could the child learn in order to reduce the likelihood of the challenging behavior occurring in the future? |

| _X_ Asking for a break
_X_ Asking for help
_X_ Requesting wants and needs | _X_ Expressing emotions (e.g., frustration, anger, hurt)
___ Expressing aversions (e.g., "No," "Stop") | _X_ Expressing preference when given a choice (e.g., "Yes, I like that," "I want the ___ one.") |

Other: _____

| 2. What social skill(s) could the child learn in order to reduce the likelihood of the challenging behavior occurring in the future? |

| _X_ Getting attention appropriately
___ Sharing—giving a toy
___ Sharing—asking for a toy
___ Taking turns
___ Beginning interactions with peers and adults
_X_ Responding to or answering peers and adults | ___ Staying on topic with peers and adults in a back-and-forth exchange
___ Offering a play idea ("You be the mommy")
___ Playing appropriately with toys and materials with peers | ___ Accepting positive comments and praise
___ Making positive comments
___ Giving praise to peers
_X_ Waiting for acknowledgment or reinforcement
___ Skills to develop friendships |

Other: _____

| 3. What problem-solving skill(s) could the child learn in order to reduce the likelihood of the challenging behavior occurring in the future? |

| _X_ Controlling anger
_X_ Controlling impulsive behavior
_X_ Strategies for calming down
_X_ Asking for help
___ Using visuals to support independent play | _X_ Self-management
_X_ Playing independently
___ Playing cooperatively
_X_ Following directions
_X_ Following schedules and routines
_X_ Accepting "no"
_X_ Managing emotions | ___ Getting engaged in an activity
___ Staying engaged in activities
_X_ Choosing appropriate solutions
_X_ Making choices from appropriate options
___ Following through with choices |

Other: _____

Additional comments not addressed:

Figure 4.2a. Timmy's PTR-F Assessment Checklist: Teach.

FORM 6

PTR-F Assessment Checklist: Reinforce

Challenging behavior: <u>Tantrums</u>   Person responding: <u>Mom and Dad</u>   Child: <u>Timmy</u>

---

1. What consequence(s) usually follow your child's challenging behavior?

___ Sent to time out	_X_ Calming/soothing	___ Gets desired item/toy/food
___ Sent to bedroom	_X_ Talk about what just happened	___ Gets access to desired activity
___ Sent to quiet spot/corner	___ Spanking	
___ Given personal space	___ Assistance given	
_X_ Delay in activity	___ Verbal warning	
_X_ Activity changed	_X_ Verbal redirect	Other: lay or sit with Timmy in bed,
___ Activity ended	_X_ Verbal reprimand/scolding	sing more songs, or read another
___ Removed from activity	___ Review house rules	story
	___ Physical guidance	
	___ Sibling/peer reaction	
	___ Physical restraint	

---

2. What is the likelihood that privileges or preferred items/activities are removed from your child following your child's challenging behavior?

__X__ Very likely	_____ Sometimes	_____ Seldom	_____ Never

3. What is the likelihood of your child's challenging behavior resulting in acknowledgment (e.g., reprimands, corrections, restating house rules) from adults and children?

__X__ Very likely	_____ Sometimes	_____ Seldom	_____ Never

4. Does the challenging behavior seem to occur in order to gain attention from other children (e.g., siblings, peers)?

___ Yes   *List specific children* _____
_X_ No

5. Does the challenging behavior seem to occur in order to gain attention from adults?

_X_ Yes   *List specific adults*   Mom and Dad _____
___ No

6. Does the challenging behavior seem to occur in order to obtain objects (e.g., toys, games, materials, food) from other children or adults?

___ Yes   *List specific objects* _____
_X_ No

7. Does the challenging behavior seem to occur in order to delay a transition from a preferred activity to a nonpreferred activity?

_X_ Yes   *List specific transitions* _____ bedtime, diapering, bath _____
___ No

(continued)

Figure 4.3a.   Timmy's PTR-F Assessment Checklist: Reinforce.

Figure 4.3a. *(continued)*

FORM 6   **PTR-F Assessment Checklist: Reinforce** *(continued)*

---

8. Does the challenging behavior seem to occur in order to terminate or delay a nonpreferred (e.g., difficult, boring, repetitive) task or activity?

_____ Yes   *List specific tasks or activities* _____
_X_ No

9. Does the challenging behavior seem to occur in order to get away from a nonpreferred child or adult?

_____ Yes   *List specific children or adults* _____
_X_ No

10. What is the likelihood of your child's appropriate behavior (e.g., participating appropriately, cooperating, following directions) resulting in acknowledgment or praise from adults or children?

_____ Very likely	_____ Sometimes	___X___ Seldom	_____ Never

11. Does your child enjoy praise from adults and children? Does your child enjoy praise from some people more than others?

_X_ Yes   *List specific people* ____Mostly Mom and Dad_____
_____ No

12. What items and activities are most enjoyable to the child? What items or activities could serve as special rewards?

_X_ Social interaction with adults	_____ High fives	_____ Small toys, prizes (e.g., stickers, stamps)
_X_ Physical interaction with adults (rough-housing, tickle, cuddle)	_X_ Praise from adults	_X_ Device time (e.g., tablet, electronic game system)
_____ Social interaction with siblings/ peers	_____ Praise from siblings/ other kids	_____ Art activities (e.g., drawing pictures, painting)
_X_ Playing a game	_____ Music	_____ Objects/toys:
_____ Parent helper	_____ Puzzles	(specify) _____
_____ Extra time outside	_X_ Books	_X_ Food:
_X_ Extra praise and attention from adults	_____ Special activity	(specify) _____
_X_ Extra time in preferred activity	_____ Special helper	
	_____ Computer time	
	_X_ Television time	

Other: _____

Additional comments not addressed:

(page 2 of 2)

FORM 7

PTR-F Assessment Summary Table

Child: Timmy   **Date:** 6/26/15

Challenging behavior: Tantrums

1. PREVENT	2. REINFORCE
During morning, evening, and bedtime During diapering, bathing, toothbrushing, bedtime, and eating out with parents	Activity delayed or changed Talk about what happened, verbal redirect, verbal reprimands Laying or sitting with Timmy in his bed, singing additional songs, or reading additional books

3. Hypothesis statement: When the bedtime routine is over and mom and dad attempt to leave the room, then Timmy tantrums (see Goal Sheet for full definition); as a result, he delays bedtime and gets extra attention from Mom and/or Dad.

Desirable behavior: Staying in his room/bed until he falls asleep

4. PREVENT	5. REINFORCE
During meals, watching TV/device, outdoor play	Praise, social and physical interaction from Mom and Dad TV/device time Books

6. TEACH

Communication: appropriately requesting wants, needs, or help; expressing emotions; expressing preference
Social skills: getting attention appropriately, responding to/answering adults, self-management, playing independently, following directions, following schedules and routines, accepting "no"

Figure 4.4a. Timmy's PTR-F Assessment Summary Table.

for up to an hour to keep Timmy from having a tantrum and waking up his brother. Basically, whatever Jodie and Phil could come up with to keep Timmy from having a tantrum, they did. They tried to just let him cry, but that only made things worse, since that is when he would scream and cry the loudest and roll around and kick his feet on the floor the most. Jodie and Phil have received a lot of advice from family, friends, teachers, and the Internet, but nothing so far has worked more than once in a while. After additional discussion with Kaci, it became more evident that Timmy was getting a lot of attention from them, and perhaps his tantrums had more to do with their attention than avoiding bedtime. The team came to a consensus that his behavior probably served both functions and would make sure to implement strategies accordingly.

Jodie and Phil knew that Timmy was trying to avoid going to bed and that he was good at getting them to stay in his room longer each night; they were not sure what they could do differently to stop his tantrums because they did not want Timmy to wake up Dakota, keep Dakota up late, or receive any more noise complaints. They felt like they had tried everything they could up until this point, with no success, and were skeptical of being able to come up with any effective strategies that they would be able to implement. Still, they were anxious for something to work.

Because Jodie and Phil were so eager to identify strategies, and Kaci was able to stay longer than was planned the team decided to identify interventions and create a behavior support plan that night instead of waiting until the following week. Jodie and Phil were not confident that they could wait that long, so they fed the boys a quick dinner, and the meeting commenced around the dinner table as the boys ate. Kaci said it would be important not to directly talk about Timmy's behavior right in front of him, so they used "code" words or terms, spelled words, or used gestures when talking about Timmy directly. Jodie and Phil were enthusiastic about this plan because they did not want to convey to Timmy that he was a bad boy or that there was something wrong with him. The discussion to identify interventions occurred with this in mind.

Desirable Behavior Goals and the Behavior Rating Scale

To begin the discussion, Kaci referred back to the PTR-F Goal Sheet and asked Jodie and Phil what desirable behavior they would like to focus on for this plan given their hypothesis statement from the PTR-F assessment. Ultimately, Jodie and Phil wanted Timmy to be able to follow the bedtime routine and go to sleep independently, in a calm and cooperative manner. The goal was identified, and an operational definition was created. (Figure 4.5a shows Timmy's completed PTR-F Goal Sheet.) The next step would be to determine how to measure Timmy's desirable behavior and create anchors for the BRS.

In their discussion about what dimension of behavior to measure, Kaci asked if it might be helpful to measure how long Timmy is staying in his room by himself each night. With an enthusiastic "Yes!" the team identified the anchors in number of minutes that Timmy stayed in his room, identifying that if he stayed in his room for up to 30 minutes, he probably would be asleep by then. Currently, he was not even making it 1 minute on his own. Kaci asked Timmy's parents to clarify whether, in order to count him as demonstrating desirable behavior, they would count his behavior as desirable if Timmy stayed in his room but still had a tantrum or if he had to stay in his room quietly (without a tantrum). Jodie and Phil agreed that if Timmy stayed in his room, regardless of what he was doing or his noise level, they would count that as demonstrating desirable behavior for now. (Figure 4.6a shows Timmy's completed BRS.)

Self-Evaluation Checklist

Although the meeting was going to continue in order to develop Timmy's behavior support plan, Kaci reviewed the PTR-F Self-Evaluation Checklist with Jodie and Phil to ensure that all the steps were followed before proceeding to the next step. The team agreed that all the steps were completed and that they could move on to creating Timmy's plan.

FORM 1 **PTR-F Goal Sheet**

Instructions:
1. Identify and write out the child's challenging behaviors to decrease and the contexts or routines where these behaviors need to improve.
2. Select ONE challenging behavior to target within family contexts or routines.
3. Operationally define this target behavior—observable (seen or heard) and measurable (counted or timed).
4. Identify and write out the child's desirable behaviors to increase.
5. Select target desirable behavior (to be completed following PTR-F assessment).
6. Operationally define the desirable behavior (to be completed following PTR-F assessment).

Child: Timmy   **Date:** 6/25/15

Goals: Challenging behaviors		
	Behaviors	*Context/routines*
Challenging behaviors to decrease	"Fits" (tantrums), especially high-pitched screaming, rolling around on the floor, kicking his legs Hitting Mom and Dad Throwing toys Saying/yelling "no" Running away/hiding	Diapering Bath time Bedtime
Target behavior	Fits/tantrums	Bedtime
Operational definition	Timmy emits a high-pitched scream (often for several seconds) and usually rolls around on the floor and kicks his legs; if someone is near, he may hit or kick whoever is close. He sometimes screams "NO!" during these episodes.	

Goals: Desirable behaviors	
Desirable behaviors to increase	Go to sleep on his own (at least stay in room) Complete routines—calm, agreeable Speak more clearly Express himself appropriately and calmly Accept when he can't have something Get along/play with brother, friends Listen to mom and dad Do what other boys his age do—age-appropriate development
Target behavior	(to be completed following PTR-F assessment) Goes to sleep on his own
Operational definition	(to be completed following PTR-F assessment) Timmy will calmly (e.g., use an inside voice, use compliant phrases and actions, walk from room to room, follow parent prompt in 30 seconds or less) participate in and complete the bedtime routine. When mom or dad completes the routine and leaves the room, Timmy will stay in his room and fall asleep independently.

Figure 4.5a. Timmy's completed PTR-F Goal Sheet.

FORM 2

PTR-F Behavior Rating Scale

Child: Timmy   Rater: Mom and Dad   Routine: Bedtime   Month: July

Date/time:

	6/26/15	6/27/15	6/28/15	6/29/15	6/30/15	7/01/15										
Desirable behavior Stay in his room	☑5 ☐4 ☐3 ☐2 ☐1	☑5 ☐4 ☐3 ☐2 ☐1	☑5 ☐4 ☐3 ☐2 ☐1	☑5 ☐4 ☐3 ☐2 ☐1	☑5 ☐4 ☐3 ☐2 ☐1	☑5 ☐4 ☐3 ☐2 ☐1										
Challenging behavior Tantrums	☐5 ☐4 ☐3 ☐2 ☐1	☑5 ☐4 ☐3 ☐2 ☐1	☑5 ☐4 ☐3 ☐2 ☐1	☑5 ☐4 ☐3 ☐2 ☐1	☑5 ☐4 ☐3 ☐2 ☐1	☑5 ☐4 ☐3 ☐2 ☐1										

Desirable behavior: Stay in his room (noise ok) until asleep

5 = 30 minutes or until asleep

4 = up to 20 minutes

3 = up to 10 minutes

2 = 1-3 minutes

1 = 1 minute or less

Challenging behavior: Tantrums - number of minutes

5 = 30 minutes or more

4 = 20-30 minutes

3 = 10-20 minutes

2 = 5-10 minutes

1 = less than 5 minutes

Figure 4.6a. Timmy's completed Behavior Rating Scale.

TEAM MEETING 2: LUCY

Review the Behavior Rating Scale

Roberta arrived at the house for the second meeting, and Marguerite answered the door. She welcomed Roberta inside and was ready to participate in the meeting with Gabby. They sat at the kitchen table, and Roberta asked Gabby how Lucy's behavior had been since her last visit and asked to see the BRS. Gabby had filled out the BRS for all but 1 day, and Lucy's behavior was stable, with ratings of 4s and 5s. Roberta commended Gabby for collecting the data so that they had something to review and use to document progress.

Roberta asked Gabby if the ratings reflected how she felt about Lucy's physical aggression and if there were any concerns with the scale or with taking the data. Gabby agreed with the ratings and felt that they were an accurate reflection of the past week. She also felt that the data collection was easy and that the form did not take much time to fill in, but the hard part was remembering to do it. Gabby said that if she did not set a reminder on her phone, she probably would have missed more days. The reason she missed a day was because she ended up falling asleep early that night and completely forgot to record the data. In thinking back to that day, Gabby thought that she could try to remember how many instances of aggression occurred. However, Roberta told her that it might be okay to fill in the missing information if it had occurred the day before, but now, because it was a few days later, to leave that day blank instead of trying to remember. Roberta explained that it is more important to record the data as reliably as possible than to be complete.

Gabby asked Roberta about her observation at the school and how Lucy did. Roberta shared that Lucy was successful in the classroom with the right supports, including a visual schedule, making sure she understands what she is supposed to do, and giving her lots of attention when she is acting appropriately. Because Roberta had obtained written permission from Gabby to record video of Lucy at school, she had a short video clip of Lucy working on an activity. Both Gabby and Marguerite were surprised to see Lucy sitting at a table and writing with a crayon, and they wanted to know how Mrs. Williams got her to do any work. They both commented that they try to get Lucy to do those kinds of things at home, but Lucy always refuses to sit with them or write anything. They were both excited at the thought of being able to do Lucy's homework packets without a struggle. They were hopeful about developing a plan to make life with Lucy easier and to have effective strategies to make progress.

PTR-F Assessment and Summary Forms

Roberta took out copies of the PTR-F assessment checklists and gave one to both Gabby and Marguerite to refer to as they went through the questions. Mrs. Williams, Lucy's teacher, also filled out the checklists and gave them to Roberta when she was at the school observing Lucy. As they went through each question, Roberta recorded the answers, incorporating information from Mrs. Williams and her observations where relevant. (Figures 4.7a–4.9a show Lucy's completed checklists.) Marguerite also contributed information, which provided several different perspectives about Lucy's physically aggressive behavior.

Once all the questions were answered, Roberta summarized the information gathered from the checklists on the PTR-F Assessment Summary Table and discussed it with Gabby and Marguerite. From this information, Roberta reviewed a possible hypothesis and asked Gabby and Marguerite for their feedback. They agreed that the function of Lucy's physically aggressive behaviors was to avoid doing something that Lucy did not want to do (nonpreferred activity) and created the hypothesis statement to record on the PTR-F Assessment Summary Table. (Figure 4.10a shows Lucy's completed PTR-F Assessment Summary Table.)

Gabby stated that she was already aware that Lucy did not want to do most of what Gabby asked of her and wondered why it took all this time to get to a conclusion or hypothesis that she already knew. She wanted to know how she could get Lucy to do

---

FORM 4

PTR-F Assessment Checklist: Prevent

Challenging behavior: <u>Physical aggression</u>   Person responding: <u>Team</u>   Child: <u>Lucy</u>

1. Are there times of the day when challenging behavior is most likely to occur?
   If yes, what are they?

___ Waking up _X_ Morning	___ Before meals _X_ Afternoon	_X_ During meals ___ Nap time	___ After meals _X_ Evening	___ Preparing meals _X_ Bedtime

Other: _____

2. Are there specific activities when challenging behavior is very likely to occur?
   If yes, what are they?

_X_ Leaving home _X_ Arriving home ___ Family celebrations ___ Church/religious activities ___ Looking at books ___ Watching television/device ___ Special event (specify): _____	___ Nap time _X_ Bedtime _X_ Toileting/diapering ___ Bathing _X_ Toothbrushing ___ Play group/classes ___ Eating out _X_ Visiting others ___ Snack	___ Interactions with sibling/child ___ Indoor play ___ Outdoor play _X_ Meals ___ In the car/bus ___ At a store ___ Park/playground	___ Taking medicine ___ Medical procedure ___ At doctor or therapist ___ At dentist ___ Children's attractions (e.g., zoo) ___ Transitions (specify): _____

Other: _____

3. Are there other children or adults whose proximity is associated with a high likelihood of challenging behavior? If so, who are they?

___ Siblings ___ Family member(s) ___ Care provider(s) ___ Other adults	Specify: _____ Specify: _____ Specify: _____ Specify: _____	_X_ Parent ___ Other children (specify): _____

Other: <u>Mostly occurs with Mom</u> _____

(page 1 of 2)

(continued)

Figure 4.7a. Lucy's PTR-F Assessment Checklist: Prevent.

Figure 4.7a. *(continued)*

FORM 4   **PTR-F Assessment Checklist: Prevent** *(continued)*

4.	Are there times of the day when challenging behavior is least likely to occur? If yes, what are they?			

____ Waking up	____ Before meals	____ During meals	____ After meals	____ Preparing meals
____ Morning	____ Afternoon	____ Nap time	____ Evening	____ Bedtime

Other: <u>As long as she is doing something she wants to do</u>

5.   Are there specific activities when challenging behavior is least likely to occur? What are they?

____ Leaving home	____ Nap time	____ Interactions with sibling/child	____ Taking medicine
____ Arriving home	____ Toileting/diapering	_X_ Indoor play	____ Medical procedure
____ Family celebrations	____ Bathing	_X_ Outdoor play	____ At doctor or therapist
____ Church/religious activities	____ Toothbrushing	____ Meals	____ At dentist
_X_ Looking at books	____ Play group/classes	____ In the car/bus	____ Children's attractions (e.g., zoo)
_X_ Watching television/ device	____ Eating out	_X_ At a store	____ Transitions (specify):
____ Special event (specify): _____	____ Visiting others	____ Park/playground	_____
	____ Snack		

Other: _____

Additional comments not addressed:

(page 2 of 2)

FORM 5

PTR-F Assessment Checklist: Teach

Challenging behavior: <u>Physical aggression</u>   Person responding: <u>Team</u>   Child: <u>Lucy</u>

1. What communication skill(s) (using words, pictures, signs, augmentative systems) could the child learn in order to reduce the likelihood of the challenging behavior occurring in the future?

X Asking for a break X Asking for help X Requesting wants and needs	X Expressing emotions (e.g., frustration, anger, hurt) X Expressing aversions (e.g., "No," "Stop")	X Expressing preference when given a choice (e.g., "Yes, I like that," "I want the ____ one.")

Other: _____

2. What social skill(s) could the child learn in order to reduce the likelihood of the challenging behavior occurring in the future?

X Getting attention appropriately ___ Sharing—giving a toy ___ Sharing—asking for a toy ___ Taking turns ___ Beginning interactions with peers and adults X Responding to or answering peers and adults	___ Staying on topic with peers and adults in a back-and-forth exchange X Giving a play idea ("You be the mommy") ___ Playing appropriately with toys and materials with peers	___ Accepting positive comments and praise ___ Making positive comments ___ Giving praise to peers X Waiting for acknowledgment or reinforcement ___ Skills to develop friendships

Other: _____

3. What problem-solving skill(s) could the child learn in order to reduce the likelihood of the challenging behavior occurring in the future?

___ Controlling anger X Controlling impulsive behavior ___ Strategies for calming down X Asking for help ___ Using visuals to support independent play	___ Self-management X Playing independently ___ Playing cooperatively X Following directions X Following schedules and routines X Accepting "no" ___ Managing emotions	X Getting engaged in an activity X Staying engaged in activities ___ Choosing appropriate solutions ___ Making choices from appropriate options ___ Following through with choices

Other: _____

Additional comments not addressed:

Figure 4.8a. Lucy's PTR-F Assessment Checklist: Teach.

FORM 6

PTR-F Assessment Checklist: Reinforce

Challenging behavior: <u>Physical aggression</u>   Person responding: <u>Team</u>   Child: <u>Lucy</u>

1. What consequence(s) usually follow your child's challenging behavior?

_X_ Sent to time out	___ Calming/soothing	___ Gets desired item/toy/food
___ Sent to bedroom	___ Talk about what just happened	___ Gets access to desired activity
___ Sent to quiet spot/corner	___ Spanking	
_X_ Given personal space	___ Assistance given	
_X_ Delay in activity	___ Verbal warning	
_X_ Activity changed	_X_ Verbal redirect	Other:
_X_ Activity ended	___ Verbal reprimand/scolding	
_X_ Removed from activity	___ Review house rules	
	_X_ Physical guidance	
	___ Sibling/peer reaction	
	___ Physical restraint	

2. What is the likelihood that privileges or preferred items/activities are removed from your child following your child's challenging behavior?

_X_ Very likely	___ Sometimes	___ Seldom	___ Never

3. What is the likelihood of your child's challenging behavior resulting in acknowledgment (e.g., reprimands, corrections, restating house rules) from adults and children?

_X_ Very likely	___ Sometimes	___ Seldom	___ Never

4. Does the challenging behavior seem to occur in order to gain attention from other children (e.g., siblings, peers)?

___ Yes   *List specific children* _____
_X_ No

5. Does the challenging behavior seem to occur in order to gain attention from adults?

_X_ Yes   *List specific adults*   <u>Mostly Mom</u>
___ No

6. Does the challenging behavior seem to occur in order to obtain objects (e.g., toys, games, materials, food) from other children or adults?

___ Yes   *List specific objects* _____
_X_ No

7. Does the challenging behavior seem to occur in order to delay a transition from a preferred activity to a nonpreferred activity?

_X_ Yes   *List specific transitions* <u>getting dressed, sitting for meals, toileting, leaving for school, bedtime</u>
___ No

(page 1 of 2)

(continued)

Figure 4.9a. Lucy's PTR-F Assessment Checklist: Reinforce.

Figure 4.9a. *(continued)*

FORM 6   **PTR-F Assessment Checklist: Reinforce** *(continued)*

---

8. Does the challenging behavior seem to occur in order to terminate or delay a nonpreferred (e.g., difficult, boring, repetitive) task or activity?

_____ Yes   *List specific tasks or activities* _____
_X_ No

9. Does the challenging behavior seem to occur in order to get away from a nonpreferred child or adult?

_____ Yes   *List specific children or adults* _____
_X_ No

10. What is the likelihood of your child's appropriate behavior (e.g., participating appropriately, cooperating, following directions) resulting in acknowledgment or praise from adults or children?

_____ Very likely	_____ Sometimes	____X____ Seldom	_____ Never

11. Does your child enjoy praise from adults and children? Does your child enjoy praise from some people more than others?

_X_ Yes   *List specific people* _____Almost anyone, definitely Mom_____
_____ No

12. What items and activities are most enjoyable to the child? What items or activities could serve as special rewards?

_X_ Social interaction with adults	_____ High fives	_____ Small toys, prizes (e.g., stickers, stamps)
_X_ Physical interaction with adults (rough-housing, tickle, cuddle)	_X_ Praise from adults	_X_ Device time (e.g., tablet, electronic game system)
_____ Social interaction with siblings/ peers	_____ Praise from siblings/ other kids	_____ Art activities (e.g., drawing pictures, painting)
_____ Playing a game	_X_ Music	_____ Objects/toys: (specify) _____
_____ Parent helper	_____ Puzzles	_X_ Food: (specify) fruit snacks, juice
_____ Extra time outside	_____ Books	
_X_ Extra praise and attention from adults	_____ Special activity	
_____ Extra time in preferred activity	_____ Special helper	
	_____ Computer time	
	_X_ Television time	

Other: _____

Additional comments not addressed:

FORM 7 · PTR-F Assessment Summary Table

Child: Lucy   Date: 8/5/15

Challenging behavior: Physically aggressive behaviors	
1. PREVENT	**2. REINFORCE**
Arriving to or leaving the house Bedtime Toileting Toothbrushing Meals Visiting others Mostly with mom	Sent to time out/given personal space Activity delayed, changed, ended, and/ or removed Verbal redirect Physical guidance Very likely to remove items/activities, result in acknowledgment, gain attention from adults, and delay transition to nonpreferred activity

3. Hypothesis statement: When Lucy is asked to do something she does not want to do, then she will engage in physically aggressive behaviors (see Goal Sheet for definition); as a result, she avoids or delays the task or activity and gets attention through verbal redirects and/or physical guidance.

Desirable behavior: Follow daily routines calmly and cooperatively	
4. PREVENT	**5. REINFORCE**
Doing something she wants to do (looking at books, watching TV, playing on cell phone, playing with preferred toys) In the car	Seldom receives acknowledgment for appropriate behavior From mom: praise, hugs, cuddling, playing together, tickling Music, TV Mom's cell phone

6. TEACH
Communication – break, help, wants and needs, expressing emotions, aversions and/or preference Social skills – get attention appropriately, respond to adults, giving a play idea, waiting for reinforcement Problem solving – controlling impulsive behavior, asking for help, playing independently, following directions, following schedules and routines, accepting "no," getting engaged in an activity, staying engaged in activities

Figure 4.10a. Lucy's PTR-F Assessment Summary Table.

things she did not want to do. Roberta explained that knowing (or hypothesizing) about the function of Lucy's behavior was important for identifying strategies to implement and that to have a successful plan, it was important to understand why the behavior was occurring and identify more appropriate skills to teach Lucy that serve the same function. Roberta told Gabby that she completely understood her frustration about taking time to get the plan together, but reminded her about following the PTR-F process in order to develop the most comprehensive and effective plan. Due to all of the current stress, Gabby was frustrated but understood the process and wanted to move forward to start identifying strategies.

Desirable Behavior Goals and the Behavior Rating Scale

Roberta brought out the PTR-F Goal Sheet to identify a goal for a desirable behavior, given the results of the PTR-F assessment. Now that they all understood that Lucy's physically aggressive behavior was used to avoid nonpreferred tasks, it was time to identify what skill would be helpful for Lucy to learn to use when she wanted to avoid nonpreferred tasks instead of displaying physical aggression. As the team reviewed the goal sheet and the list of behaviors that Gabby identified to increase, being able to communicate better (or say more words) seemed like the best way to provide Lucy with a replacement for physical aggression to avoid nonpreferred tasks. Lucy knows how to say "no" and says it often when she does not want to do something, but Gabby wanted to know what they would do if "no" is not an option. What if Lucy needed to get dressed for the day to get to school and she did not want to? In this case, following the routine should not be a choice.

Gabby agreed that communication is an important goal for Lucy, but perhaps getting her to follow the daily routines would be a better place to start because that is what was important to Gabby and what would make the day go more smoothly and calmly. Gabby also believed that she could still work on increasing Lucy's verbal language at the same time in this process. The team agreed to develop a plan to get Lucy to follow daily routines more calmly and cooperatively and to actively participate in the routines. (Figure 4.11a shows Lucy's completed PTR-F Goal Sheet.)

The next step was to return to the BRS to develop the anchors for the identified desirable behavior. Roberta briefly reviewed the different dimensions of behavior that could be measured and had Gabby think about the best way to track whether or not Lucy is making progress. After some discussion between Gabby and Marguerite, Gabby ultimately decided that keeping track of how much Lucy was following the routine on her own would be the most helpful to document (using a prompt hierarchy). Because Lucy's plan was going to be developed across multiple routines, Roberta asked if she wanted to keep track of the routines across the day like she was documenting for physically aggressive behaviors, or if there might be another way to record Lucy's progress. Gabby asked if it would be okay to just keep track of how Lucy is doing during the morning routine, since it is extremely stressful trying to get Lucy to school during the week. Gabby still wanted to work on the other routines at the same time, but could figure out a better way to track those later. Roberta agreed that if it would be more beneficial to collect data on the morning routine only (for now); Gabby could try that for a couple of weeks to see how that was going, and they could always adjust the BRS if there were problems. The prompt hierarchy was developed for the anchors, and Roberta recorded these on the BRS (see Figure 4.12a). A score of 5 meant that Lucy could complete a task independently with little prompting or few reminders and that she was cooperative and calm, whereas a score of 1 meant that mom had to fully prompt her through most steps of the routine.

After finalizing the BRS, Gabby wanted to continue the meeting to start identifying strategies. Roberta informed Gabby that there would not be enough time to get through all of them today, but that they could get started and see how much they could accomplish before Roberta had to leave.

FORM
1

PTR-F Goal Sheet

Instructions:
1. Identify and write out the child's challenging behaviors to decrease and the contexts or routines where these behaviors need to improve.
2. Select ONE challenging behavior to target within family contexts or routines.
3. Operationally define this target behavior—observable (seen or heard) and measurable (counted or timed).
4. Identify and write out the child's desirable behaviors to increase.
5. Select target desirable behavior (to be completed following PTR-F assessment).
6. Operationally define the desirable behavior (to be completed following PTR-F assessment).

Child: Lucy   **Date:** 7/29/15

Goals: Challenging behaviors		
	Behaviors	*Context/routines*
Challenging behaviors to decrease	Hitting Kicking Biting Scratching Taking her clothes off Running away/hiding Screaming/yelling	Getting dressed Meals—grazes, likes snacking Toileting Going to school Ending preferred activities Bedtime
Target behavior	Physically aggressive behaviors	Getting ready for the day Meals
Operational definition	When Lucy is physically aggressive, she may hit, slap, kick, bite, scratch, pull on clothes/hair, scream/yell, or try to take her clothes off.	

Goals: Desirable behaviors		
Desirable behaviors to increase	Follow daily routines calmly (without resisting) Follow directions—listen to Mom Eat at the table Eat a more complete meal Say more words—communicate better Play more independently Play with toys appropriately (vs. throwing, breaking)	
Target behavior	(to be completed following PTR-F assessment) Follow daily routines calmly and cooperatively	
Operational definition	(to be completed following PTR-F assessment) When Lucy is told that it is time for a daily routine, she will actively participate in the routine calmly (and eventually independently) by following Mom's directions for the routine, attempting to complete or completing the specific task, and/or initiating the next steps of the routine.	

Figure 4.11a. Lucy's completed PTR-F Goal Sheet.

FORM 2

PTR-F Behavior Rating Scale

Child: _Lucy_   Rater: _Mom_   Routine: _Throughout the day_   Month: _August_

Date/time: _____

	7/29/15	7/30/15	7/31/15	8/1/15	8/2/15	8/3/15	8/4/15	8/5/15	8/6/15	8/7/15	8/8/15	8/7/15	8/8/15	8/9/15	8/10/15	8/11/15	8/12/15	8/13/15	8/14/15	8/15/15
Desirable behavior	5 4 3 2 1	5 4 3 2 1	5 4 3 2 1	5 4 3 2 1	5 4 3 2 1	5 4 3 2 1	5 4 3 2 1	5 4 3 2 1	5 4 3 2 1	5 4 3 2 1	5 4 3 2 1	5 4 3 2 1	5 4 3 2 1	5 4 3 2 1	5 4 3 2 1	5 4 3 2 1	5 4 3 2 1	5 4 3 2 1	5 4 3 2 1	5 4 3 2 1
Morning routine – calm and cooperative																				
Challenging behavior	5 ☑4 3 2 1	☑5 4 3 2 1	5 ☑4 3 2 1	☑5 4 3 2 1	5 ☑4 3 2 1	5 4 3 2 1	5 4 3 2 1	5 4 3 2 1	5 4 3 2 1	5 4 3 2 1	5 4 3 2 1	5 4 3 2 1	5 4 3 2 1	5 4 3 2 1	5 4 3 2 1	5 4 3 2 1	5 4 3 2 1	5 4 3 2 1	5 4 3 2 1	5 4 3 2 1
Aggressive behaviors																				

Desirable behavior: _Morning routine - calm and cooperative_

5 = 1 or 2 steps calm, cooperative, indept.

4 = Only 1 or 2 steps partially prompted

3 = Most steps partially prompted

2 = Only 1 or 2 steps fully prompted

1 = Most steps fully prompted

Challenging behavior: _Aggressive behaviors_

5 = 8 or more times

4 = 6–7 times

3 = 3–5 times

2 = 1–2 times

1 = 0

Figure 4.12a. Lucy's completed Behavior Rating Scale.

Self-Evaluation Checklist

The meeting continued in order to make progress toward a fully developed plan for Lucy, but before moving to the next step, Roberta reviewed the PTR-F Self-Evaluation Checklist with Gabby to ensure that all the steps were followed before proceeding further. Gabby and Roberta agreed that all the steps were complete and that they could continue moving forward.

PTR-F Intervention

5

The previous chapter discussed the process of assessment and gathering information for developing a behavior support plan. This chapter outlines the behavior support planning process, moving from gathering information in the assessment process to developing a feasible and practical behavior support plan that is a good fit for both the child and the family.

IMPLEMENTATION OF UNIVERSAL PRACTICES

Before discussing how to identify individualized strategies to create the behavior support plan, it is important to revisit universal practices for addressing the behavior of young children in the home, which were introduced in Chapter 2 of this manual. As mentioned previously, these practices have been shown to improve behavior regardless of function, and when they are in place, conditions are most optimal for implementing successful behavior support plans. As a reminder, these practices include the following: 1) providing high rates of positive attention, 2) establishing and maintaining predictable daily schedules, 3) including consistent patterns of activities within daily routines, and 4) defining behavioral expectations and the differences between desirable behavior and challenging behavior.

We recognize that many families already use these practices, at least to some extent. That is, many families follow schedules that occur on most days, have regular sequences of activities within routines, attempt to engage their children in positive interactions, and describe rules for their children's behavior. However, maintaining these practices and using them with precision and consistency can be extremely difficult when family life is disrupted by frequently occurring challenging behaviors. Still, studies have shown that efforts to implement these practices as regularly as possible can lead to great improvements in behavior (Fixsen, Blase, Naoom, & Wallace, 2009). Indeed, we have often seen that implementing these universal parenting practices can lead to such improvements that the use of relatively effortful, individualized interventions such as the Prevent-Teach-Reinforce for Families (PTR-F) model becomes unnecessary. For this reason, we recommend that families adopt the universal practices as soon as they can. It is not necessary to wait for the PTR-F assessments to be completed before putting these practices into place. These universal practices can be implemented before and during the individualized process of PTR-F. In some cases, families will see that behaviors have improved to the point that use of the individualized strategies is not so urgent as initially believed, or they find that the individualized strategies become easier to use and even more effective than they would be without the universal practices in place. How to implement the four universal strategies is described in greater detail in the following sections.

TIP *Consistent use of universal practices may make additional individualized planning unnecessary. However, if one or more universal practices is lacking and the frequency or severity of behavior warrants, the team can still choose to go ahead with planning and incorporate specific strategies to address deficient universal practices within the scope of the behavior support plan.*

Provide High Rates of Positive Attention and Acknowledge Occasions in Which the Child Is Behaving Appropriately

As noted in Chapter 2, we recommend that families seek to provide at least a 5:1 ratio of positive attention to corrective feedback. This 5:1 ratio is based on research demonstrating improved child behavior when adults spend the majority of their time attending to desired behaviors (Kazdin, 2012; Kontos, 1999; Zanolli, Saudargas, & Twardosz, 1997). Positive attention primarily consists of family members spending extended periods of quality time engaged with their child in positive, fun activities and offering encouragement and compliments. Also, recall that positive attention also includes "catching the child being good" and providing praise and other forms of acknowledgment when special acts of desirable behavior occur. We understand that establishing such a high rate of positive interaction can seem daunting and even artificial at first, but with practice, most families can come close to or even exceed this ratio. Providing positive attention also gets easier as the child's behavior becomes more favorable, especially when all family members partake in acknowledging and praising the child.

Establish and Maintain Regular and Predictable Daily Routines

For a child to be successful in any environment, it is vital that there is some consistency in the routine and that the child has some idea of what will come next in the day. Without this predictable schedule, the child may be in a state of some anxiety about what will happen next, or the child may be concerned that an important or valued activity will not occur. This often makes challenging behavior more likely.

In family homes, there are usually activities that occur, or could occur, on a daily basis and that can be built into a daily schedule. These activities may include getting dressed, having breakfast, getting ready to go to a program or school, lunch, playtime, dinner, bathing, and getting ready for bed. Specific activities and the way in which they are carried out may vary quite a bit from family to family, but every family should have general expectations for a set of activities in their home. Once a schedule is put together, it can be conveyed to the child in a number of ways. For children with communication or developmental disabilities, a visual schedule can be helpful in framing this discussion with the child.

When setting up a visual schedule with the family, there are several considerations that will maximize the effectiveness of this practice: 1) use both words and pictures (drawings or photographs, depending on what would be the best fit for the child and family); 2) make sure that the schedule is at eye level and located where the child can see and access it; 3) review the schedule consistently and often (many times per day in the beginning and always at least daily); 4) provide ample warning for changes that might occur in a day's schedule and use the schedule to talk about these changes; 5) refer to the schedule when all is going well, not just when the child is becoming upset; and 6) include some allowance for variation in the schedule. This variation should include fun activities and not just potentially aversive activities.

Include Consistent Patterns of Activities within Daily Routines

Although a daily schedule of activities does provide children with some consistency, this level of structure is not sufficient for children to be successful in all routines throughout the day. Many routines (e.g., bathing, mealtime, bedtime, getting ready to leave the house) may need to be more defined for the child. This additional scaffolding, or building routines within routines, is the third universal practice. Establishing a consistent sequence of activities within everyday routines helps children predict and participate in the steps of the routines and reduces challenging behaviors.

Some activity routines can be simple. For example, a family may have a bath time sequence that begins with having a child make a choice between a bubble bath or a regular bath, take off his or her clothes, and then choose two toys to play with in the bath. Other activity sequences might be more elaborate, with more activities or activity steps, and some may be supported by visual schedules of picture sequences. For instance, an activity sequence or *task analysis* of a toothbrushing routine might involve seven steps: 1) pull out toothbrush and toothpaste, 2) add toothpaste to toothbrush, 3) wet toothbrush, 4) brush teeth with up-and-down motion, 5) rinse out mouth, 6) rinse toothbrush, and 7) return items. Such a task sequence helps not only with predictability but also with teaching an important self-care skill.

Clearly Define Behavioral Expectations and the Differences Between Desirable and Challenging Behaviors

Children must be taught the difference between acceptable and unacceptable behavior and the fact that behavioral expectations sometimes differ across settings and across routines. Although many behavioral expectations will be the same across most family routines, some will be different. For instance, it may be appropriate to yell and run during outdoor play, but these behaviors are not welcomed during indoor block play. To effectively teach these different expectations for behavior, the adults in the family first need to know the differences between what is expected in various routines and settings and be able to agree consistently on these distinctions. This is not always as straightforward as it may seem. Therefore, it is vital for parents and other relevant family members to discuss and agree upon, for example, acceptable touching versus unacceptable hitting, indoor versus outdoor voices, and the time allotted for responsiveness to adult requests. When these distinctions are well understood by supervising adults, they can then be taught to the child.

Children can learn differences in behavioral expectations quite readily if they are explained and if the consequences for desirable behavior and undesirable behavior are administered consistently. As indicated in the first universal practice, acknowledgment (such as sincere praise) for desirable behavior should be much more frequent than corrections for undesirable behavior. Sometimes, especially as children are learning the difference between acceptable and unacceptable behavior, activities need to be engineered in such a way that desirable behavior will be much more likely to occur. This can be accomplished in many ways—for example, by including more preferred materials and activities or by making less preferred routines shorter than usual. The point is that the emphasis should be on reinforcing the child's desirable behavior, with challenging behavior viewed as a mistake and an opportunity for gentle, corrective guidance.

INDIVIDUALIZED INTERVENTIONS AND THE BEHAVIOR SUPPORT PLAN

If challenging behavior continues even with these general strategies in place, more intensive, individualized intervention may be a prudent course of action. We recognize that some of these universal parenting strategies can take time for families to implement and that families may not be able to wait for these strategies to work before they need to acquire more individualized support. In that case, we recommend that an individualized plan be developed and implemented as the family works on these general parenting strategies. Developing an individualized behavior support plan can help to augment universal parenting practices and can provide more scaffolding for the family in implementing both general and individualized strategies for promoting desirable behavior. For example, if the team notes that the family needs assistance in breaking up activities into more consistent routines, the problematic routine can be delineated in the plan as well as taught as a general strategy.

A facilitator needs to possess certain skills in order to develop an effective behavior support plan. Although this manual provides a prescriptive approach to planning and offers an array of options for building a behavior support plan, an understanding of learning principles and applied behavior analysis will help the facilitator to apply the strategies (and help the family apply the strategies) in a manner that is most responsive to the information in the PTR-F assessment and that ensures that intervention strategies are properly aligned with the perceived function of the behavior. It is useful, and often essential, for the facilitator to be well versed in instructional practices, such as those recommended by the Division for Early Childhood of the Council for Exceptional Children (Division for Early Childhood, 2014). In particular, it is important for the facilitator to be experienced with general behavioral principles, including reinforcement and antecedent and contextual influences (as discussed in Chapter 1).

TIP *Every behavior support plan needs to include multiple strategies to both reduce challenging behaviors and increase desired behaviors, including at least one prevent strategy, at least one teach strategy, and all of the core reinforce strategies. Be sure that all strategies contained within the behavior support plan are aligned with the identified function of the behavior as determined by the PTR-F assessment.*

A plan developed with the PTR-F model always includes multiple strategies, with at least one drawn from the array of prevent strategies, at least one drawn from teach strategies, and specific procedures for arranging consequences (reinforce). Including strategies from each of these categories allows for an intervention plan that is more robust than single-component interventions and addresses factors that precipitate a behavior (prevent), the functions of the behavior (teach), and the consequences that strengthen or weaken the behavior (reinforce). In the following sections, we will first review the general procedures and considerations for designing and implementing the behavior support plan and then describe each of the intervention components: prevent, teach, and reinforce.

Intervention Procedures

The PTR-F Intervention Menu (see Table 5.1) provides a list of strategies for families to consider in developing the behavior support plan. The Intervention Guide at the end of the

Table 5.1. PTR-F Intervention Menu

Prevent strategies	Teach strategies	Reinforce strategies
• Provide choices • Intersperse difficult or nonpreferred tasks with easy or preferred tasks • Embed preferences into activities • Enhance predictability with calendars and schedules • Use timers and other visual/auditory supports for added structure • Alter physical arrangement of environment/ activity area • Remove triggers for challenging behavior • Modify what is explicitly asked of your child • Change how instructions are delivered • Reduce distractions or competing events or materials • Use safety signal to inform your child of follow-up activities • Use scripted social stories to describe problematic situations and potential solutions	• Teach appropriate ways to communicate/functional communication training • Teach social skills • Teach self-monitoring • Tolerate delay of reinforcement • Teach independence with visual schedules and calendars • Teach active participation	All plans must: 1. Identify a functional reinforcer(s) 2. Provide reinforcer for desirable behavior 3. Remove reinforcement for challenging behavior

book describes these strategies in detail, and the facilitator should be familiar with all of the options before supporting the family in making decisions about components to include in the behavior support plan. Although the menu is not exhaustive of all the evidence-based practices for addressing challenging behavior, the list is composed of the most common and most effective strategies in a majority of circumstances. We encourage teams to be flexible and creative when designing behavior support plans, and there are certainly additional practices that families or the facilitator could suggest that would be worthwhile to include. However, any practice strategy included in the support plan should: 1) fit within one of the three components—prevent, teach, or reinforce—with team members agreeing on which category the strategy will fit in; 2) be consistent with the overall logic and assessment data of the PTR-F model; 3) be evaluated with careful, objective data to be sure that it is effective; and 4) be respectful of contextual fit and family preferences.

There are several important considerations that need to be followed for the plan to be aligned with the principles of PTR-F. First, the plan needs to have at least one strategy from the components of prevent and teach, and it needs to include the core strategies of the reinforce component. Second, this set of strategies needs to be consistent with the findings of the assessment and address the function as stated in the hypothesis statement. Finally, family members implementing the behavior support plan in the home need to be able and willing to consistently implement all the intervention strategies within the routines where challenging behavior occurs. Whether intervention strategies are implemented by one parent, two parents, or multiple family members, all involved parties need to be comfortable with the intervention procedures and should receive support so that they can use the strategies with reasonable consistency and precision.

TIP *Strategies included in a plan should be both evidence based and efficient for use in home and community settings. Make sure that plans are written in language that makes sense to the family members who will be using the plan. Break more complex strategies down into smaller steps that can be easily followed.*

Choosing strategies that address or honor the functions of the challenging behavior is not always an easy task. If there was a clear and simple method for developing a perfect behavior support plan, then the process would be much easier to convey, and children probably would exhibit fewer challenging behaviors. However, the process of selecting intervention strategies can be a bit complicated. There are many things to take into account. The strategy should be supported by research that shows demonstrated effectiveness with similar challenges, and it should make sense in light of the information unveiled by the functional behavioral assessment (PTR-F assessment). The strategy should be not only effective, but also reasonably efficient, meaning that implementation of the intervention should not require extensive time or effort in relation to the anticipated benefits. And, just as important, the strategy must be congruent with a family's values and preferences, and it should be able to be implemented within the ongoing context of the family's life. This latter point is what we mean by *contextual fit* (Albin et al., 1996). Without contextual fit, the plan would not be worth much because it most likely would not be implemented over any extended period of time.

The good news is that a behavior support plan does not have to be perfect to be effective. There are many intervention components to choose from. So, if the ideal strategy is not one that is acceptable for a particular family, it is probable that an alternative strategy will be effective. This is part of the reason for the PTR-F requirement that multiple strategies (at least one from each of the prevent, teach, and reinforce categories) be included. In the following sections, we describe considerations for selecting intervention strategies from each of the three components. Complete descriptions of the strategies and how they should be implemented are provided in the Intervention Guide at the end of the book.

Prevent

The evidence-based strategies available for the prevent category are listed in the left column of the PTR-F Intervention Menu (see Table 5.1) and are described in detail in the Intervention Guide at the end of the book. As with the other categories, the selection of prevent strategies should be based on information gained from the PTR-F assessment in Chapter 4. These assessment procedures should have provided information about the stimuli, events, and activities that are associated with high rates of challenging behavior. Information should also have been obtained about those antecedent stimuli, events, and activities associated with high rates of desirable behavior. The essential idea behind prevent interventions is to remove or ameliorate the stimuli associated with challenging behaviors and add or enhance those stimuli, events, and activities associated with desirable behavior. The intervention options on the Intervention Menu basically offer strategies to accomplish these objectives.

Many of the prevent strategies involve manipulation of antecedent variables that are associated with or that may even trigger the occurrence of challenging behavior. These triggers may vary considerably, and thus, any strategies developed should be tied closely to the findings in the assessment. Such antecedent manipulations (such as adding or removing cues) often involve changing the behavior of parents, siblings and others who might influence the child's challenging behavior. It is important to recognize that there are some antecedent events that cannot simply be removed. For example, a mother's call that the child needs to get ready to take a bath cannot be eliminated entirely, but the transition might be ameliorated by having the mother ask the child whether she wants bubbles in her bath or wants to play with a new bath toy.

Although we recommend that at least one prevent strategy be used as part of the behavior support plan, it is acceptable, and often advantageous, to use multiple prevent strategies to address a single behavior within a routine (see Timmy's case example at the end of this chapter, in which two prevent strategies are suggested to address tantrums during the bedtime routine). It is important that the selected strategies are logical steps to take in the context of the routine, that they correspond to the developmental level of the child, and that they are a good fit with the family. Also keep in mind that each of the prevent strategies can be adapted to fit the needs of the child and family. For example, if Lucas's family notes that Lucas responds poorly to being asked if he wants to stop playing and get ready for dinner, the team should choose "change how instructions are delivered," because this strategy has a logical connection to the challenging behavior. If the team decides that this prevent strategy is a good fit for the child and family, the team then needs to determine specific details as to how, when, where, and by whom the modified instructions are to be delivered. These details should all be evident in the plan, as described in subsequent chapters.

Prevent strategies can often have powerful and immediate effects (Dunlap & Kern, 1996; Kern & Clemens, 2007; Kern, Sokol, & Dunlap, 2006). However, their effects are not expected to be as long-lasting as instruction. Therefore, it is always important to accompany prevent strategies with well-chosen practices from the teach and reinforce categories.

Teach

Teach strategies in PTR-F are listed in the middle column of Table 5.1. The facilitator should help the team to connect the identified function of the behavior to the appropriate strategy. In the majority of cases, the team will conclude that the child needs to learn skills to communicate wants and needs appropriately. This is frequently the case because most challenging behavior is, in fact, a form of communication, and the most urgent need is to help the child use appropriate forms of communication instead of the challenging behavior. The trick here is to first identify the specific function of the challenging behavior within specified routines (via the assessment procedures described in Chapter 4). Recall that the function can be to get something, such as attention, assistance, a toy, physical contact, food, or drink, or to get rid of something, such as a request or demand, an unwanted play partner, a transition to a less preferred activity, or even some physiological discomfort. When the function is clear, the next step is to identify an appropriate replacement behavior that will serve the same function (purpose) as the challenging behavior. The replacement behavior usually involves some words, but for nonverbal children, it can take the form of gestures, signs, pictures, or anything else that will be effective in soliciting desired action on the part of a parent or other family member. When the replacement behavior is selected, the procedure involves prompting and reinforcing the desirable behavior while ignoring the challenging behavior. This intervention strategy is known as *functional communication training* (Carr & Durand, 1985; Durand & Moskowitz, 2015), and it is the most thoroughly researched and essential procedure in the entire field of behavior support (aside from the general use of positive reinforcement). Functional communication training is described in detail in the book's Intervention Guide, and it is recommended as the primary choice in the teach column of the Intervention Menu.

The Intervention Menu includes other teach strategies that can be used in addition to functional communication training or, in some cases, as the primary instructional practice. For example, if a child is seen to display extreme challenging behaviors in the context of sibling interactions, a teach strategy might focus on the social skills of turn taking, appropriate ways to express frustration, and sharing. Other children might benefit greatly from instruction on how to engage in activities with greater independence, and some might need to learn how to wait for a desired item or activity to become available, which we refer to as tolerating a delay of reinforcement.

After prevent and teach strategies are selected, the team must follow effective procedures for reinforcing behavior as part of the reinforce component of PTR-F, described next.

Reinforce

As shown in Table 5.1, the reinforce menu differs from the prevent and teach menus in that the intervention process must include each of the following strategies: 1) identify valued, functional reinforcer(s); 2) provide reinforcer for desirable behavior; and 3) remove reinforcement for challenging behavior.

Identify Valued, Functional Reinforcers

It is essential that the reinforcers for replacement behaviors or other desired behaviors are at least as valuable to the child as what he or she currently gets from engaging in challenging behavior. If a replacement behavior is reinforced, but the child does not find the consequence to be as rewarding as what he or she was getting out of the challenging behavior, then the child will not find value in adopting the proposed alternative behavior and will try to find another way to get what was previously obtained through the behavior of concern. Reinforcers for desired behavior must be sufficiently powerful or the desired behavior will not increase and the intervention will be ineffective. A great deal of the efficacy of PTR-F, or any other behavior support approach, depends on the strength of the reinforcer and the timeliness with which the reinforcer is delivered (Miltenberger, 2008).

 It is not enough to provide or increase reinforcement for desired behavior. For behavior support to be effective, access to reinforcement must also be minimized when a child engages in challenging behavior. Keep in mind that what is considered a reinforcer for one child may not be a reinforcer for another child. A reinforcer is defined by how the child responds to the item or activity in a particular context.

It is always best to use reinforcers that are as natural as possible. Praise, hugs, high fives, and applause are consequences that occur naturally in family interactions, so these are good consequences to use. Sometimes, these are sufficiently powerful to change difficult behavior if they are used consistently and immediately when desired behavior occurs. However, there are times when these natural consequences need to be augmented by something more powerful, at least for a period of days or weeks until clear behavior change has been seen. More special reinforcers might be stickers, special treats, extra special physical engagement, or access to a special toy. For an example, see Lucy's case example at the end of this chapter, in which fruit snacks are offered as a special reinforcer in addition to praise and attention from Mom. It is important to appreciate that not everything will work as a reinforcer, and the only way to be sure is to observe the change in behavior that occurs when the reinforcer is used. It is also good to remember that a special reinforcer is only special if it is earned only by engaging in the desired behavior that is part of the support plan. If the special reinforcer is easily available at other times, it will no longer be as powerful as it would be if reserved for needed behavior change.

Provide Reinforcer for Desirable Behavior

Once a valued reinforcer is identified, the facilitator helps the family to set up the routine so that this reinforcer is earned when the child engages in the desired behavior. In addition, this contingent reinforcement must be provided at least as quickly and as consistently as the response that the child was getting for engaging in the challenging behavior. This is a crucial element. The effectiveness of the reinforcer is influenced by its connection to the desired behavior, and consistency and immediacy are vital in establishing that connection.

Remove Reinforcement for Challenging Behavior

For reinforcement of desired behavior to be effective, it is necessary to remove reinforcement for the challenging behavior, or reduce the reinforcement as much as possible. Remember that challenging behavior occurs because it has been (inadvertently) reinforced. The most certain way to reduce or eliminate challenging behavior is to remove the reinforcers, but that is not always easy to do because the reinforcers almost always involve some kind of attention, and severe challenging behavior can be difficult or impossible to ignore. Even corrective feedback is a form of attention and can be reinforcing. However, it is much easier to remove reinforcement for challenging behavior when the same reinforcers are available for desired behaviors.

Once again, the critical consideration in this stage of the reinforce procedures is correctly identifying the reinforcer that has been maintaining the challenging behavior. This takes us back to the PTR-F assessment and the vital importance of identifying the function of the challenging behavior within the routine. The function is the reinforcer. Removing the reinforcer means breaking the connection between the behavior and its function. If the behavior no longer functions as it once did, it will be weakened and will eventually disappear. However, as we emphasized previously, this is hard to do unless the same function can be achieved through effective reinforcement of alternative, desired behaviors.

Developing the Behavior Support Plan

The behavior support plan is developed in a team meeting during which the assessment data and the hypotheses are reviewed, and discussion focuses on selection of strategies to include in the plan. We have given an overview of the prevent, teach, and reinforce strategies, described in detail in the Intervention Guide at the end of this book. The facilitator and the team should review all these possible strategies. Usually, the facilitator offers general guidance to help the family select strategies, but since the family members will be responsible for implementing the strategies, they must make the final decisions about what to include in the behavior support plan. To make informed decisions, the family must have accurate information about what exactly is involved in implementing the strategies. Team discussions need to consider any support that might be needed and what coaching support can be provided (see Chapter 6), any materials that might be required, and the time and diligence needed for implementation and data collection.

Once the team has agreed upon the strategies, the intervention components must be laid out in a plan that describes the intervention in enough detail to provide a roadmap for implementation. The plan will need to include detailed information about materials (if materials are needed) and how these materials will be used, the specific steps for roll-out of intervention strategies, which individuals will be responsible for carrying out the intervention, and the specific procedures for carrying out each intervention component. Because it is important to describe the plan in detail, some plans can be lengthy; however, having the previously mentioned details in place will help to ensure that the family is prepared to implement the plan and aware of and ready for any potential issues in implementation. Sample behavior support plans for Timmy and Lucy are included at the end of this chapter.

 TIP *Foster a collaborative atmosphere in which input is sought from family members and other team members throughout the planning process. This will help to garner commitment to the behavior support plan and ensure that all family members are aware of their roles and are comfortable in carrying out the intervention strategies.*

Because of the complexity of an intervention plan, the PTR-F Behavior Support Plan Summary (see Figure 5.1), used as a cover page or first page of the behavior support plan, serves as a quick reference guide for families that summarizes the key components of the behavior support plan. Families can choose to place multiple copies of this reference guide in easy-to-access locations in rooms of the house that see the most activity. We should stress that the PTR-F Behavior Support Plan Summary should not be used without regularly reviewing the whole plan. This document only serves as a quick reference and reminder for family members who are implementing the plan.

This PTR-F Behavior Support Plan Summary begins with a checklist of the universal practices that are described in the first section of the chapter. This list serves as a reminder for parents to use the universal strategies, and those practices that are especially relevant to the situation or to the child's and parent's behavior can be highlighted or circled to provide additional emphasis. The rest of the form is devoted to child-specific prevent, teach, and reinforce strategies. The first row divides the strategies into these three components, with room to list and describe multiple strategies per component as dictated by the plan. The second row of the form provides room for a brief description of the intervention strategies, with space in the third row for parents to add notes. The notes section provides a space for parents to quickly record observations related to the strategies as well as potential variations, embellishments, or special considerations. These notes can then provide a cue to parents when revisiting the plan with the facilitator.

Moving from Planning to Implementation

An important part of developing the support plan is to consider how to initiate implementation and the kinds of support that families might need to implement the plan with precision and comfort. The process of implementation will vary greatly from family to

FORM
9
PTR-F Behavior Support Plan Summary

Child: _____   Date: _____

Practices for all children:
- ❑ Provide high rates of positive attention.
- ❑ Establish and maintain predictable daily schedules.
- ❑ Include consistent patterns of activities within daily routines.
- ❑ Define behavioral expectations and difference between desirable and challenging behavior.

Hypothesis statement: _____
_____

Intervention strategies:

	Prevent	Teach	Reinforce
Strategies			All plans must: 1. Identify valued, functional reinforcer(s) 2. Provide reinforcer for desirable behavior 3. Remove reinforcement for challenging behavior
Brief description			
Implementation notes			

Figure 5.1.   PTR-F Behavior Support Plan Summary.

family, depending on time available, the complexity of the plan, the severity of the challenging behaviors, the number of conflicting responsibilities, and other factors. With some cases, implementation will be fairly straightforward and, hopefully, behavior change will be rapid. With other families, the early stages of implementation will be hectic. Decisions might be made to introduce different strategies gradually, especially if certain strategies are complicated and key family members are uncertain about their abilities to implement with fidelity. This is understandable. Many of the specific intervention practices require adults to adopt unfamiliar behaviors and ways of responding and relating to their child. These can require instruction and practice. This process is referred to as coaching, and we devote the following chapter to the details of this stage. A vital role of the facilitator is to serve as the coach.

SUMMARY

As with previous steps, intervention planning and development of the behavior support plan conclude with team members completing self-evaluation using the Self-Evaluation Checklist: PTR-F Intervention (see Figure 5.2).

Behavior change requires a concerted effort. The effort is important and worthwhile, but we appreciate that it requires focus and dedication. Although ultimately the goal is to improve the behavior of a child, it is the family's behavior that needs to change first. The behavior support plan describes the changes that the family will adopt, and it is these changes that will work to help the child to establish a new trajectory of social and behavioral development.

FORM
10

Self-Evaluation Checklist: PTR-F Intervention

		Yes	No
1.	Has the team carefully assessed the status of general parenting strategies, and have steps been taken to improve the implementation of these strategies?	❏	❏
2.	Did the team members review the descriptions of the required intervention strategies for reinforce and the possible intervention strategies for prevent and teach (listed in the PTR-F Intervention Menu)?	❏	❏
3.	Did the team decide on intervention strategies to include in the child's behavior support plan?	❏	❏
4.	Did the team complete the PTR-F Behavior Support Plan Summary?	❏	❏
5.	Did the team determine next steps for implementing the behavior support plan and the schedule for training and support?	❏	❏

Figure 5.2.   Self-Evaluation Checklist: PTR-F Intervention.

APPENDIX
Case Examples

TEAM MEETING 3: TIMMY

PTR-F Intervention

Once the Prevent-Teach-Reinforce for Families (PTR-F) assessment was complete, a desirable behavior goal was selected, and a plan for collecting data on the desirable behavior was in place, the next step was to identify strategies and create the behavior support plan. Kaci took out the PTR-F Intervention Menu and gave a copy to Jodie and Phil to look at while they reviewed the strategies. Because Kaci knew all of the strategies well, she briefly described each of the prevent strategies and how each strategy could possibly look for Timmy. After all the strategies were briefly reviewed, Kaci referred back to the PTR-F Assessment Summary Table and hypothesis statement and asked Jodie and Phil which interventions they would like to consider for preventing Timmy's tantrums during bedtime. She reminded them that the strategies should honor the functions of Timmy's tantrums: avoiding bedtime and getting attention. In between helping the boys eat their dinner, Jodie and Phil went down the list of prevent strategies and were able to rule out several of the strategies, thinking that they would not be effective for Timmy or would not honor the function of Timmy's behavior. After some discussion among the team, Jodie and Phil decided to implement the following two prevent strategies: enhance predictability with calendars and schedules and use timers and other visual and auditory supports for added structure.

The team quickly identified how the strategies would be implemented, and Kaci helped Jodie and Phil break down the two strategies into specific discrete steps. Once those details were finalized, they looked at the teach strategies. Jodie and Phil were quickly able to identify tolerating delay of reinforcement as the strategy they wanted to implement but were clueless about how they would do that. Kaci mentioned several ideas, including teaching Timmy to stay in his room by himself for increasing amounts of time, using a sticker chart or having Timmy earn tokens, or giving him a certain number of "passes" to limit how many times he could leave his room during the night. After some discussion, Jodie and Phil decided that teaching Timmy to stay in his room for increasing amounts of time would probably be the most effective, given his age. Plus, Timmy did not seem to care much about stickers anyway.

Next, the team began to determine how they would teach Timmy to delay reinforcement (e.g., avoiding bedtime, attention from Mom or Dad). Incorporating a visual schedule and using a timer to help Timmy stay in his room, Jodie and Phil agreed on starting with getting Timmy to stay in his room for 1 minute and increasing the time from there, since he could hardly make it that long. Phil was initially concerned that they would need to stay by Timmy's room all night until he fell asleep, but as they worked through the next steps, Phil felt more comfortable with the idea and was starting to gain confidence that they might see some relief in the very near future!

The next step was to identify how they would reinforce Timmy's desirable behavior, and Kaci walked Jodie and Phil through the reinforce steps. Jodie and Phil first identified functional reinforcers for Timmy (superhero books, a list of Timmy's favorite songs, lying with Timmy and/or snuggling, and tickling/rough-housing). Because they were all related to attention from Mom or Dad, Kaci encouraged them to identify additional toys or activities that would help Timmy stay in his room and would only be available during bedtime.

The team then laid out a plan for how they would reinforce Timmy for staying in his room. The first couple nights would take the most time, but with the detailed plan that they devised, Kaci assured Jodie and Phil that there was likely to be improvement within the first few days. Kaci explained that she would typically be with them the first time they implemented the plan, but because they wanted to start on a Friday night and it was a holiday weekend, she would not be available to provide direct coaching for that first session or the weekend due to previously scheduled obligations. Also, because there were materials that were needed to implement the plan, they would not be able to start that night, when Kaci was already there. Jodie was unsure about how things would go that first night and contemplated rescheduling, but she decided to stick with the original plan and work toward making progress as soon as possible. To provide additional support, Kaci agreed to talk with Jodie on Saturday morning by phone, if she wanted, to review how bedtime went on Friday night and make any adjustments for Saturday night if needed. (Figures 5.1a and 5.2a show Timmy's PTR-F Behavior Support Plan and PTR-F Behavior Support Plan Summary, respectively.)

It was past the boys' bedtime, so Jodie and Phil quickly got them ready for bed. Phil put Dakota to bed, and Jodie put on a movie for Timmy so they could finish creating the plan. Timmy usually stays in bed and falls asleep when a movie is playing. Jodie did not like Timmy

---

PTR-F Behavior Support Plan

Child: Timmy

Team members: Jodie (Mom), Phil (Dad), Kaci (PTR-F facilitator)

Date of plan: July 2, 2015

Target behavior to increase: Goes to sleep on his own

Operational definition: Timmy will calmly (e.g., use an inside voice, use compliant phrases and actions, walk from room to room, follow parent prompt in 30 seconds or less) participate in and complete the bedtime routine. When Mom or Dad completes the routine and leaves the room, Timmy will stay in his room and fall asleep independently.

Target behavior to decrease: Tantrums

Operational definition: Timmy emits a high-pitched scream (often for several seconds) and usually rolls around on the floor and kicks his legs; if someone is near, he may hit or kick whoever is close. He sometimes screams "NO!" during these episodes.

Hypothesis statement: When the bedtime routine is over and Mom and/or Dad attempt to leave the room, then Timmy tantrums; as a result, he delays bedtime and gets extra attention from Mom and/or Dad.

Prevent strategy: Enhance predictability with calendars and schedules; use timers and other visual/auditory supports for added structure

Materials needed: Pictures of the steps of the bedtime routine in the correct order, digital timer

Steps for implementing the strategy:

1. Five minutes before it is time for Timmy to begin his bedtime routine, Mom will make sure to have Timmy's attention and tell him, "Five more minutes until bedtime. I'm going to set the timer." Briefly review the steps for bedtime with Timmy and set the timer. The timer will be kept out of Timmy's reach.
2. When the 5 minutes are over and the timer is beeping, Mom will take the timer to Timmy and ask, "What time is it?" (pause to wait for response from Timmy – if he does not respond or gives an incorrect answer, Mom will say) "It's time to get ready for bed."
3. Mom will show Timmy the picture of the first step of the bedtime routine (pick out pajamas) and say, "What do we do first?" (pause to wait for response from Timmy – if he does not respond or gives an incorrect answer, Mom will say) "We pick out pajamas."
4. Timmy will walk to his room and pick out pajamas.

(continued)

Figure 5.1a. Timmy's completed PTR-F Behavior Support Plan.

Figure 5.1a.   *(continued)*

5. As Timmy completes each step (pajamas, potty, brush teeth, pick out two books, read books, say goodnight), Mom will provide descriptive verbal praise (e.g., "Thank you for walking with Mommy," "I like when you listen to Mommy") for each of the steps (even if Mom has to help Timmy complete the steps at first).
6. When the second story is almost over (last few pages), provide Timmy with a verbal warning that the book is almost over and it will be time to go to sleep.

Teach strategy: Tolerate delay of reinforcement

Materials needed: Pictures of Timmy in his bed and of the basket of superhero books, digital timer

Steps for implementing the strategy:

1. When the bedtime routine steps are complete, show Timmy the next step in the schedule, which is him lying in his bed. Mom will say, "Stay in bed and mommy will come back to read you a special story."
2. Set the timer for 1 minute.
3. Say "Goodnight" and leave the room.
4. When Timmy stays in his bed (or at least in the room), follow step 2 of Reinforce Plan; when Timmy leaves the room, follow step 3 of Reinforce Plan.
5. Repeat these steps until Timmy falls asleep.

Reinforce plan: 1) Identify functional reinforcers, 2) provide reinforcer for desirable behavior, and 3) remove reinforcement for challenging behavior

Materials needed: Special superhero books in Timmy's room, out of his reach

Steps for implementing the strategy:

1. Select special superhero books that Timmy can only access for successfully staying in his bed/room.
2. When Timmy stays in his bed (or at least in the room) until the timer starts to beep, provide descriptive praise to Timmy (e.g., "Good job staying in your bed"), allow him to pick a special superhero book, and read it to him. When the story is over, say "Goodnight" again and leave the room.
3. If Timmy leaves his room before the timer starts to beep, calmly tell him one time, "It's time for bed," put him back in bed, and walk out of the room. Reset the timer for 1 minute. If he does not stay in his bed/room, continue to follow this step until he stays in bed for 1 minute (then follow step 2, above).

Data collection: Continue to collect data using the PTR-F Behavior Rating Scale. Data will be reviewed with the facilitator, and decisions will be made based on the data.

FORM
9
PTR-F Behavior Support Plan Summary

Child: Timmy   Date: July 2, 2015

Practices for all children:
- ☑ Provide high rates of positive attention.
- ❏ Establish and maintain predictable daily schedules.
- ❏ Include consistent patterns of activities within daily routines.
- ❏ Define behavioral expectations and difference between desirable and challenging behavior.

Hypothesis statement: When the bedtime routine is over and Mom and/or Dad attempt to leave the room, then Timmy tantrums; as a result, he delays bedtime and gets extra attention from Mom and/or Dad.

Intervention strategies:

	Prevent	Teach	Reinforce
Strategies	1. Enhance predictability with calendars and schedules 2. Use timers and other visual/auditory supports for added structure	1. Tolerate delay of reinforcement	All plans must: 1. Identify valued, functional reinforcer(s) 2. Provide reinforcer for desirable behavior 3. Remove reinforcement for challenging behavior
Brief description	1. Give 5-minute warning. 2. "What time is it?" 3. Show picture schedule. 4. Provide descriptive praise for completion of steps in getting ready for bed. 5. Give warning for end of story.	1. Show picture of Timmy in bed: "Stay in bed and Mommy will come back to read you a special story." 2. Set timer for 1 minute. 3. "Goodnight." 4. If stays in room, follow Reinforce step 2; if he leaves room, follow Reinforce step 3. 5. Repeat until Timmy falls asleep.	1. Select special books and keep out of reach. 2. When stays in bed/room until timer, provide praise, and have him pick a book to read. 3. If Timmy does not comply, say, "It's time for bed," put him back in bed, reset timer, and walk out.
Implementation notes	Use bedtime routine pictures, timer Descriptive praise examples: "Thank you for walking with Mommy!" "I like when you listen to Mommy's words!" "Great job saying good night!"	Need pictures of Timmy in his bed, basket of books, timer	Need basket of books (out of reach), mom and dad's love Descriptive praise examples: "Good job staying in your bed!" "I like it when you stay in your room like a big boy!"

Figure 5.2a. Timmy's PTR-F Behavior Support Plan Summary.

falling asleep to movies, but some nights that was the only way to get him to sleep at a decent time without a fight. While Jodie and Phil got the boys ready for bed, Kaci worked on writing up the details they discussed for the behavior support plan.

Once the boys were in bed (with Timmy watching a movie), the team finalized the behavior support plan. They wrote out what they would do if Timmy left his room and/or had a tantrum. Jodie and Phil admitted that it would be difficult to ignore Timmy's tantrums because of the noise, but Kaci asked if that was something they were willing to try for at least three nights. They agreed to try it out and hoped it would not be too disruptive to Dakota, who would likely be sleeping. They also discussed talking with their neighbors to let them know that they would be working on this plan and that it might get noisier for the next few nights. Because it would be the weekend, perhaps it would not be as disruptive because the boys would be able to sleep later since they did not have to attend childcare in the morning, and it might be easier for the neighbors to accommodate as well.

The team reviewed the plan and identified what materials were needed. Jodie would take pictures of specific items related to bedtime tonight and would get them printed out the next day to put in a small photo album in the correct order. A timer would be kept in Timmy's room, along with the special superhero books that would only be for bedtime when Timmy stays in his room. Kaci would complete the PTR-F Fidelity of Strategy Implementation Form (see Chapter 6) in the morning and e-mail it to Jodie and Phil so they could use it to reflect on their plan implementation. Tonight, they would let Timmy fall asleep to a movie and would be ready to implement the plan tomorrow night. Before leaving, the team did a quick role-play to walk through all the steps and make sure everyone was clear about what to do and what was needed.

Jodie and Phil agreed to implement the strategies over the weekend, and if no progress was made or the plan fell apart, Jodie would call Kaci for assistance. Kaci agreed to come back on Monday for an observation and coaching session of bedtime. Kaci took pictures of their written plan and agreed to finish typing out the plan and the summary form to e-mail with the PTR-F Fidelity of Strategy Implementation Form.

Self-Evaluation Checklist

Before ending their long meeting, Kaci reviewed the PTR-F Self-Evaluation Checklist with Jodie and Phil. They all agreed that they completed each of the steps and could continue with implementing their plan. As Kaci left, she reminded Jodie and Phil to keep the function of Timmy's behavior in mind at all times, follow the plan, and support each other. She also reassured them that they were on the path to smoother nights!

TEAM MEETING 3: LUCY

PTR-F Intervention

Gabby was anxious to identify strategies to improve Lucy's behavior, so this process began during the PTR-F assessment meeting and would continue at a subsequent meeting until the PTR-F Behavior Support Plan was completed. Roberta gave a copy of the PTR-F Intervention Menu to Gabby and Marguerite to reference and said that they might not complete the whole plan today. Gabby was okay with doing what they could with the time that they had left. Roberta started with the hypothesis statement and asked Gabby and Marguerite to think about prevent strategies that would address Lucy's avoidance of the daily routine. Roberta gave a brief description of each of the prevent strategies, identifying potential strategies that were discussed when they were completing the PTR-F Assessment Summary Table. When the review of the strategies was complete, Roberta listed the ones that were possibilities to discuss further.

Because a visual schedule was being used successfully at school and because she had tried it before unsuccessfully, Gabby was interested in getting help to effectively use a visual schedule at home to prevent Lucy's physically aggressive behavior. Also, because Gabby wanted Lucy's behavior support plan to include multiple routines across the day, a visual schedule could eventually be provided for each of the routines. Roberta had an additional suggestion. Because Lucy frequently says "No!" when Gabby asks her to do things she does not want to do, Roberta suggested adding an additional prevent strategy to provide choices. Lucy is clear about communicating in situations where she does not want to do something, and Roberta wondered whether providing choices could prevent Lucy's refusals. Gabby thought that it would be worth a try if Roberta could help her create an easy way to enact the strategy.

Not much time was left in the meeting, so Roberta suggested that they create a plan to work on the visual schedule, because that would need to be put together before they could implement the prevent strategies. Roberta asked Gabby if she wanted to use computer icons, line drawings, actual photographs, magazine pictures, or other kinds of drawings. Gabby decided to use photographs, saying she could take them on her phone and print them at the store. She felt that Lucy would be more interested if real photographs were used instead of other types of pictures. Roberta helped Gabby create a list of the pictures she would need to take of the daily routines and what should be included in the pictures. Roberta agreed to bring the materials to put the schedule together, and they scheduled the next meeting to identify the teach and reinforce strategies, write the behavior support plan, and assemble the visual schedule. As Roberta was leaving, she reminded Gabby to continue to collect the BRS data, even recording the morning routine if possible. She also encouraged Gabby to keep up the great work and assured her that, by the next meeting, they would have a full behavior support plan ready to implement. Roberta would bring her laptop so they could write out the behavior support plan while she was at the house and then she could send it to Gabby by e-mail so Gabby would have a copy immediately.

Roberta arrived for the next meeting with her laptop and schedule materials in hand. Marguerite was not able to join them today because she was at a doctor's appointment with Hector, but Gabby was ready with the pictures. Roberta asked how things had been going and wanted to see the BRS. Gabby had recorded data points for both the challenging and desirable behaviors, and Roberta congratulated her for continuing to collect the data. Roberta told Gabby that because they would be completing the PTR-F behavior support plan today and probably starting the intervention, they would be able to compare the data she had collected so far with the data starting that day to monitor progress. Lucy's data were pretty clear and straightforward at this point, and hopefully they would be able to start to see some progress within the next week. Gabby was definitely anxious to get the behavior support plan in place.

Roberta suggested they write the behavior support plan first and then assemble the schedule in case they ran out of time. They started by writing out the steps for the prevent strategies (enhance predictability with calendars and schedules and provide choices). Roberta and Gabby talked through how Gabby would present the schedule, which helped them figure out how the schedule would look and be organized. Once the steps were written out, they did a quick role-play with Roberta pretending to be Lucy so Gabby could practice what it would be like to use the schedule. Once Gabby felt comfortable with how she would use the visual schedule and provide choices with the schedule activities, they decided to move on to identifying teach and reinforce strategies.

Roberta handed a copy of the PTR-F Intervention Menu to Gabby and briefly reviewed the teach strategies. Gabby was interested in teaching active participation in the daily routines and teaching appropriate ways to communicate. Roberta mentioned that if both skills were something Gabby wanted to incorporate, she could help Gabby create and implement a behavior support plan that included both teach strategies. Gabby was motivated and ready to do whatever would help Lucy become more independent and make the days go more smoothly. Also, if these strategies were working well at school, Gabby knew that she would be able to do them at home with Lucy now that she had support from Roberta.

Following the same process, Roberta and Gabby talked through how Gabby would teach Lucy to actively participate, with Roberta typing as they talked. They incorporated ways to teach communication through this process as well, providing opportunities for Lucy to verbalize what they would be doing next. Once the steps were written out, they performed another quick role-play with Roberta pretending to be Lucy while Gabby went through the steps to make sure they were clear and complete. When Gabby felt comfortable with how she would be enacting the strategies with Lucy, they moved on to creating the plan for the reinforce strategy.

Referring to the PTR-F Assessment Checklist: Reinforce, Roberta and Gabby looked at potential reinforcers for Lucy. Roberta noted that they would need to identify powerful reinforcers and multiple options to ensure that Lucy would quickly learn to use the desirable behaviors. Roberta asked Gabby what she thought would be the most powerful or motivating reinforcers for Lucy when teaching the new skills of actively participating in the routine and using more appropriate communication. Lucy loves fruit snacks and juice, or basically anything with sugar, but she really loves Gabby's attention the most. Roberta shared that when she observed Lucy at school, Lucy responded so well to the adults' attention that they rarely used tangible reinforcers (e.g., food items, stickers, stamps).

Roberta asked Gabby if she thought that would work at home as well, and Gabby agreed that her attention and affection would be the best reinforcer and would be easy to give. As Roberta began recording the steps of the reinforce strategy, she asked Gabby where she might be able to incorporate giving Lucy either a little drink of juice or a couple of fruit snacks for cooperating and participating in the routines, so that she could solidify Lucy demonstrating these behaviors at home. Roberta noted some times throughout the day when Gabby could consider giving Lucy juice or fruit snacks along with Gabby's positive feedback and attention for participating in the routine. Roberta discussed what Gabby should do when Lucy engaged in physically aggressive behavior so that it was clear to Gabby how she should handle her daughter in those situations. Those steps were included in Lucy's behavior support plan as well. Again, Roberta and Gabby did a quick role-play to help ensure that they had all the details identified and that Gabby would be comfortable with implementing these strategies. (Figure 5.3a shows Lucy's completed PTR-F Behavior Support Plan.)

Once the behavior support plan was complete and Gabby felt comfortable being able to implement all the strategies, they spent the rest of their time assembling the visual schedule for Gabby to use. Roberta had a picture of what the visual schedule looked like at school, so they could make the visual schedule used at home look similar. At school, the visual schedule included the day's main activities in a series of vertical pockets, and when an activity was finished, the "schedule helper" would turn the picture over so it was blank. Roberta brought a laminated file folder for Lucy's schedule and attached a strip of Velcro vertically on one side of the file folder. The other side of the file folder had strips of Velcro to hold the additional pictures. Velcro was attached to both sides of each picture so it could be turned over while staying attached to the file folder. Roberta completed the PTR-F Behavior Support Plan Summary while Gabby worked on putting the visual schedule together. Roberta had to leave before it was completely assembled, but Gabby would continue to work on it and get it ready to use. They scheduled their first four coaching sessions, with Roberta agreeing to observe and provide coaching on the morning routine for at least the first two sessions because this was currently the most problematic routine.

Roberta noted on the BRS that implementation was starting and reminded Gabby to continue to collect the data each day. Roberta advised Gabby to post the PTR-F Behavior Support Plan Summary (see Figure 5.4a) somewhere convenient where she could review it each day as a reminder of all the steps in the plan. Roberta also encouraged Gabby to share the plan with her mother and enlist her help when possible.

Self-Evaluation Checklist

As their meeting came to an end, Roberta reviewed the PTR-F Self-Evaluation Checklist with Gabby, and they both agreed that they had completed all the steps. Gabby was anxious to begin implementing the plan and was happy to finally be at this stage.

PTR-F Behavior Support Plan

Child: Lucia "Lucy"

Team members: Gabby (Mom), Marguerite (grandma), Roberta (PTR-F facilitator)

Date of plan: August 12, 2015

Desirable behavior to increase: Follow daily routines calmly and cooperatively

Operational definition: When Lucy is told that it is time to start a daily routine, she will actively participate in the routine calmly (and eventually independently) by following Mom's directions for the routine, attempting to complete or completing the specific task, and/or initiating the next steps of the routine. Lucy will participate without exhibiting any challenging behaviors (see challenging behavior definition).

Target behavior to decrease: Physically aggressive behaviors

Operational definition: When Lucy is physically aggressive, she may hit, slap, kick, bite, scratch, pull on clothes/hair, scream/yell, or try to take her clothes off.

Hypothesis statement: When Lucy is asked to do something she does not want to do, then she will engage in physically aggressive behaviors (see definition); as a result, she avoids or delays the task or activity and gets attention through verbal redirects and/or physical guidance.

Prevent strategy: Enhance predictability with calendars and schedules; provide choices
Materials needed: Visual schedule with real photos of the routine/activity
Steps to implementing the strategy:

1. When it is time for a particular routine/activity, approach Lucy with the visual schedule in hand, prepared with the correct activities in the correct order.
2. Tell Lucy, "It is time for (routine/activity). What do we do first?" while showing her the schedule and pointing to the first picture. For routines/activities where a choice can be offered, you can say, "Lucy, it is time for (routine/activity). Do you want to do (option A) first or (option B) first?"
3. If Lucy starts to move in the correct direction or clearly indicates she is calm and compliant (within 5 seconds), provide descriptive praise for following the initial direction (e.g., "That's right Lucy, it's time to go to the bathroom," "Good job listening to Mommy and putting your clothes on!").
4. If Lucy does not respond within 5 seconds, provide the instruction again. If she does not respond the second time, gently provide physical guidance for that step. Provide descriptive praise for cooperating with parts of the routine/activity as much as possible (e.g., "Good standing up like a big girl!" "Thank you for opening the door by yourself").

Teach strategy: Teach active participation, teach communication skills; this strategy is used in conjunction with the prevent strategy
Materials needed: Visual schedule with pictures needed for the routine/activity
Steps for implementing the strategy:

1. When the visual schedule is first being used, start with the prevent strategy steps 1–4 (where applicable), above.
2. When it is time for the next step of the routine/activity, point to the next picture and ask, "What do you do next?"
3. Wait up to 5 seconds for Lucy to respond with a verbal response to your question. If she makes any kind of verbalization, provide descriptive praise (e.g., "Good words!" or repeat what she says). If she does not respond verbally, say the step (e.g., "Wash hands") while showing her the picture. Then move to the next step.

(continued)

Figure 5.3a.   Lucy's completed PTR-F Behavior Support Plan.

Figure 5.3a. *(continued)*

4. Repeat these steps for the rest of the routine/activity, asking, "What do you do next?" and providing descriptive praise for each of the steps, even if only partially completed calmly and cooperatively, especially when Lucy is first learning these steps.

Reinforce plan: 1) Identify functional reinforcers, 2) provide reinforcer for desirable behavior, 3) remove reinforcement for challenging behavior

Materials Needed: Mom, fruit snacks, juice

Steps for Implementing the Strategy:

1. Create a list of verbal and nonverbal ways Mom can provide attention/affection when Lucy is demonstrating desirable behaviors.

2. When Lucy participates in routines, follows directions, and is calm and cooperative (demonstrates desirable behaviors), provide descriptive praise and/or physical affection. About 3–5 times throughout the day, provide a small amount of juice or a few fruit snacks when Lucy demonstrates desirable behaviors.

3. When Lucy engages in challenging behaviors, ignore her; do not say anything to her and turn your face and/or body slightly away if necessary. Point to the relevant picture on the visual schedule to prompt her to start or participate in the next step of the routine/activity. As soon as she begins to comply with the routine or request, follow step 2 to reinforce the desirable behavior.

Data collection: Continue to collect data using the PTR-F Behavior Rating Scale. Data will be reviewed with the facilitator, and decisions will be made based on the data.

FORM 9 **PTR-F Behavior Support Plan Summary**

Child: Lucy   Date: August 12, 2015

Practices for all children:
- ❏ Provide high rates of positive attention.
- ☑ Establish and maintain predictable daily schedules.
- ❏ Include consistent patterns of activities within daily routines.
- ❏ Define behavioral expectations and difference between desirable and challenging behavior.

Hypothesis statement: When Lucy is asked to do something she does not want to do, then she will engage in physically aggressive behaviors (see definition); as a result, she avoids or delays the task or activity and gets attention through verbal redirects and/or physical guidance.

Intervention strategies:

	Prevent	Teach	Reinforce
Strategies	1. Enhance predictability with calendars and schedules 2. Provide choices	1. Teach active participation 2. Teach communication skills	All plans must: 1. Identify valued, functional reinforcer(s) 2. Provide reinforcer for desirable behavior 3. Remove reinforcement for challenging behavior
Brief description	1. Present visual schedule. 2. "It is time for ____. What do we do first?" or "Do you want to do ____ or ____ first?" 3. Provide descriptive praise. 4. If she doesn't respond, give instruction again.	1. Start with prevent strategy steps. 2. "What do you do next?" 3. Wait up to 5 seconds; if Lucy verbalizes, provide descriptive praise; if she doesn't verbalize, repeat the step. 4. Repeat steps 2 and 3 until all steps of the routine are complete.	1. Refer to list of verbal/nonverbal ways to provide attention/affection when Lucy is demonstrating desirable behaviors. 2. Provide descriptive praise when Lucy participates. 3. Ignore challenging behaviors.
Implementation notes	Descriptive praise examples "That's right Lucy, it's time to go to the bathroom!" "Good job listening to Mommy and putting your clothes on!" "Great sitting at the table like a big girl!"	Descriptive praise examples "Good words!" "Nice talking!" "Great job trying to say ___!"	Provide as much descriptive praise as possible!

Figure 5.4a. Lucy's PTR-F Behavior Support Plan Summary.

Coaching the Family to Implement Plans with Fidelity

6

Coaching is an integral part of the Prevent-Teach-Reinforce for Families (PTR-F) process that helps to ensure that the family will implement all aspects of the behavior support plan with fidelity. Once the PTR-F behavior support plan has been completed, the facilitator is responsible for coaching family members to implement the plan, with a focus on ensuring that the family has the skills to implement the interventions (i.e., competence) and the confidence to use the intervention strategies within daily routines. Coaching provides family members with guided practice, feedback, and opportunities to ensure that they can implement the strategies with precision and consistently over time. Coaching sessions allow the team to examine the child's responsiveness to the intervention strategies and identify whether additional strategies should be used or whether adjustments to strategy implementation should be made. The goal is to ensure that family members will be able to continue implementing the plan with fidelity as the facilitator reduces assistance.

UNDERSTANDING IMPLEMENTATION FIDELITY

Even the best quality intervention plan will not be effective if it is not implemented with fidelity. Fidelity means that each step of each intervention strategy within the plan is carried out consistently and accurately. For this reason, we have included a tool for assessing and attending to fidelity. It is crucial that fidelity is measured regularly, especially at the outset, to ensure a solid implementation of the behavior support plan and to catch mistakes and omissions before they become part of the new routine.

In the coaching process, the facilitator will take an active role in monitoring fidelity as part of observations, coaching, and performance feedback. The PTR-F Fidelity of Strategy Implementation Form (see Figure 6.1) was designed to provide a systematic method for identifying the steps of the intervention strategies that were implemented and the steps that were missed, and it is a source of important data that will inform discussions about how to ensure the faithful completion of all steps in the intervention process. For instance, the tool can be a springboard for conversation and troubleshooting if there are steps that are routinely missed. This form should be completed by the facilitator in every coaching observation, and the data should be discussed during reflection and feedback with the family. For examples of how to use this form during coaching, see the completed PTR-F Fidelity of Strategy Implementation Forms for Timmy and Lucy in the case examples at the end of this chapter.

The PTR-F Fidelity of Strategy Implementation Form should be prepared before implementation of the behavior support plan. To prepare the form, the team lists the steps for each of the three individualized intervention strategies (prevent, teach, and reinforce) that are part of the behavior support plan. When the form is used, the person tracking fidelity documents the following information:

▲ Were all steps implemented as intended? If any steps were not implemented as listed on the fidelity form, then those steps should be marked "No." If the listed step was implemented during the routine, the box should be marked "Yes."

109

FORM 11 PTR-F Fidelity of Strategy Implementation Form

Child: _____ Routine: _____

Date: _____ Person implementing: _____

Strategy steps	Were the steps implemented as intended?	Did your child respond as intended?	Was the strategy implemented as frequently as intended?
Prevent strategy:		❑ Yes ❑ No	❑ Yes ❑ No
1.	❑ Yes ❑ No		
2.	❑ Yes ❑ No		
3.	❑ Yes ❑ No		
4.	❑ Yes ❑ No		
5.	❑ Yes ❑ No		
Teach strategy:		❑ Yes ❑ No	❑ Yes ❑ No
1.	❑ Yes ❑ No		
2.	❑ Yes ❑ No		
3.	❑ Yes ❑ No		
4.	❑ Yes ❑ No		
5.	❑ Yes ❑ No		
Reinforce strategy:		❑ Yes ❑ No	❑ Yes ❑ No
1.	❑ Yes ❑ No		
2.	❑ Yes ❑ No		
3.	❑ Yes ❑ No		
4.	❑ Yes ❑ No		
5.	❑ Yes ❑ No		

Figure 6.1. PTR-F Fidelity of Strategy Implementation Form.

▲ Did the child respond as intended? The team must have an expected response that they are trying to elicit through the intervention. For example, if referring to a picture schedule with the verbal prompt, "All done washing our hands! Now it is time to sit at the table for dinner," then there is an expectation that the child will respond to the direction. If the child responded as desired, this box is marked "Yes." If the child did not respond as desired, whether the child engaged in the challenging behavior or a different behavior, the box is marked "No."

▲ Was the strategy implemented as frequently as intended? The behavior intervention plan should have a specific recommended frequency for intervention strategies. The frequency might vary considerably between categories. Prevent strategies are typically used only in the prescribed routine. Teaching and reinforcement strategies might be used whenever the opportunity presents itself. Reinforcement, in particular, may be quite frequent during, before, and after routines. Mark "Yes" if the frequency of implementation met or exceeded the frequency specified in the plan and "No" if it did not meet this level of frequency.

We advise that the family have a copy of the fidelity form and that they are encouraged to use the form as a self-check for their implementation integrity. The fidelity form can be a useful tool for troubleshooting implementation issues. With additional information about the child's response, the tool becomes more powerful and can also be used to assess strategy effectiveness and fit for the child as well as the family. If all strategies are being implemented with fidelity and the child is not responding to the intervention, then the intervention may not be a good fit for the child or the hypothesis about the function of the behavior may be incorrect. If strategies are not being implemented with fidelity and the child's behavior does not improve, the team cannot evaluate whether or not the plan was effective.

WHAT IS COACHING?

Coaching for the goal of implementing practices or intervention strategies has been described as "an adult learning strategy that is used to build the capacity of a parent or colleague to improve existing abilities, develop new skills, or gain a deeper understanding of practices for use in current and future situations" (Rush & Shelden, 2008, p. 1). Coaching has been identified as an essential step for promoting adult learning and assisting adults with the implementation of new practices. The provision of coaching typically involves the following: 1) establishing the coaching partnership; 2) developing a plan that will serve as the foundation for the coaching activity; 3) observation; 4) practice; 5) reflection; and 6) feedback.

Coaching should be provided from only one member of the team that is supporting the family—the facilitator. The delivery of coaching support by one person in the role of facilitator will strengthen the relationship with the family, help the family become comfortable with the coaching process, and provide continuity so that the family receives consistent coaching guidance as they implement the behavior support plan.

Coaching is often thought of as being associated with athletics or sports. When the facilitator describes the coaching process to the family, it might be useful to draw an analogy between coaching to support an athlete and the coaching that will be provided to the family for plan implementation. The facilitator's coaching will be similar to that of an athletic coach who provides instruction and pointers, watches the athlete perform, and provides feedback on performance. The facilitator might also share that the athlete already knows how to participate in the sport or play the game, but the coach's role is to assist the athlete in sharpening his or her skills and helping the athlete use his or her strengths to be successful. Similarly, the facilitator's role in PTR-F will be to make sure that the family member can use the behavior support plan with the timing and accuracy needed to make a difference with his or her child. Thus, the facilitator will observe the family member implementing the strategies and provide feedback on how to use them in the most effective manner. Coaching observations will also allow the facilitator and the family to work through how the intervention strategies will be optimally used within the context of the family's routines.

Another aspect of coaching that should be acknowledged and discussed with the family is that implementing the behavior support plan can be emotionally challenging. Families often find that it is difficult to change how they respond to the child, especially when the child has challenging behavior. When a child is having a difficult time and displaying challenging behavior, it can trigger reactions by adults that might not be part of the behavior support plan. The facilitator should express to the family that a goal of coaching will be to support the family in becoming comfortable and confident in the use of the plan strategies.

At this point in the PTR-F process, the facilitator should have established a strong relationship with the family by engaging in the collaborative process of developing a plan, and he or she should have a good understanding of the family's preferences, routines, values, and goals for their child. This will be extremely important to the coaching process. The family must view the facilitator as warm, trustworthy, reliable, and respectful to engage in the intimate work of coaching for plan implementation. Although the facilitator brings important expertise to the process and will have a clear idea about how targeted strategies should be used, the facilitator should make sure that all interactions with the family are collaborative, respectful, and flexible. Remember that the goal of this process is to have a behavior support plan that works for both the child and the family and will be implemented with fidelity over time. The following principles will be important for a successful coaching relationship:

1. Coaching is systematic—Coaching is most effective when the facilitator systematically uses research-based coaching practices to guide the family in knowing how to use the intervention strategies and implement the behavior support plan with fidelity.

2. Coaching focuses on building capacity—The explicit goal of coaching is for the family to be confident and competent in the implementation of the behavior support plan. Coaching will be provided until the goal of family confidence and competence is achieved.

3. Coaching is a collaborative process—The coaching process should be a collaborative endeavor that considers family needs and preferences and should support the family's decisions about what works best for their child and family.

4. Coaching emphasizes the family's strengths—Coaching interactions reinforce specific behaviors that are aligned with the intervention or that help ensure success of the child.

Before beginning coaching, it is helpful to describe the coaching process to the family, talk about the structure of the coaching session and the strategies that might be used, and discuss the expectations of the coaching sessions. In addition, the facilitator should map out a schedule for coaching visits and identify the family member who will be coached within these routines. Although the family might ultimately want all family members to be able to implement behavior support with a specified routine (e.g., bedtime), the facilitator will focus on the primary person who is most likely to be involved in the routine. However, there might be some routines that involve multiple family members (e.g., dinner), and all family members who are present might have some role in the behavior support plan. Figure 6.2 provides an information sheet on what is entailed with the PTR-F coaching sessions, with answers to frequently asked questions. This can be used as a handout in the coaching discussions with families.

PTR-F Family Coaching Information Sheet

Coaching describes the process that will be used by your facilitator to help you know how to implement the behavior support plan with your child and become confident in the use of the strategies in the plan. The most common questions that family members have about coaching are addressed below.

Q: Why do I need coaching? Can't I just implement the plan after we figure out what interventions I might use and call you if I need more help?

- We find that coaching sessions are essential for making sure the intervention plan will work for the family. During the coaching session, the coach will learn more about your routine and how your child reacts to the interventions, and he or she can tweak the strategies to make sure they fit you and your child.

- Coaching sessions maximize the likelihood that the plan will be successful. It is important that you and your child are successful and that challenging behavior can be addressed quickly. When families try to implement plans without support, they often become frustrated if the plan is difficult to implement or the child continues to struggle with challenging behavior.

Q: What will happen in a coaching session?

- Your facilitator (coach) will schedule the coaching session for the time of day when a family member would naturally conduct the target routine with the child.

- In the first coaching session, the session will begin with a review of the plan and a discussion about how to implement the strategies within the routine. After that, coaching will begin with a review of the child's progress (you can share the data you have collected) since the last time the facilitator was with you for a coaching session, and then there will be a brief review of the strategies. This is a good time for you to ask questions about any strategies or to problem solve with your facilitator to address strategies that are not working for you or with your child.

- After discussing the plan, the facilitator will watch you implement the plan with your child within the target routine. During the observation, the facilitator will be taking notes on the steps you implement using the PTR-F Fidelity of Strategy Implementation Form and how your child responds to the strategies. The facilitator might also provide modeling or side-by-side guidance or use a video recorder or other strategies to help you. These strategies will only be used if you agree that you will be comfortable with their use during the routine.

- After the observation of the routine, you and your facilitator will talk about what happened and how your child responded to the intervention strategies. During this discussion, you will be encouraged to share your perspectives about how the plan works, ask questions to clarify how to use strategies, and raise any concerns about the plan. Your facilitator will give you feedback about your implementation and work with you to ensure that the plan will be effective for your child.

Q: How do I prepare for my coaching visit?

- Make sure that the family member who is most likely to conduct the routine and has agreed to be coached will be present for the entire coaching session. Although you will probably want all family members to be knowledgeable about the behavior support plan, the facilitator will be working with one family member to implement the plan in the target routine. Of course, all family members can participate in the review of your child's progress, the plan strategies, and discussions about the implementation of the plan.

- The coaching visit requires your focused attention. We recommend that you minimize the likelihood that there will be distractions or interruptions during the coaching session. This might mean that you turn off the television, don't take phone calls, and limit visitors during the coaching visit. When you schedule the coaching session with your facilitator, discuss how long the session might last and make sure you can be available for the duration.

Figure 6.2. PTR-F Family Coaching Information Sheet.

Figure 6.2. *(continued)*

FORM 12 **PTR-F Family Coaching Information Sheet** *(continued)*

- It is helpful if you are organized and ready for the coaching session. You will want to have completed Behavior Rating Scales ready to share and have a list of any questions or concerns that you might want to review with your facilitator.

- Don't worry about entertaining your facilitator or cleaning up the house for company! The coach is there to support you and your family and does not want these coaching sessions to cause additional stress for your family. It will be important for the facilitator to see how your normal routine works for you and your child.

Q: How long is the average coaching session?

- The duration of the coaching session will depend on a couple of variables. First, you should expect that initial coaching sessions might last longer because you will be reviewing plan steps and strategies in detail before you use the plan in the routine. In addition, the duration of the routine that you are working on with your coach will be a factor in determining the length of the coaching session. For example, if the coach is there to work with you on addressing behavior during mealtimes, and the routine is 30 minutes, your coaching session might be longer than a session that is focused on dressing or some other shorter routine. You and your coach should discuss the start time, end time, and what will occur within the coaching session as you set the appointment for your coaching sessions.

Q: How frequently will coaching sessions occur?

- It is likely that the frequency of coaching sessions will be determined by the agency that is providing you with coaching support and their service guidelines. Regular coaching sessions (e.g., weekly) are important, and we strongly encourage families to make sure that they can schedule activities so that coaching visits occur as planned.

THE PTR-F COACHING PROCESS

In this section, we describe the coaching process, structure of a coaching session, and coaching practices that might be used by the facilitator to support the family. The coaching phase begins once the plan and the supports are developed and ready for implementation by the family. Thus, it might take a few days for visual materials to be developed or materials to be gathered to use for plan implementation. The PTR-F materials that will be needed by the facilitator and family for the coaching sessions are the behavior support plan, behavior support plan summary, fidelity checklist, and Behavior Rating Scale (BRS).

TIP *The PTR-F process involves several forms that the family will need to have organized and ready to use in their implementation of the plan. It is helpful if the facilitator organizes these in a folder or notebook for the family so that they are in one place and easy to access.*

Coaching sessions should be scheduled for times when the family can engage in the target routine or routines where the behavior support plan will be used. For some families, the facilitator might be able to provide coaching for several routines in a visit, whereas other families might need multiple visits to provide coaching on routines that occur at different times of the day. Although it might not be feasible to coach every routine each week, it is important that at least one coaching session for each routine is provided during the time that the routine naturally occurs. In planning the scheduling of the coaching session, the facilitator should confirm who will be coached during the routine. As stated previously, it is desirable to consistently coach the same primary family member for a given routine across coaching visits. However, other family members can be present for these sessions, participate in the plan review, and contribute to discussions about the child's progress and the implementation of the plan.

Before conducting a coaching session, the facilitator should prepare the family for what will occur during the session. The instructions might include statements such as,

> "The next time we meet, we will start the coaching process. I would like to schedule our session for the time of day that you can implement the plan with your child. When I arrive, we will talk about how your child is doing and review the plan. You will implement the plan during the routine while I watch. Once the routine is completed, we will talk about how the plan worked and how your child responded. Together, we will decide what might be the next steps for plan implementation."

We recommend that coaching sessions always involve the following: 1) a review of progress, 2) a review of the behavior support plan, 3) observation, 4) reflection, 5) feedback, and 6) planning. Each of these elements is described in the following sections.

TIP *When the facilitator arrives for a coaching session, it is helpful to restate the plan for what will happen in the session. Restating the sequence for the coaching session activities will help the family member remain focused and feel more comfortable about expectations.*

Review of Progress

All of the coaching sessions (except perhaps the family's first one) should begin with a review of the child's progress since the last time the facilitator met with the family. This review of progress includes asking for the family members' impressions on how the child has been responding to the plan, gauging the family members' comfort in using the plan, and reviewing the data that the family has collected. A review of progress can be initiated by asking, "Tell me about how (name the routine) has been for you and (child's name) since I saw you last week." The facilitator might also ask, "Were you able to implement the steps in the plan?" In asking these questions, the goal is for the family members to share as much as possible about plan implementation, the child's responses, and issues related to using the plan. In response to these questions, the facilitator should not jump prematurely into giving advice or offering new information. Instead, the facilitator should use open-ended questions to encourage the family member to share what has happened since the last visit. Sample questions that might yield important information include the following:

▲ How did your child respond to the use of the (state the strategy)?

▲ What worked well in the routine?

▲ What strategies did not seem to work?

▲ Were there any steps in the plans that were difficult to implement?

After asking for the family members' impressions and encouraging the family members to describe the implementation of the plan, the facilitator should ask to see the data that have been collected. The review should begin by first reinforcing the family heavily for collecting the data, even if data collection is inconsistent (e.g., "Great! We have data we can review. This is helpful to reflect on how things have been going"). Collecting data systematically is challenging for busy adults, and we want to encourage the family to continue these efforts. After the facilitator expresses enthusiasm for the data, the facilitator should ask the family member to describe what appears on the BRS (e.g., "I see you have data for a couple of days; tell me about your ratings"). Asking the family member to share the ratings and provide his or her interpretations will establish that these ratings belong to the family and can be used by the family (versus a form that is completed for the facilitator). If the family has not collected any data, the facilitator should help the family determine what actions might be needed to make it easier for the family to complete the BRS. Suggestions for improving data collection might include setting a reminder on the parent's phone, placing the BRS in a prominent location or with the materials used in the routine, or taking a current routine and adding the completion of the BRS as a step (e.g., after putting the child to bed, the family member completes the BRS that is posted on the child's bedroom door bulletin board). In making these suggestions, the facilitator should consider what the barriers are to data collection and identify a strategy that will work best for the family.

The review of the BRS with the family will allow for a discussion about the child's progress in the routine. If there are only a few data points on the BRS, the facilitator might need to guide the family to not make assumptions from the data until the plan has been implemented for multiple days and there are more data in which to identify a pattern (as will be demonstrated in the case example of Timmy at the end of this chapter). If the family member is discouraged by the data, the facilitator might need to point out the overall positive trend (while not becoming distracted by 1 or 2 days where the child ratings are less encouraging) or provide feedback related to why the child is not progressing more quickly. If the data show a positive trend, the facilitator can note the pattern and point out to the family that the intervention effort is resulting in incremental improvements for the child (although the family might wish the improvements were more dramatic or occurred more quickly).

Review of the Behavior Support Plan

In preparation for observing the routine, the facilitator should review the behavior support plan briefly with the family member. In the first coaching sessions, this review will be conducted in a more intensive and focused way as the facilitator spends time walking through each step of plan implementation. If there are supports that will be used with the plan (e.g., a visual schedule or modified materials) or the environment needs to be arranged to support plan implementation, the family should be encouraged to get out the materials or make those arrangements as the facilitator talks through the behavior support plan steps. The facilitator should end the review by asking the family member if he or she has any questions or is concerned about any of the steps. After the plan review, the facilitator should remind the family member that he or she will be watching the routine while the family member supports the child. At this point, the facilitator should also confirm with the family member what coaching strategies might be used during the observation to support the family member in plan implementation. In the discussion of the observation procedures that follows, strategies that might be used to assist the family as they implement the plan are described. It is important that the family member anticipates what strategy might be used and is on board with the use of any strategies that might be perceived as intrusive (e.g., modeling, environmental arrangements, video recording).

TIP *Once the family member knows the behavior support plan well, the plan review can be brief and should be prompted by the facilitator with a question such as, "Before we start, can you restate the plan steps for this routine?"*

During the behavior support plan review, the family might raise questions or need support to understand exactly how the strategy will be implemented. In addition to verbally describing how to use a strategy, the facilitator might use role-playing or environmental arrangements, or he or she might engage in a problem-solving discussion to assist the family member in understanding the use of an intervention strategy. For example, the coach might role-play with the family how a visual schedule is used, help the family move toys from the toy box to a toy shelf so that the child can access choices more readily (i.e., environmental arrangements), or think through how to prompt the child to take a bath while keeping the younger sibling engaged (i.e., problem solving).

Observation of Plan Implementation

The observation of plan implementation will allow the facilitator to see how the family member implements the plan and the child's response to intervention strategies. As the facilitator watches, the fidelity checklist will be used to record what strategies are implemented and identify the strategies that might need improvement or adjustments. In addition to watching the family member, the facilitator might use coaching strategies to support the family member during the routine. As stated previously, these strategies are described to the family prior to use so that the family member understands the strategy and agrees to its use during the routine. Possible coaching strategies are as follows:

▲ Video recording—The facilitator uses a video-recording device to record the intervention routine so that it can be viewed by the family member and facilitator for reflection.

▲ Modeling—The facilitator demonstrates how to use the intervention strategy with the child during the intervention routine.

▲ Side-by-side support—The facilitator provides verbal (e.g., reminders, instructions) or gestural cues (e.g., pointing) during the intervention routine to remind the family member to use an intervention strategy.

▲ Problem-solving discussion—The facilitator discusses a challenge related to the routine, use of the intervention strategy, or child's response to the intervention plan with the family. The family member and facilitator generate ideas and propose options for addressing the issue and then identify what they will try as a potential remedy.

▲ Environmental arrangements—The facilitator might rearrange the physical space, move materials, or hand the family member materials to support the use of intervention strategies.

▲ Role-playing—This strategy might be used when reviewing the behavior support plan before observation or after the observation to practice plan or intervention strategy implementation. Role-playing involves simulating the situation, with the facilitator and the family member each taking a defined role (family member or child) to learn or practice the intervention strategy.

The selection of the coaching strategies to use during the observation will be based on factors related to the nature of the routine (e.g., you might not use video recording in a community environment, and modeling is unlikely to be used for a routine like bedtime or bathing), family comfort with the strategy, and the nature of the intervention strategies that have been selected. When using any of these coaching strategies, the facilitator should monitor the family member's reaction to their use and address any discomfort that might be observed during the reflection phase of the coaching process.

TIP *When observing the family member implement the plan within a routine or activity, the facilitator should hang back and try to stay in the background. It is important that the facilitator does not become a part of a family activity by interacting with the child. Although there might be some occasions where the facilitator will use modeling for the caregiver, this strategy should be used minimally because it changes the nature of the routine for the child.*

Reflection

After observing the implementation of the routine and behavior support plan, the facilitator will discuss the observation with the family member. As the facilitator observes the routine, the process of reflection begins by noting how well the family member implemented the behavior support plan, how the child responded, the strategies that worked, and the strategies that did not appear to be effective. Before sharing his or her own reflections of the observation with the family, the facilitator should first guide the family member in also reflecting on the routine and the behavior support plan. The facilitator can promote the family's reflection by asking, "Tell me how you thought it went," and then follow with other questions such as, "How do you think it worked for your child?" "What seemed to work well?" and "What was difficult?" The goal in guiding reflection is to build the family member's capacity to look back and assess his or her behavior and the child's reactions. The ability to reflect and critically assess difficult situations will be an important skill for the family member to continue to use when the facilitator is not present in the routine and providing direct support. Questions that might be used to guide reflection include the following:

▲ How are you feeling?

▲ What worked well?

▲ What are your thoughts about the plan?

▲ How did your child respond?

▲ What did you notice during the routine?

▲ How was this different than before?

▲ Why do you think it went well?

If video recording was used as part of the observation, it can be used in the reflection process. The video should be viewed by the facilitator and the family member together and then followed by a conversation about the observation. The facilitator might start the conversation by asking the family member to reflect on how the child responded to the intervention strategies. We advise that the facilitator begin by guiding the family member's reflections on how the child responded to increase the family member's comfort with evaluating what is seen in the video. Once the family member reflects on the child's engagement in the routine and responses to the strategies, the facilitator should shift the reflections to what the family member did in the routine, immediately offering supportive feedback about his or her observations of the family member. This feedback can include acknowledging the family member for remembering to use the behavior support plan steps, praising the family member for his or her persistence with an intervention strategy or for using a strategy effectively, or any other comments that acknowledge or encourage the family member's effort. We recommend moving quickly from the family member's reflections on the child to providing encouraging feedback during the review of the video because we want to decrease the discomfort that might be associated with having the family member watch and evaluate his or her implementation of the plan. After offering the encouraging feedback, the facilitator can prompt the family member to reflect on his or her actions and share his or her perspectives about plan implementation. The next section discusses providing feedback in more detail, including how to phrase feedback statements.

Feedback and Problem Solving

After the family member shares reflections, the facilitator will provide his or her reflections and feedback. Feedback should include providing acknowledgment and reinforcement for the family's and child's strengths and capacities (positive feedback) and providing guidance or suggestions that might improve intervention implementation (constructive feedback).

Positive feedback should be meaningful, descriptive, and delivered with enthusiasm. When delivering feedback, the facilitator should state exactly what the family member did and why it was effective. For example, rather than saying, "You did great; you really implemented the plan well," the facilitator might say, "You did great; you used the visual schedule to prompt her a few minutes before the transition, and she really seemed to understand that bath time was next." When descriptive information is added in this manner, the family member is guided to a deeper understanding of the plan strategies and why they might be effective. See the case examples at the end of this chapter to learn how facilitators Kaci and Roberta gave descriptive, specific feedback to Timmy's and Lucy's families.

Data that have been gathered with the fidelity checklist during the observation are used in the feedback session; however, facilitators should be cautious about how those data are shared and reviewed. Some families might respond well to examining the data and reflecting on the steps that were not implemented as intended or the child's response to the strategy, whereas others might feel uncomfortable with being "rated" by the facilitator. The facilitator should share these data in a manner that is supportive and portray the data as information for discussion versus data that are evaluative. For example, the facilitator might say, "Would you like to see the fidelity form? It provides information on what steps worked and what steps we might need to work on."

Although providing reflections on and feedback about strategy use can be relatively straightforward, the facilitator will also want to address issues that are occurring with behavior support plan implementation that might be more complex. This will include addressing the family member's comfort or confidence with the use of the behavior support plan, distractions or disruptions that interfere with the delivery of the routine, or the need to modify the environment or materials to fit with the needs of the family or child.

If the family member seems uncomfortable or states that he or she is not confident about the implementation of the plan, the facilitator should reflect on what was observed or expressed and engage in problem-solving discussions to address the issue if needed. Keep in mind that it is common for family members to initially express discomfort or a lack of confidence, and these concerns might be addressed by acknowledgment (e.g., "It is often awkward when you are doing something new") or encouragement (e.g., "I think the routine went pretty smooth. I couldn't tell you were nervous") and might not require problem solving. If needed, the problem-solving discussion involves identifying the issue, collaboratively generating options to address the problem, and deciding on a course of action for implementation. If a problem-solving discussion results in a decision to change the behavior support plan, the facilitator should revise the written plan to include those changes. In addition, the facilitator and the family member should evaluate the effectiveness of the changes in the next coaching visit.

Another coaching strategy that might be used to address the family member's comfort or confidence about the implementation of the plan is role-playing. In role-playing, the facilitator and family member practice the implementation of the plan in a simulated situation. For example, the facilitator might say, "I will be (child's name), and you use the schedule to prompt me to leave my toy and come to the table." Or, the role-play might begin by having the facilitator demonstrate the strategy and having the family member play the child (if this is selected as the first step, the facilitator should make sure to role-play again with the roles switched so that the family member has an opportunity to practice using the strategy).

Finally, problem solving might also be needed to address issues related to reducing distractions or minimizing disruptions that are problematic in the routine. For example, if the child does not move easily to the dinner table because she is distracted by the television, the coach might suggest that the television is turned off before prompting the beginning of the routine. Other times, problem-solving discussions involve identifying changes in the routine steps or environment to enhance the effectiveness of the behavior support plan (see how Roberta proposes changes to the breakfast routine to support Lucy's success at sitting at the table in Lucy's case example at the end of this chapter). Once a change has been proposed for the behavior support plan or the routine, the facilitator might need to demonstrate the use of the strategy or walk through the changes in the plan. These discussions and demonstrations provide an opportunity for the family member to reflect on the change and ask any questions or raise additional concerns.

Planning and Next Steps

The facilitator will end the coaching session by summarizing the changes that are being made to the behavior support plan or strategies and reminding the family member about implementation steps to focus on for improvement. After the summary, the facilitator should encourage the family member to raise any additional questions or concerns. Before leaving, the facilitator should confirm that the family member has the forms and materials that will be needed for plan implementation and discuss how and when needed materials might be delivered (e.g., e-mailing an updated written behavior support plan, dropping off a new visual support). The facilitator should communicate how the family member might make contact, if needed, before the next coaching session and confirm the date and time of the next coaching visit. In addition, the facilitator might restate the plan for the next coaching visit (e.g., "I will bring the video recorder and observe dinner," or "In our next session, I will go to the grocery store with you and we can work on the intervention for your shopping routine"). The facilitator's final words before departure should be an expression of confidence in the family about their ability to continue with implementation.

If the family uses e-mail, the facilitator should e-mail a summary of the coaching session to the family with a confirmation of the date, time, and activities of the next coaching session. In addition, if the family uses texting, the facilitator can text the family messages of encouragement before the next visit and text a message to confirm the appointment before the next session.

The PTR-F Coach Planning and Reflection Log (see Figure 6.3) is provided for facilitators to organize their coaching plans, record progress notes, plan coaching strategies to use, and designate plans for follow-up with the family. In addition, the form provides a place to record notes when conducting the observation. The log is designed to guide the

PTR-F Coach Planning and Reflection Log

FORM 13

Family name: _____   Coaching session date: _____

Target routine	Time of routine	Family member to coach

A. Progress review (notes from your discussion with family):

B. Review of intervention plan (notes from your discussion with the family):

C. Observation of routine:

In addition to completing the PTR-F Fidelity of Strategy Implementation Form, record your reflections from the observation

What I observed	What I want to share

D. Reflection/feedback (notes from your discussion):

(continued)

Figure 6.3. PTR-F Coach Planning and Reflection Log.

Figure 6.3. *(continued)*

FORM 13   **PTR-F Coach Planning and Reflection Log** *(continued)*

Coaching strategies

The form below allows the facilitator to indicate whether a particular strategy was used during observation (with parent consent), during plan review, or during reflection and feedback.

Coaching strategies	Used in observation	Used in plan review	Used during reflection and feedback	Notes
Observe				
Model				
Side-by-side support				
Video recording				
Problem-solving discussion				
Environmental arrangement				
Role-playing				

Next steps:

Follow-up to family:

❏ E-mail   ❏ Phone call   ❏ Skype call   ❏ Material provision   ❏ Other

Day/time for next session:

Focus for next session:

facilitator on systematically implementing the coaching process and provides a record of coaching that can be used for reflection about child and family progress in the PTR-F process. Examples of completed coaching logs are found in the case examples at the end of this chapter.

STAGES OF COACHING IN PTR-F

The number of coaching sessions that will be needed will largely be determined by the complexity of the behavior support plan, the number of routines that are the focus of intervention, and the family's confidence with and capacity to implement the behavior support plan. The facilitator will use the implementation fidelity data as a guide for determining how much coaching might be needed and when to phase out coaching support.

As stated previously, it is important to provide at least one coaching session for each routine that is being addressed by the family. During the coaching support stage, the observation of the behavior and plan implementation during the routine provides critical information for fine-tuning the plan and the support provided to the family. For many families, coaching might only need to occur for three to five sessions before they are able to implement the plan with fidelity. Once the family knows how to implement all strategies and can demonstrate that they can use the strategies in support of the child, the facilitator can move from coaching support to maintenance support.

Maintenance support might include additional in-person meetings with the family that occur less frequently (e.g., monthly for two or three additional check-ins), e-mail exchanges, phone conversations, or remote video calls using Web technology (this might allow for a more personal contact). Maintenance support sessions should include a review of child progress, an examination of data that has been collected, family reflection about the intervention strategies, and discussions about any changes that might need to be made in the behavior support plan.

TIP *As the child becomes able to use new skills and problem behavior is reduced, the plan might be modified for the caregiver to use in a maintenance phase. Modifications might include various actions such as reducing the number or nature of the prompts that are used, changing how and when reinforcement is delivered, or changing how much support is provided by the adult. The facilitator should discuss how these changes should be made and create new materials (e.g., a new version of the plan or a new fidelity checklist) that will help the caregiver continue to be systematic in supporting the child.*

If the child seems to be having new issues or is not responding to the behavior support plan during the maintenance phase, the facilitator might need to schedule an additional session to observe plan implementation or the routine where challenging behavior is occurring. The family might need this booster session to restore implementation of the behavior support plan and use of the strategies as designed, or the child might have new issues that will require additional supports.

Coaching support and the PTR-F process end when there is an effective behavior support plan in place and the family members are confident and competent in the implementation of the plan. We want to caution facilitators to avoid terminating the process prematurely (e.g., when a plan is developed) and encourage facilitators to continue coaching until the family is able to implement the support plan with fidelity.

SUMMARY

In this chapter, we have described the coaching approach used in PTR-F in order to assist and encourage families in implementing the behavior support plan. We have repeatedly stressed the importance of implementing all intervention strategies in the behavior support plan with fidelity, or consistently and precisely implementing each step as outlined in the plan. To better monitor and assess fidelity of implementation, we provided the PTR-F Fidelity of Strategy Implementation Form as way to gauge whether any steps were missed or not being implemented accurately. This form plays an important role in coaching sessions with families, which are crucial in helping to ensure fidelity of implementation. All coaching sessions should be supportive, encouraging, and collaborative, with a focus on the family's strengths. During each coaching session, the facilitator discusses the child's progress, reviews the behavior support plan, and then observes the family implement intervention strategies in the context of a specific family routine, using coaching strategies to guide the family through the implementation as needed. After this observation, the family and facilitator reflect on the child's responses and the way the plan was implemented, and the facilitator offers both positive and constructive feedback. Together, the team problem solves issues and makes any necessary changes to help ensure the successful implementation of the behavior support plan and improved behavior of the child. The following chapter describes how to use data to monitor the child's behavioral improvements and adjust the behavior support plan as needed to ensure progress.

APPENDIX

Case Examples

COACHING SESSIONS: TIMMY

Implementing the Plan

Coaching Session 1   Kaci never received a call from Jodie over the weekend, so she sent an e-mail to both Jodie and Phil on Monday morning to remind them she would be coming that evening. She would arrive a little bit prior to bedtime to review what happened over the weekend, observe bedtime, and stay for a few minutes after bedtime to debrief on how it went. Later that evening, Kaci arrived at the house and began the visit by asking how things had gone over the weekend. She also asked to review the Behavior Rating Scale (BRS).

Jodie and Phil stated that things were not great and that they had not been able to do everything that they had agreed upon for the behavior support plan or fill out the PTR-F Fidelity of Strategy Implementation Form. Jodie told Kaci that she did not call over the weekend because she felt bad about bothering her. In particular, Jodie was not sure if she was implementing the teach strategy correctly and was thinking that she might still be spending too much time in Timmy's room and wondered if that was going to make things worse. Although Timmy's tantrums were not worse than last week, he was still having them but had 1 day with less than 30 minutes of tantrum time. Kaci asked Phil and Jodie to look at the data and reflect on what they saw represented. Jodie stated that although it was a hard weekend, it did look like Timmy was starting to spend more time in his room on his own. Kaci asked Jodie how she felt about Timmy's progress, and Jodie reflected that she did feel that Timmy was making progress, even though the BRS data did not show a huge improvement. Kaci reminded her that it had only been 3 days, and even though the BRS data did not show a huge improvement, there was a little bit of improvement to celebrate, along with collecting the data and implementing the plan as much as she did.

After reflecting on the data, Kaci suggested they review the steps of the plan again before Jodie started the bedtime routine. She and Jodie agreed that it would be best if Kaci hung back and observed without using any other coaching strategies, as it would be disruptive to the routine. Kaci would use the PTR-F Fidelity of Strategy Implementation Form to track Jodie's implementation of steps and provide coaching support after the bedtime routine was over. Phil put Dakota to bed so he could observe the bedtime routine as well. Jodie role-played the bedtime routine with Kaci to review the steps and prepare for getting Timmy to bed.

Once Dakota was settled in bed, Jodie began Timmy's bedtime routine. She got out the pictures showing the order of the steps, reviewed them with Timmy, and set the timer for 5 minutes to indicate when it was time to start getting ready for bed. Kaci reviewed the steps with Jodie and Phil, and when the timer went off, Jodie showed Timmy the schedule and asked Timmy, "What time is it? It's time to get ready for bed." Jodie flipped to the next picture, which was Timmy's open drawer of pajamas.

Jodie went through the steps of getting Timmy ready for bed, and he followed most of the steps without a problem. When Jodie was finishing reading the last book and getting ready to say goodnight, she told Timmy, "Three more pages and the book will be all done. Mommy will say goodnight and give you a kiss." Jodie finished the book, gave Timmy a kiss, and showed him the picture of him lying in his bed. Jodie reminded Timmy that if he stayed in his room, she would come back in and read him one of the books from the basket (superhero books that Timmy could only earn when he stayed in his room), and then she set the timer for 1 minute. Hesitant, Jodie left Timmy's room and joined Phil and Kaci, who were waiting around the corner. Jodie indicated that Timmy started to whine when she gave him the warning that the story was almost over, but she did not respond to it and kept reading.

She thought for sure that Timmy would follow her out of the room or "blow up" because she left, but she was surprised that he was still in his room after a minute. When the minute was up and Timmy was still in bed, Jodie and Phil were in shock and wanted to wait longer to see how long Timmy would stay in his room. Because they were still so early in the teaching process, Kaci reminded them that they should be reinforcing Timmy's behavior right away, to make sure that he continues to stay in his room. Jodie reported that she had not been doing that because she was just so excited that he was staying in his room, and that it was probably part of the reason that Timmy was having such a hard time staying in his room and going to sleep.

Jodie went into Timmy's room and told Timmy, "You're such a big boy for staying in your bed!" Jodie got the basket with Timmy's special books, allowed him to pick one, and read him the book. When Jodie was finished reading, she said, "Okay, Timmy, time to go to sleep. See you in the morning. Sweet dreams." Timmy curled up in his bed and waved. Surprised, Jodie walked out of Timmy's room and back around the corner, where she found Phil and Kaci. Jodie described how easily things went with Timmy, and she was sure that he would be coming out of his room at any minute.

After a few minutes of quiet with Timmy still in his room, Kaci asked Jodie to reflect on how things went, including what was different about tonight than previous nights. Jodie reflected that Timmy had done well the past week until the timer went off, but because he was staying in his room, Jodie would wait to see how long he would stay in there. Usually within a couple of minutes of the timer going off, he would wander out of his room and look for Jodie, and she would proceed to put him back in his bed, sometimes kicking and screaming. Then, because it took him a while to calm down, she had to stay in his room for a long time until he was quiet. Kaci reflected that she was impressed by how naturally Jodie used the visual schedule and the confident manner in which she gave Timmy instructions. She followed the statement by suggesting that they review the plan again and examine a few of the elements that needed more focus.

The team reviewed the plan again, and Kaci reiterated how important it is to reinforce Timmy's desirable behavior, especially at the beginning of implementation. Kaci shared that it is tempting and common to want to fade any supports as soon as a child demonstrates some success, but for that new behavior to be maintained, it needs to be reinforced immediately and contingently during the early part of implementing a new strategy. Plus, as Timmy gets more consistent with staying in his room, there will be a plan for how to increase the amount of time he can stay in his room on his own. Kaci talked with Jodie and Phil about staying with the 1-minute requirement for the next week and continuing to keep data to see how Timmy does. Kaci assured Jodie that if the plan continued to go well and the data represented consistent behavior, they could talk next week about increasing the time Timmy was staying in his room. Kaci confirmed that Jodie would be able to commit to reinforcing Timmy for staying in his room at bedtime after 1 minute for the next week. Jodie and Phil both agreed, and they happily recorded that night's data on the BRS. (Figure 6.1a shows Timmy's completed PTR-F Coach Planning and Reflection Log for the first coaching session, and Figure 6.2a shows Timmy's PTR-F Fidelity of Strategy Implementation Form.)

Coaching Session 2   On the morning of the second coaching session, Kaci sent a reminder by text message for their appointment later that evening. Kaci arrived and found Jodie and Phil excited and proud of Timmy's progress. Jodie reported that Timmy had consistently stayed in his room for 1 minute every night and that his whining after the timer had diminished quite a bit. Jodie shared the BRS data with Kaci and pointed out the trend showing Timmy's progress. She stated that she was hoping that the time could be increased to a few minutes.

Kaci asked how other parts of the bedtime routine were going, and Jodie reported that overall, bedtime was a lot smoother, although not perfect. Jodie had filled out the PTR-F Fidelity of Strategy Implementation Form on a couple of nights the past week and shared them with Kaci. Jodie reflected that she was not always following all of the steps, but Timmy

FORM
13

PTR-F Coach Planning and Reflection Log

Family name: __Jodie and Phil__   Coaching session date: __July 6, 2015__

Target routine	Time of routine	Family member to coach
Bedtime	7 pm	Mom

A. Progress review (notes from your discussion with family):

First 3 nights of implementation "okay," not able to implement complete plan or fidelity forms

Mom wondering if spending too much time in Timmy's room—didn't call, felt it would be a bother

One day with tantrums less than 30 min.; Timmy starting to spend more time in room on his own.

B. Review of intervention plan (notes from your discussion with the family):

Reviewed all steps and did quick role-play with Jodie.

C. Observation of routine:

In addition to completing the PTR-F Fidelity of Strategy Implementation Form, record your reflections from the observation.

What I observed	What I want to share
Provided warning, reviewed schedule, set timer Time up, provided prompt to "get ready for bed" and showed picture of pajamas Timmy followed most of routine cooperatively End of story warning—started whining, Mom ignored	Natural use of visual schedule Confidently giving instructions Important to provide immediate reinforcement; don't fade supports so quickly

D. Reflection/feedback (notes from your discussion):

Stay with 1-minute requirement for wait time for this week.
Continue to follow plan.
Continue to collect data.
Keep up the great work!

(page 1 of 2)

Figure 6.1a.   Timmy's completed PTR-F Coach Planning and Reflection Log.

Figure 6.1a. *(continued)*

FORM 13   **PTR-F Coach Planning and Reflection Log** *(continued)*

Coaching strategies

The form below allows the facilitator to indicate whether a particular strategy was used during observation (with parent consent), during plan review, or during reflection and feedback.

Coaching strategies	Used in observation	Used in plan review	Used during reflection and feedback	Notes
Observe	✗			
Model				
Side-by-side support	✗			
Video recording				
Problem-solving discussion			✗	
Environmental arrangement				
Role-playing		✗		

Next steps:

Follow-up to family:

☑ E-mail   ❑ Phone call   ❑ Skype call   ❑ Material provision   ❑ Other

Day/time for next session:
7/13/15; 11:30 a.m.

Focus for next session:
Reinforcing desirable behavior immediately and contingently

PTR-F Fidelity of Strategy Implementation Form

FORM 11

Child: Timmy

Date: 7/6/15

Routine: Bedtime

Person implementing: Mom

Strategy steps	Were the steps implemented as intended?	Did your child respond as intended?	Was the strategy implemented as frequently as intended?
Prevent strategy:			
1. Five minutes before it is time for Timmy to begin his bedtime routine, Mom will make sure to have Timmy's attention and tell him "5 more minutes until bedtime. I'm going to set the timer." Briefly review the steps for bedtime with Timmy and set the timer. The timer will be kept out of Timmy's reach.	☑ Yes ☐ No		
2. When the 5 minutes are over and the timer is beeping, Mom will take the timer to Timmy and ask, "What time is it? It's time to get ready for bed."	☑ Yes ☐ No		
3. Mom will show Timmy the picture of the first step of the bedtime routine—pick out pajamas.	☑ Yes ☐ No	☑ Yes ☐ No	☑ Yes ☐ No
4. Timmy will walk to his room and pick out pajamas.	☑ Yes ☐ No		
5. As Timmy completes each step (pajamas, potty, brush teeth, pick out two books, read books, say goodnight), Mom will provide descriptive verbal praise for each of the steps (even if Mom has to help Timmy complete the steps at first).	☑ Yes ☐ No		
6. When the second story is almost over (last few pages), Mom will provide Timmy with a verbal warning that the book is almost over and it will be time to go to sleep.	☑ Yes ☐ No		

(page 1 of 2)

(continued)

Figure 6.2a. Timmy's completed Fidelity of Strategy Implementation Form.

Figure 6.2a. *(continued)*

FORM 11   **PTR-F Fidelity of Strategy Implementation Form** *(continued)*

Teach strategy: 1. When the bedtime routine steps are complete, Mom will show Timmy the next step in the schedule—him lying in his bed. Mom will say, "Stay in bed and Mommy will come back to read you a special story." 2. Set the timer for 1 minute. 3. Say "goodnight" and leave the room.	☑ Yes ☐ No ☑ Yes ☐ No ☑ Yes ☐ No	☑ Yes ☐ No	☑ Yes ☐ No
Reinforce strategy: 1. Select special superhero books that Timmy can only access for successfully staying in his bed and/or room. 2. When Timmy stays in his bed (or at least in the room) until the timer starts to beep, provide descriptive praise to Timmy, allow him to pick a special superhero book, and read it to him. When the story is over, say "goodnight" again and leave the room. 3. If Timmy leaves his room before the timer starts to beep, calmly tell him one time "It's time for bed," put him back in bed, and walk out of the room. Reset the timer for 1 minute. If he does not stay in his bed or room, continue to follow this step until he stays in bed for 1 minute (then follow step 2, above).	☐ Yes ☑ No ☐ Yes ☑ No ☐ Yes ☑ No	☑ Yes ☐ No	☐ Yes ☑ No

(page 2 of 2)

seemed to be responding consistently well. After reviewing the BRS and fidelity forms, the team agreed that Timmy might be ready for an increase in the amount of time he is required to stay in his room. Kaci asked Jodie and Phil what amount of time they were considering and what would be realistic given the progress with Timmy so far. Although they wanted to be able to jump to 10 minutes, they knew that was not the best idea. After a quick discussion, the team agreed on increasing the time to 2 minutes, wrote the new time on the BRS, and made a note on the behavior support plan. They would consider increasing to 3 minutes the following week if Timmy's behavior remained consistent.

Kaci asked Jodie to reflect on implementing the plan over the past week, and Jodie talked about how much of a difference she could see in Timmy when she was consistently responding to him after the 1 minute on the timer was up. She shared that she had stayed outside his room, out of sight, until the timer went off, instead of going to the kitchen to help with getting lunches ready for the next day or trying to do anything else—1 minute went fast. Jodie shared that she was trying to squeeze too much in and trying to push Timmy's behavior too quickly, and that it was clear to her this past week that responding to him when he was being appropriate had a positive impact. She also thought that putting him to bed a little bit later than usual was helpful because she felt Timmy was more tired and would fall asleep more quickly.

Jodie felt confident that she and Timmy were on the road to success and calm bedtimes. Phil even implemented the plan with Timmy last night, and things went smoothly as well. In fact, Phil reported that he felt that Timmy did better with him, reflecting that Timmy did not even whine when it was time to go to sleep. As Jodie was preparing to put Timmy to bed, Phil wanted to complete the PTR-F Fidelity of Strategy Implementation Form, so Kaci handed him the form. Jodie and Phil quickly reviewed the steps, with a reminder that they would have Timmy stay in his room for 2 minutes instead of 1. Phil put Dakota to bed when Jodie set the timer for Timmy.

Jodie completed the bedtime routine with Timmy without a fuss, and Phil completed the fidelity form. When Timmy fell asleep, Jodie completed the BRS and reflected on bedtime with Phil. Kaci was present to observe and facilitate as needed, but Jodie and Phil were able to reflect on the routine together. Kaci provided positive feedback to Jodie for completing all the steps of the behavior support plan and to Phil for completing the fidelity form. She commented on how well they worked together to implement the plan and reflect on the routine and process afterward.

The team celebrated their success thus far and agreed to meet the following week. Kaci reminded them that they would follow the same process for the next coaching session, adding that they would consider increasing the amount of time Timmy stays in his room next week if his behavior remained consistent. Jodie and Phil agreed to continue collecting BRS data and filling out the fidelity form.

Coaching Session 3   At the next coaching visit, Jodie and Phil were prepared with the BRS and were excited to share Timmy's continuing progress with Kaci. Timmy was doing great staying in his room, seemed to be getting more sleep during the night, and was falling asleep earlier than he has before. The entire bedtime routine was going well, and the nights had been calmer than ever. Kaci reviewed the BRS and fidelity forms with Jodie and Phil, who reflected on the past week with confidence and were proud to report that Timmy was continuing to spend more time in his room on his own. Kaci commented on how well they were doing with continuing to collect BRS data, using the data and fidelity forms for reflection, and sticking to the behavior support plan even though it was tempting to try to move faster. One of the critical features of their success was that they were supporting each other through this process and helping to address Timmy's behavior together. Jodie and Phil commented that they were able to have more positive conversations about Timmy and were getting better about providing positive feedback to him when he was following directions or engaging in other appropriate behaviors.

Because the bedtime routine was continuing to improve and Timmy was staying in his room for longer periods of time without tantrums, Jodie and Phil asked Kaci about increasing Timmy's wait time to 5 minutes. They decided to try it that night to see how Timmy would respond, and Kaci would be present to help with any troubleshooting, if needed. Based on the BRS and fidelity data, it was clear that Jodie was implementing the plan with fidelity and that Timmy was continuing to spend longer amounts of time in his room on his own. Timmy's tantrums had also diminished and were continuing to improve.

Phil asked Kaci how long it might take to get to their goal of having Timmy stay in his room until he fell asleep or for at least 30 minutes. Kaci could not provide a definitive answer but shared that Timmy's behavior would let them know when he was ready to be completely independent at bedtime. Kaci also shared that it was typical for 2-year-olds to not always go to bed independently. Phil admitted that he was anxious about how much longer they would need to continue implementing the behavior support plan. Kaci encouraged Phil to stick with the plan and focused the conversation back on the progress that Timmy had made in such a short amount of time. She reminded Phil of when she first met with them and how difficult this level of progress seemed at that time. Kaci encouraged Phil to continue with the hard work of supporting Timmy's needs and assured him that Timmy would continue to make progress if they continued to follow the plan. Kaci agreed to discuss a plan for increasing the amount of time after observing the bedtime routine.

Phil was putting Dakota to bed, and Jodie set the timer to start the bedtime routine with Timmy. Jodie quickly reviewed the steps with Kaci, with the change of extending the wait time to 5 minutes. Jodie followed all the steps of the behavior support plan, and Timmy did well waiting for 5 minutes in his room without whining or having a tantrum. After Jodie read Timmy his book, she joined Kaci and Phil and was excited that Timmy did well waiting for 5 minutes. Phil was also surprised and impressed, hopeful that they would be able to make quicker progress to get to their goal of Timmy being able to independently go to sleep at night.

Jodie noted the new time requirement on the BRS and recorded the data for that night. Jodie and Phil were both interested in increasing the amount of wait time and felt confident in their ability to continue to follow the behavior support plan. Kaci asked Jodie and Phil to reflect on how bedtime went that night and how things had been over the past week with Timmy, including what was contributing to their progress. They reflected that things at night were calmer overall and that they had been able to increase the amount of positive responses they were giving to the boys. They really felt that providing positive feedback on a regular basis was making a positive impact across the board, but especially during bedtime. Phil commented that they also felt more confident in being able to make progress toward reaching their goal of getting Timmy to fall asleep independently. The increase in positive interactions and the progress made in the bedtime routine were both contributing to having better days overall.

After celebrating how well things were going and all the work that was being put into successfully implementing a behavior support plan, Jodie and Phil began talking with Kaci about a plan to increase the wait time for the next week. The team discussed criteria for increasing the wait time, specifically, how many nights Timmy would need to be successful before the time was extended. The team agreed that if Timmy did well with the 5-minute wait for 3 nights in a row, they could increase the time to 8 minutes. Kaci reminded Jodie and Phil to monitor the data to determine when to move forward in getting closer to their 30-minute goal.

Coaching Session 4 Kaci returned for the fourth coaching session to discover that Timmy had made exponential progress over the past week. Jodie and Phil were enthusiastic to share their progress, the fidelity checklists, and BRS data, reporting that Timmy had been staying in his room and that they were now up to 10 minutes of wait time! Jodie reviewed the data sheets with Kaci, showing her that Timmy met the wait time goal each night for the past week. After three nights in a row of successfully waiting for 5 minutes, they then increased the time to 8 minutes. Timmy then successfully waited for 8 minutes for the subsequent three nights and was successful last night with waiting for 10 minutes. Jodie and Phil were eager to discuss a plan to continue to increase Timmy's wait time.

Jodie prepared for and started the bedtime routine with Timmy. Jodie implemented all of the steps, and Timmy stayed in bed without any tantrums. Jodie and Phil reported that Timmy was not having tantrums at night and that bedtime was going smoothly and calmly. They discussed next steps for moving forward and increasing Timmy's wait time. They agreed that if Timmy was successful with 10 minutes, they could move to 15, 20, and then 30 minutes. The team also agreed to meet for the next coaching session in 2 weeks instead of 1 week because Jodie was consistently implementing the steps of the behavior support plan and Timmy was responding by staying in his room and following the expected bedtime routine.

Coaching Session 5 Kaci arrived for the scheduled coaching session 2 weeks later. Jodie and Phil were eager to share their progress and reviewed their data with Kaci. Bedtime for the past 2 weeks had continued to go well, and Timmy was falling asleep on his own almost every night. Jodie and Phil reported that Timmy was often falling asleep around 20 minutes after being put to bed, so they had not even had an opportunity to work up to a 30-minute wait time with Timmy. Phil also reported that he put Timmy to bed a couple of nights in the past week without any problems.

Because Phil had been putting Timmy to bed successfully, Kaci observed Phil for the coaching session, and Jodie completed the PTR-F Fidelity of Strategy Implementation Form. The bedtime routine went smoothly, and Timmy fell asleep after about 15 minutes. Kaci asked Phil and Jodie if they had any concerns about the current bedtime routine, and they did not. They reflected that bedtime was continuing to go smoothly and were thankful for all of Kaci's support and expertise. Kaci reiterated that they were the ones who did all the work and that they needed to really congratulate themselves.

Their goal for getting Timmy to fall asleep in his room independently had been accomplished, so Kaci suggested they meet again in 2 weeks to continue to monitor Timmy's progress and possibly discuss next steps and any other goals. Kaci encouraged Jodie and Phil to continue implementing the plan and collecting BRS and fidelity data.

COACHING SESSIONS: LUCY

Implementing the Plan

Coaching Session 1 Roberta arrived the morning after the behavior support plan was finalized for the first observation and coaching session. She arrived before Lucy was awake to review the behavior support plan and make sure Gabby was prepared to begin implementation. Roberta also reviewed the coaching process, and Gabby prepared to wake Lucy up to get ready for school.

Roberta observed as Gabby woke Lucy up and got her out of bed. Once Lucy was awake, Gabby showed Lucy the schedule and told her that she was going to "go potty, get dressed, brush her hair, eat breakfast, and then go to school." Lucy said "No!" and then pushed away the schedule and sat on the floor. Gabby then told Lucy it was time to go to the bathroom and asked her if she wanted to sit on the big potty or little potty (full-size toilet or smaller child toilet) while showing her the pictures of the two toilets. Lucy lightly touched the picture of the full-size toilet, and Gabby walked her over to the bathroom, helped her pull down her pants, take off her nighttime diaper and throw it away, and then sit on the toilet. Lucy sat on the toilet for a minute, but did not use it. She got off the toilet on her own and pulled up her pants. She started to walk toward the door, but Gabby stopped her and lightly guided her toward the sink. She had a picture of Lucy washing her hands taped to the mirror and said, "Lucy, it is time to wash your hands" while pointing to the picture of her washing her hands. Gabby had to help Lucy wash her hands because Lucy wanted to play in the water, but she cooperated with Gabby to scrub her hands, rinse off the soap, and dry her hands. Then it was time to get dressed for the day.

Gabby presented the schedule, showing Lucy it was time to get dressed, and asked her which one of two shirts she wanted to wear. Lucy took one, said "this one," and started to try to put it on. She was struggling to get her shirt on, and Gabby pulled the shirt over Lucy's head and lightly guided Lucy's arms to get them in the sleeves. Lucy needed similar help with the rest of her clothes, and Gabby did a wonderful job of providing help to Lucy as needed, but not doing everything for her. Once Lucy was dressed, it was time to brush her hair.

Gabby brushed Lucy's hair in her room to avoid having to go back to the bathroom and to prevent issues with getting to the bathroom and/or leaving the bathroom. Lucy seemed to really like having her hair brushed because she could see herself in the mirror and talk with Mom at the same time. Lucy was very cooperative with this part of the morning routine, and Gabby quickly brushed her hair. When Gabby was finished, she let Lucy know that it was time for breakfast and to go to the kitchen.

Lucy raced into the kitchen and opened the refrigerator, swinging the door open quickly, hitting the wall, and making a loud sound. Gabby scolded Lucy for hurting the refrigerator and making so much noise and had her sit at the table. Gabby proceeded to get Lucy yogurt and a piece of toast, and while the bread was in the toaster, Lucy wandered away from the table. When the toast was ready, Gabby turned around to see that Lucy had left the kitchen. Gabby found Lucy going into Hector's room (where he was sleeping) and picked her up to take her back to the kitchen. Lucy let out a loud squeal and squirmed around trying to get down and out of Gabby's hold. Gabby was able to keep hold of her and get her to the table, but Lucy continued to struggle and resisted sitting at the table to eat her breakfast. Gabby asked Lucy if she wanted some juice for getting dressed, which she did, so Lucy ended up sitting at the table and Gabby got her some juice. Lucy ate her breakfast, and Roberta took a few minutes to talk with Gabby about her observations.

Before Gabby had to leave to get Lucy to school, she wanted to address giving Lucy the juice after she ran from the table. Roberta suggested that perhaps Gabby should give the juice to Lucy right when she sits down at the table the first time, or she could make having juice a part of the routine of going to the kitchen and sitting down at the table. Roberta reviewed that giving reinforcers right after any behavior makes it more likely that the behavior will happen again; so, it is important to reinforce desirable behaviors as soon as possible. She also suggested that she could have Gabby's breakfast ready before she wakes her up so that when they get to the kitchen, Lucy can sit right down and start eating. Roberta noted that waiting with nothing to do provided an opportunity for Lucy to find something less desirable to do. Gabby liked the suggestions and said that she would implement those changes tomorrow.

Lucy finished her breakfast, and Gabby wanted to get her to school so they would not be late. Roberta wanted to complete their coaching session and provide additional feedback to Gabby, so Gabby agreed to call Roberta later in the morning when she was back home from taking Lucy to school.

Later that morning, Gabby called Roberta to finish their coaching session and discuss next steps. Roberta first asked how this morning was in comparison to a typical morning. Gabby reported that it was pretty similar to how it had been going in the morning, but that Lucy was much more cooperative this morning than usual. Roberta commented that Gabby did a great job implementing most of the steps of the strategies, especially noting how well Lucy does when Gabby brushes her hair. Roberta pointed out how attentive and cooperative Lucy was during this time, and Gabby commented how natural and fun it was to sit and brush Lucy's hair. Lucy did love looking at herself in the mirror, and Roberta asked if there were other times when Gabby could use the mirror as a reinforcer for Lucy's desirable behaviors. Gabby said she could give Lucy a little mirror for some of the other routines too, and Roberta reminded her to keep the mirror for key times when Lucy might need it the most. Roberta added a mirror to the list of Lucy's reinforcers on the behavior support plan and discussed when and how the mirror could be used as a reinforcer throughout the day. Gabby's biggest concern was getting Lucy to give her the mirror back in a calm and cooperative manner.

Roberta then talked with Gabby about using the schedule. She reminded Gabby to review only one or two activities or steps and ask Lucy "What's that?" while referring to the schedule instead of telling her what was next. Roberta noticed that if Gabby asked Lucy to identify what the picture was, she seemed to be more cooperative for that part of the routine. Roberta mentioned that at school, even though the whole day's schedule might be posted, Mrs. Williams only reviews one or two activities at a time. Roberta also reminded Gabby to use the schedule at every change in activity because she did not use the schedule when it was time to brush her hair or go to the car.

Roberta wrote up brief reminders of their coaching session and sent them to Gabby by text message. Roberta had written coaching feedback to give to Gabby at their next session, and she e-mailed that to her as well. They reviewed the behavior support plan again briefly, highlighting the feedback from that morning. Figure 6.3a is a completed PTR-F Coach Planning and Reflection Log for the first coaching session with Gabby, and Figure 6.4a is the first completed PTR-F Fidelity of Strategy Implementation Form.

Coaching Session 2   Roberta arrived for the second observation and coaching session in the morning before Gabby got Lucy up in order to review progress from the previous week. Gabby was prepared to show Roberta the BRS and was pleased to note more progress over the past week for the morning routine. Lucy was starting to have fewer tantrums overall and was doing better with the morning routine. Gabby really appreciated Roberta's feedback from the last observation and was able to implement the advice she provided. Gabby was thankful to have those reminders as a text message, because they were easily accessible and she could refer to them whenever she needed. Roberta asked Gabby if she wanted to review the behavior support plan before she woke Lucy up, but Gabby stated that she knew the steps and was ready. She had Lucy's breakfast out at the table, including a small cup of juice, and had the schedule prepared for the morning.

Gabby went into Lucy's room to wake her up and discovered that she was already awake, just lying in her bed. As Gabby entered the room, Lucy smiled and sat up in her bed. As Gabby approached, with the schedule in hand, Lucy got out of her bed and headed toward the bathroom. Surprised, Gabby told Lucy, "What a big girl going to the potty by yourself!" Lucy walked into the bathroom, stood up on the stool at the sink, and began playing with her reflection in the mirror. Gabby entered and just pointed toward the toilet, and Lucy slowly stepped down off the stool and started pulling her pants down. She still struggled with getting her pants down over the overnight diaper, so Gabby helped her maneuver her pants, take the overnight diaper off, and put it into the trash.

Roberta continued observing the rest of the morning routine, with prompts from Gabby to complete the steps of the routine. For the most part, Lucy cooperated and increasingly participated in the routine. Twice, Roberta provided a quick prompt to Gabby to present the visual schedule, which she did, even though it did not seem to make much of a difference with getting Lucy to participate in the morning routine. When Lucy sat right down to eat her breakfast, Roberta had an opportunity to provide some feedback to Gabby. She was impressed with how well Gabby was implementing the steps of the strategies and how well Lucy was responding to Gabby's instructions. Gabby felt confident with the morning routine now, and the mornings were much calmer than they had been in a long time. Now, Gabby could envision when Lucy would be mostly independent with getting ready in the morning.

Roberta asked Gabby for any feedback she had about the behavior support plan and how things were going thus far. Gabby was extremely happy with the progress that she was making with Lucy and mentioned that her mom was starting to notice a difference as well. Roberta observed that when Gabby implemented all of the steps of the behavior support plan, Lucy seemed to start making more progress in a shorter amount of time. Roberta shared the fidelity form and encouraged Gabby to stick with the current plan until Lucy's desirable behavior becomes more consistent and reliable. They discussed the next two coaching sessions, and

FORM 13

PTR-F Coach Planning and Reflection Log

Family name: _Lucy and Gabby_   Coaching session date: _August 13, 2015_

Target routine	Time of routine	Family member to coach
Morning	7:30 am	Mom
Mealtimes	8:00 am, 12:30 pm, 6:00 pm	Mom
Toileting	Throughout day	Mom

A. Progress review (notes from your discussion with family):

   Gabby collecting Behavior Rating Scale data

B. Review of intervention plan (notes from your discussion with the family):

   Reviewed and role-played plan with Gabby

C. Observation of routine:

   In addition to completing the PTR-F Fidelity of Strategy Implementation Form, record your reflections from the observation.

What I observed	What I want to share
Schedule review—reviewed too many steps Ask Lucy about the next step instead of telling her—seemed more cooperative when asked, "What's that?" Didn't use schedule for brushing hair or going to the car Overall, followed the steps pretty closely	Nice job implementing most of the steps Lucy seems to love when Gabby brushes her hair—attentive and cooperative

D. Reflection/feedback (notes from your discussion):

   Gabby thankful for the feedback (sent via text)—only review one or two activities on the schedule, provide reinforcement for desirable behaviors as immediately as possible

(page 1 of 2)

Figure 6.3a.   Lucy's completed PTR-F Coach Planning and Reflection Log.

(continued)

Figure 6.3a. *(continued)*

FORM 13   **PTR-F Coach Planning and Reflection Log** *(continued)*

Coaching strategies

The form below allows the facilitator to indicate whether a particular strategy was used during observation (with parent consent), during plan review, or during reflection and feedback.

Coaching strategies	Used in observation	Used in plan review	Used during reflection and feedback	Notes
Observe	✗			
Model				
Side-by-side support				
Video recording				
Problem-solving discussion	✗	✗	✗	
Environmental arrangement				
Role-playing				

Next steps:

Follow-up to family:

❑ E-mail   ☑ Phone call   ❑ Skype call   ❑ Material provision   ☑ Other

Day/time for next session:
8/20/15; 2:00 p.m.

Focus for next session:
More verbal praise—timely and contingently

FORM 11 PTR-F Fidelity of Strategy Implementation Form

Child: Lucy   Routine: Morning

Date: August 13, 2015   Person implementing: Mom

Strategy steps	Were the steps implemented as intended?	Did your child respond as intended?	Was the strategy implemented as frequently as intended?
Prevent strategy:			
1. When it is time for a particular routine/activity, approach Lucy with the visual schedule in hand, prepared with the correct activities in the correct order.	☐ Yes ☑ No		
2. Tell Lucy, "It is time for (routine/activity). What do we do first?" while showing her the schedule and pointing to the first picture. For routines/activities where a choice can be offered, you can say, "Lucy, it is time for (routine/activity). Do you want to do (option A) first or (option B) first?"	☐ Yes ☑ No		
3. If Lucy starts to move in the correct direction or clearly indicates she is calm and compliant (within 5 seconds), provide descriptive praise for following the initial direction (e.g., "That's right Lucy, it's time to go to the bathroom," or "Good job listening to Mommy and putting your clothes on!").	☐ Yes ☑ No	☐ Yes ☑ No	☐ Yes ☑ No
4. If Lucy does not respond within 5 seconds, provide the instruction again. If she does not respond the second time, gently provide physical guidance for that step. Provide descriptive praise for cooperating with parts of the routine/activity, as much as possible (e.g., "Good standing up like a big girl!" "Thank you for opening the door by yourself").	☐ Yes ☑ No		

(page 1 of 2)

Figure 6.4a. Lucy's Fidelity of Strategy Implementation Form.

(continued)

Figure 6.4a. *(continued)*

FORM 11   **PTR-F Fidelity of Strategy Implementation Form** *(continued)*

Teach strategy:			
1. When the visual schedule is first being used, start with the prevent strategy steps 1–4 (where applicable), above.	☐ Yes ☑ No		
2. When it is time for the next step of the routine/activity, point to the next picture and ask, "What do you do next?"	☐ Yes ☑ No		
3. Wait up to 5 seconds for Lucy to respond with a verbal response to your question. If she makes any kind of verbalization, provide descriptive praise (e.g., "Good words!" or repeat what she says). If she does not respond verbally, move to the next step but repeat what the step is using the same label as is on the picture schedule.	☐ Yes ☑ No	☐ Yes ☑ No	☐ Yes ☑ No
4. Repeat these steps for the rest of the routine/activity, asking "What do you do next?" and providing descriptive praise for each of the steps, even if only partially completed calmly and cooperatively, especially when Lucy is first learning these steps.	☐ Yes ☑ No		
Reinforce strategy:			
1. Create list of verbal and non-verbal ways Mom can provide attention/affection when Lucy is demonstrating desirable behaviors.	☑ Yes ☐ No		
2. When Lucy participates in routines, follows directions, and is calm and cooperative (demonstrates desirable behaviors), provide descriptive praise and/or physical affection. About 3–5 times throughout the day, provide a small amount of juice or a few fruit snacks when Lucy demonstrates desirable behaviors.	☐ Yes ☑ No	☐ Yes ☑ No	☐ Yes ☑ No
3. When Lucy engages in challenging behaviors, ignore her; do not say anything to her and turn your face and/or body slightly away if necessary. Point to the relevant picture on the visual schedule to prompt her to start or participate in the next step of the routine/activity. As soon as she begins to comply with the routine or request, follow step 2 to reinforce the desirable behavior.	☐ Yes ☑ No		

(page 2 of 2)

Roberta was interested in observing during a time when she could see two different routines in a fairly short amount of time.

Gabby identified coming home from school and having lunch as the routines to observe for the next two coaching sessions. Roberta encouraged Gabby to keep up the great work of implementing Lucy's behavior support plan for the morning routine and continuing to collect BRS data. Gabby told Roberta that she was thankful for her help so far and that she was looking forward to getting feedback on using the schedule and teaching Lucy to actively participate in coming home from school and making and eating lunch.

Coaching Session 3   Roberta arrived as Gabby and Lucy were getting home from school. Lucy waved to Roberta and followed Gabby into the house. Gabby did not have the visual schedule with her, but as they walked into the house, Gabby verbally reviewed that they would put Lucy's backpack away and then make lunch. Gabby had Lucy put her backpack by the door in her room, and they went to the kitchen. As they were walking, Gabby asked Roberta if she could help her identify ways to encourage Lucy's active participation in getting lunch ready, as well as ways to incorporate more appropriate communication. Roberta asked Gabby if she could make lunch with them and try some ways to get Lucy to participate more as Gabby was giving instructions. Gabby was happy to have any help that Roberta could provide, because Lucy tends to get silly during this time and does not follow directions as well. Gabby was not sure how much she could have Lucy participate in meal preparation and in the use of large utensils.

Gabby started by showing Lucy the schedule and telling her it was time to make some lunch. Gabby showed Lucy two options for lunch that she could choose from: a sandwich or a quesadilla. Lucy touched the picture of the quesadilla, and said, "That one," which is what she said for most things. Roberta provided some modeling by prompting Lucy to say "quesadilla." Lucy did not respond, so Roberta prompted Lucy again to ask for a "quesadilla." When Lucy did not respond again, Roberta had Gabby prompt her, "Lucy, you want a quesadilla? Tell mama 'quesadilla.'" Lucy replied "Mama 'dilla," and Gabby was excited, saying, "Yes, mama will make quesadilla!" Gabby prompted Lucy to help get the ingredients out of the refrigerator and put them on the counter. Gabby assisted Lucy in getting each of the items out of the refrigerator, with Lucy actively participating as long as Gabby helped. Although Gabby did not want Lucy participating with putting items on the stove, she had Lucy count with her, sing songs, or label what she was doing. While Gabby made the quesadilla, Lucy stood near Gabby, sometimes singing along with her mother and using quite a few words either on her own or with prompting from Gabby. Once the quesadilla was ready, Gabby cut it and put it on a plate. She helped Lucy carefully take it to the table, and Lucy sat down to eat.

Roberta and Gabby sat with Lucy at the table while she ate and reviewed what had occurred. Referring to the PTR-F Fidelity of Strategy Implementation Form, Roberta shared her observations of what Gabby did well, including using the schedule and providing positive feedback when Lucy was exhibiting appropriate behavior and communication. Gabby asked Roberta the following questions: "Do I *always* have to use the visual schedule, or can I just say what we are going to do? What if I want Lucy to verbalize and she doesn't, like she did with you? How many times should I be asking her to verbalize? Is there anything else I can do to teach active participation?"

Roberta began by answering the first question, saying it would be best to use the visual schedule until Lucy's physically aggressive behavior was consistently absent, which would be determined by reviewing the BRS data. Roberta was hesitant to get rid of the visual schedule altogether because the data were not satisfactory at this point, but she told Gabby that if verbally listing the next steps of the routine was working, then she could use that as part of the strategy if the schedule was not readily available. Roberta encouraged Gabby to continue to prepare the schedule and have it ready each day for at least another couple of weeks. Although Lucy was making progress, Roberta did not want the supports to be faded or removed too quickly, especially since using the schedule was successfully reducing Lucy's physically aggressive behavior. Gabby agreed to continue to use the schedule as much as possible and to make more of an effort to have it ready each day. Roberta understood that it took extra time and effort but believed that this investment should pay off in the long run with more consistent appropriate behavior from Lucy.

Roberta then addressed Gabby's second question about how much to push Lucy to verbalize. Roberta recommended that Gabby should continue to encourage Lucy to use words more often but not to force it at this time. Similar to pushing the schedule, if Gabby pushed Lucy too hard regarding using language, Lucy might start to refuse more, and unlike physical movements, Gabby could not force Lucy to say anything. Roberta encouraged Gabby to say as many words throughout the day as possible, especially when they were going to be doing something fun or something that Lucy likes to do. If Gabby saved verbal requests for something fun, it would be more likely that Lucy would be motivated to talk in order to start the activity or step. Roberta reminded Gabby to consider what behavior she is reinforcing and when she is providing reinforcement. Gabby was thankful for this feedback and was relieved to not have to "force" Lucy to talk throughout the day. She also thought it was a good idea to capitalize on the opportunities when Lucy would be motivated by the particular activity.

As for Gabby's final question about ways she can incorporate more active participation, Roberta did not have much to add to what Gabby was already doing. If there were safety concerns (like being close to the stove), Roberta encouraged Gabby to identify what steps Lucy would be able to do with assistance (e.g., getting materials from the refrigerator, taking something to the table) and what steps she could do independently (e.g., getting materials from the cupboard, getting a fork for herself). Also, the more Lucy could do independently, the more Gabby would feel comfortable having her participate even further. Roberta encouraged Gabby to identify when there were additional steps or parts of the routine that she would like Lucy to actively participate in, figure out how she could participate, and then teach her how. After this discussion, Gabby felt comfortable with being able to continue to teach Lucy to actively participate in more of the daily routines. Gabby admitted that it is often easier to just do things for Lucy because it takes so long to work with Lucy to do things independently. Roberta reminded Gabby that if she wanted Lucy to become more independent, then she would need to provide more opportunities for Lucy to practice these skills and then provide positive feedback to Lucy about her behavior.

Lucy was finishing her lunch, and Roberta wrote up her coaching notes and reminders for Gabby. She complimented Gabby on her implementation of the behavior support plan and acknowledged the progress documented on the BRS. Roberta quickly reviewed the BRS one more time, pointing out how much progress Lucy has made in such a short amount of time and attributing that to Gabby's hard work. Gabby was also very happy with Lucy's progress and was committed to making life more calm and predictable for both of them. They decided to keep the next coaching session for the same time and routines for the following week.

Coaching Session 4   When Roberta arrived, she found Lucy, Gabby, and Marguerite just sitting down to have lunch together. Roberta thought she was late, but Gabby reported that it has been much easier to get Lucy in the car to come home from school, so they have been getting home a little earlier than before. Also, Lucy has been helping a lot with choosing and preparing lunch, so that has sped up the process as well. Gabby had the BRS ready to show to Roberta, as she was excited to share Lucy's amazing progress over the past week. Using Roberta's feedback from last week, Gabby had been able to implement the steps of the behavior support plan across the daily routines (at least most of the steps most of the time). The daily routines were continuing to get better, with Lucy actively participating more and more. The positive feedback was definitely the most powerful reinforcer that Gabby could use, which was improving her relationship with Lucy as well as Lucy's relationships with other family members, including her grandparents. Lucy was thriving with this type of consistent positive feedback, and Mrs. Williams was noticing more improvement at school as well.

Roberta was pleased with Lucy's progress and again commended Gabby for being responsible for all of the improvement. Roberta suggested that they continue with the current plan and then plan to meet again in 2 weeks to see how things continued to progress. She shared that if progress continued, they could discuss fading elements of the behavior support plan or adding next steps. Roberta asked Marguerite for her observations and feedback, and she was pleased and proud of the growth that both Lucy and Gabby have made over the past few weeks. It was difficult for everyone under the circumstances of living together and having their lives disrupted, but now they were on a good path to move forward. Although their lives were still stressful, getting a handle on Lucy's behaviors was a big part of making life calmer and easier.

Roberta asked whether there were other issues that they needed to discuss about the behavior support plan or if there was anything in particular they wanted to focus on for the next 2 weeks, but neither Gabby nor Marguerite had any concerns or questions at this time. Roberta scheduled to follow up with Gabby in 2 weeks during the later afternoon, including for playtime and making dinner. Lucy was doing so much better now with structured activities and with adult interaction, but she was still not doing well with playing on her own or being left alone. Gabby wanted to know how she could use the behavior support plan strategies to help Lucy learn to play by herself.

Coaching Session 5   When Roberta arrived for her observation and coaching session, Lucy was sitting in the middle of the floor with toys scattered around her. Late afternoon is usually difficult because Gabby does not always have something to do with Lucy, who does not do well being left alone. Lucy typically throws toys or ends up breaking them instead of playing with them. Roberta sat out of Lucy's view to observe how she played, and she told Gabby to do what she normally would be doing if she was not there. Gabby was trying to get some cleaning done around the house to help her mom, so she was vacuuming, doing laundry, and trying to clean the bathrooms and kitchen; she would then try to start preparing dinner. Gabby passed through the room often without interacting with Lucy. Gabby knew this was problematic, but she also had household chores to do and needed time when Lucy could play by herself. Gabby wanted to know how to incorporate the behavior support plan strategies into this playtime.

After observing for about 20 minutes, Roberta asked Gabby if she could sit and talk about her observations. Gabby had shown Lucy the schedule, told her it was playtime, and said she could play with any of the toys in the family room. When she walked through the room, she provided positive feedback to Lucy for playing with toys, even if Lucy was not really playing with the toys in a purposeful way. Gabby also had to enter the room to intervene if she heard toys being thrown, heard Lucy playing with something that she was not allowed to play with (e.g., TV remote, telephone, Marguerite's knickknacks), or had other indications that Lucy was not playing with her toys. For the most part, Gabby was following the behavior support plan strategies except for teaching active participation. Gabby knew this was where the plan was falling apart, but she did not know how she should be teaching Lucy to play.

Roberta talked with Gabby about teaching Lucy how to play with toys like she would teach Lucy to do anything else. Referring back to the behavior support plan and what has worked so far, Roberta reminded Gabby that Lucy would demonstrate the appropriate behaviors when they are taught to her and she is reinforced for them. In terms of toys, they should be reinforcing so that it would not be necessary for Gabby to give Lucy feedback about playing with them; but for now, it would be important to first find toys that Lucy is really interested in. It might still be necessary to teach Lucy how to play or interact with the toys, so Roberta started by asking Gabby about the toys Lucy currently has (which were not many). Gabby commented that Lucy seemed to like the blocks, but that once she was bored with them, she would often start throwing them around the room, and she was worried that Lucy would break something. Lucy did not seem to like any other toys, and no other toys held her interest for more than a few minutes.

Roberta helped Gabby brainstorm any other activities that Lucy could do on her own or could do if no one was around. Gabby could not think of activities that Lucy would engage in for more than a few minutes, so Roberta worked with Gabby to plan out how to increase the amount of time that Lucy is actively playing or engaging with her toys.

Roberta observed that Lucy did not seem to really know how to play with the toys, so she talked with Gabby about playing with Lucy so that she could show her how to play with the different toys and demonstrate different things that she could do with them beyond her usual activities. Roberta said it would be just like teaching Lucy anything else, but that teaching a child how to play is a little more difficult because there usually is not only one way for a toy to be used. Although Gabby really wanted Lucy to be able to play by herself, she understood that Lucy needed to be taught how to play with many of her toys. Roberta assured Gabby that these were valuable skills and could be beneficial for when Lucy is with her cousins or peers from school. Those types of play and social skills, although not an original target for Lucy's behavior support plan, would be a good next step to focus on with Lucy.

Roberta asked about how the other routines were going, especially the morning routine and Lucy's overall tantrums. Gabby went to get the BRS to review, which showed that Lucy was continuing to demonstrate sustained progress. Because Lucy was maintaining progress and Gabby was successfully able to support Lucy's continued success, Roberta suggested they consider moving on to the next steps of Lucy's behavior support plan, particularly after the conversation that day about explicitly teaching social and play skills. Roberta scheduled to meet with Gabby the following week when Lucy was in school so they could start planning without distractions.

Using Data and Next Steps

This chapter deals with monitoring the Prevent-Teach-Reinforce for Families (PTR-F) behavior support plan implementation and using data to make informed decisions about what steps to take depending on how the child's behavior responds to the behavior support plan. Sometimes, the behavior support plan works perfectly, and the data show immediate improvements that continue until challenging behavior is no longer an issue and the child has shown dramatic growth in positive social interactions. However, sometimes this is not the case. At times, change is not evident, and change sometimes is too gradual to make the difference that is needed. In this chapter, we address these possible scenarios and suggest steps that the team can take to make revisions and ensure further progress.

IMPLEMENTATION AND PROGRESS MONITORING

To review, before implementation is initiated, the following should have occurred: 1) a team has been assembled (which may include, for example, only a facilitator and parent); 2) goals have been defined; 3) data have been obtained on the baseline levels of a targeted challenging behavior and a targeted desirable behavior; 4) a PTR-F assessment has been completed; 5) a behavior support plan has been developed; and 6) necessary training and coaching have been arranged. These are the steps that have been described in previous chapters. The important step that we would like to emphasize at this point is the collection of progress monitoring data.

Prior to implementing the carefully designed behavior support plan, there should be at least 3 days of data that have been collected and summarized on a simple graph. It is best if there is more than a week of data, but 3 days is the minimum, and the data should be collected in the form of the Behavior Rating Scale (BRS; as described in Chapter 3). The data that have been collected prior to implementing the behavior support plan will reveal important information. These data are called *baseline data*. The baseline data on challenging behavior will reveal one of the following possible patterns:

1. High, stable levels of challenging behavior. In this pattern, the data confirm that the level of challenging behavior is unacceptably high and that it appears as if it will continue at a high rate unless something is done (see Figure 7.1). With this pattern, the behavior support plan should be implemented right away. The behavior support plan should also be implemented right away if the pattern shows that the challenging behavior is getting worse (see Figure 7.2).

2. Low levels of challenging behavior. This pattern (see Figure 7.3) indicates that the level of challenging behavior is quite low and brings into question the purpose of the behavior support plan. There are a number of possible explanations. One explanation is that the behavior, in fact, has decreased to the point that it is no longer a concern requiring an individualized intervention, at least at the present time. This may be because improved parenting practices had a beneficial effect, or perhaps a different change has occurred that somehow resulted in improved behavior. The team should

		1	2	3	4	5	6	7	8	9
						Days				
Desirable behavior		5	5	5	5	5	5	5	5	5
Safe use of toy		4	4	4	4	4	4	4	4	4
		3	3	3	3	3	3	3	3	3
		2	2	2	2	(2)	2	(2)	2	2
		1	1	1	1	1	(1)	1	(1)	(1)
Challenging behavior		5	(5)	5	5	(5)	(5)	5	(5)	(5)
Throwing toys		(4)	4	(4)	(4)	4	4	(4)	4	4
		3	3	3	3	3	3	3	3	3
		2	2	2	2	2	2	2	2	2
		1	1	1	1	1	1	1	1	1

Figure 7.1. High, stable levels of challenging behavior.

decide if more days of data should be collected and if the behavior support plan should be placed on hold.

Another explanation is that the behavior is actually still continuing at an alarming level but, for some reason, the data are not reflecting what is happening. This could be because the definition of the behavior needs to be improved or the data are not being collected at the appropriate time. Either way, if the data are not capturing

		1	2	3	4	5	6	7	8	9
						Days				
Desirable behavior		5	5	5	5	5	5	5	5	5
Engage		4	4	4	4	4	4	4	4	4
		3	3	3	3	3	3	3	3	3
		2	2	2	2	2	(2)	2	2	2
		1	1	1	1	(1)	1	(1)	(1)	(1)
Challenging behavior		5	5	5	5	5	5	(5)	5	(5)
Looking away/ not responding		4	4	4	4	(4)	(4)	4	(4)	4
		3	3	3	(3)	3	3	3	3	3
		2	(2)	2	2	2	2	2	2	2
		(1)	1	(1)	1	1	1	1	1	1

Figure 7.2. Increasing levels of challenging behavior.

	1	2	3	4	5	6	7	8	9
					Days				
Desirable behavior	5	5	5	5	5	(5)	5	(5)	(5)
	4	4	4	4	(4)	4	(4)	4	4
Follow the morning routine	3	3	3	3	3	3	3	3	3
	2	2	2	2	2	2	2	2	2
	1	1	1	1	1	1	1	1	1
Challenging behavior	5	5	5	5	5	5	5	5	5
	4	4	4	4	4	4	4	4	4
Tantrum	3	3	3	3	3	3	3	3	3
	2	(2)	2	2	(2)	2	(2)	(2)	2
	(1)	1	(1)	(1)	1	(1)	1	1	(1)

Figure 7.3. Low levels of challenging behavior.

the behavior of concern, then the data collection strategy needs to be revised. For example, teams may need to expand their operational definitions to include all of the possible behaviors the target behavior might include as opposed to a limited number of behaviors. Or, after collecting data for a number of days, teams might note that the challenging behavior occurs more frequently or more intensively during a routine in which they are not collecting data. The team may decide that the family should collect data during the other routine or during both routines to more accurately track the behaviors over time. Sometimes the anchors of the BRS need to be changed because they are too high or too low, and at other times, it might make sense to alter the dimension of the behavior (i.e., frequency, duration, intensity) that is being tracked if another dimension of the behavior would more accurately reflect what is happening during the routine. Such a revision should be accomplished immediately, and data should be obtained until the levels of the data are consistent with the levels reported anecdotally by the parent and other team members.

3. Decreasing trend of challenging behavior. Sometimes, challenging behavior occurs at high levels when data collection begins, but then it decreases over time (see Figure 7.4). This could be because of a positive change that has occurred in the home or in the way that parents are interacting with the child. In this case, data should continue to be collected, but implementation of the behavior support plan should be postponed until the data indicate that the behavior is again a significant concern.

4. An inconsistent pattern of challenging behavior. Another pattern is one in which the challenging behavior appears to be high on some days but nonexistent on other days (see Figure 7.5). If this pattern persists, then two actions should occur. First, the team should try to find out what is different on the good and bad days that might be responsible for the differences in behavior. Often this pattern signifies that some kind of stressor (or "setting event") has occurred that has affected the child during the day so that otherwise innocuous events come to serve as triggers setting off challenging behavior. It is possible that such stressors might have been missed during the

	1	2	3	4	5	6	7	8	9
					Days				
Desirable behavior	5	5	5	5	⑤	5	⑤	⑤	⑤
	4	4	4	4	4	④	4	4	4
Ask nicely again when told "No"	3	3	3	3	3	3	3	3	3
	2	2	2	2	2	2	2	2	2
	1	1	1	1	1	1	1	1	1
Challenging behavior	⑤	5	⑤	5	5	5	5	5	5
	4	④	4	4	4	4	4	4	4
Yelling "NO!"	3	3	3	③	③	3	3	3	3
	2	2	2	2	2	②	②	2	2
	1	1	1	1	1	1	1	①	①

Figure 7.4. Decreasing levels of challenging behavior.

functional behavioral assessment. If so, the team might wish to expand on the behavioral assessment to identify what the stressor might be. For example, the stressor might be exhaustion due to inadequate sleep, or it might be a difficult exchange during the early morning hours. If the event can be identified, then it might be possible to eliminate it, or if not, it might be possible to provide for accommodations in the family routine.

	1	2	3	4	5	6	7	8	9
					Days				
Desirable behavior	5	5	5	5	5	⑤	5	⑤	⑤
	4	4	4	4	④	4	④	4	4
Safe use of toy	3	3	3	3	3	3	3	3	3
	2	2	2	2	2	2	2	2	2
	1	1	1	1	1	1	1	1	1
Challenging behavior	5	⑤	5	5	5	⑤	5	⑤	5
	4	4	4	④	4	4	4	4	4
Throwing toys	3	3	3	3	3	3	3	3	3
	2	2	2	2	②	2	②	2	2
	①	1	①	1	1	1	1	1	①

Figure 7.5. Inconsistent levels of challenging behavior.

TIP *Data patterns might also be noted in intervention data and can be used for progress monitoring and data-based decision making while the team continues to implement the behavior support plan. For example, teams can inspect patterns in intervention data to determine if the intervention is working (e.g., the BRS would indicate that challenging behavior levels are decreasing and that desirable behavior levels are increasing). Teams can also inspect data patterns to determine if it is an appropriate time to begin fading behavior support plan supports (e.g., the BRS indicates that consistent, low levels of challenging behavior and consistent, high levels of desirable behavior are occurring). More information about this topic can be found in the Data-Based Decision Making section of this chapter.*

The second action that should occur is that the team should implement the behavior support plan as planned, with special emphasis on those days that had been a problem. The behavior support plan should proceed unless the data indicate that no progress is being made or that the behavior is getting worse over time. If limited progress or increased challenging behavior is noted, the team should engage in the data-based decision-making process that is described next.

Data-Based Decision Making

Baseline data that are collected prior to implementation will help determine the extent to which the intervention is effective. A useful way to separate baseline from intervention is to draw a vertical line on the graph at the end of baseline (see Figure 7.6) and then to continue collecting data during intervention in exactly the same way as was done when collecting the data before intervention.

Data-based decision making depends on comparing the data trends that occur in intervention with the data that were collected in baseline. Obviously, intervention should result in lower levels of challenging behavior and higher levels of desirable behavior. The speed with which this change can be expected to occur varies from child to child and from behavior support plan to behavior support plan. Sometimes it takes a while for a child to learn new desirable behaviors, and this depends on the child's characteristics as well as the quality of the parent–child interactions and the frequency with which intervention occurs during the day. The higher the quality and the more frequent the intervention, the more rapid should be the behavior change.

In PTR-F, some improvement in challenging behavior should be evident in the first few sessions or days. This is because the behavior support plan in PTR-F includes multiple components. The change in reinforce strategies often produces improvements more rapidly than the teach strategies, and the prevent strategies can result in changes that are almost immediate. Therefore, families can expect to see favorable changes quite rapidly in most cases of PTR-F implementation. We hasten to add here that just because the prevent or reinforce strategies might help change occur quickly, this does not mean that the teach component is less important. On the contrary, the teach component is probably the most important component for long-term, durable improvement. Indeed, *all* components are considered to be essential in the PTR-F model.

As teams review the data during intervention, some will see encouraging trends, whereas other teams will see trends that do not represent adequate progress. In the following sections, we describe what to do under these different scenarios.

What to Do if Progress Is Good

When the data show favorable progress, the immediate, short-term plan should be to keep doing what is working! In our experience, one of the most common mistakes made with challenging behavior interventions is that implementers are too quick to reduce the supports that have produced behavior change in the first place. As a general

FORM 2 — PTR-F Behavior Rating Scale

Child: Mia   Rater: Mom   Routine: Bedtime   Month: September

Date/time: _____

	Baseline						Intervention												September
	9/1/15	9/2/15	9/3/15	9/4/15	9/5/15	9/6/15	9/7/15	9/8/15	9/9/15	9/10/15									
Desirable behavior — Complete steps of bedtime routine	5 4 3 2 1	5 4 3 2 1	5 4 3 2 1	5 4 3 ☑2 1	5 4 3 2 1	5 4 3 2 1	5 4 ☑3 2 1	5 4 ☑3 2 1	5 4 ☑3 2 1	5 ☑4 3 2 1	5 4 3 2 1	5 4 3 2 1	5 4 3 2 1	5 4 3 2 1	5 4 3 2 1	5 4 3 2 1	5 4 3 2 1	5 4 3 2 1	5 4 3 2 1
Challenging behavior — Tantrums	5 4 3 2 1	5 4 3 2 1	5 4 3 2 1	5 4 3 2 1	5 4 3 2 ☑1	5 4 3 2 ☑1	5 4 3 2 1	5 4 3 2 1	5 4 3 2 1	5 4 3 2 1	5 4 3 2 1	5 4 3 2 1	5 4 3 2 1	5 4 3 2 1	5 4 3 2 1	5 4 3 2 1	5 4 3 2 1	5 4 3 2 1	5 4 3 2 1

Desirable behavior: Complete steps of bedtime routine

5 = Completes steps of the routine with verbal prompts

4 = Completes steps with verbal AND gesture/point/model

3 = Completes steps with verbal AND partial physical assistance

2 = Completes steps with verbal AND full physical assistance

1 = Runs away, drops to the floor, hides

Challenging behavior: Tantrums

5 = Tantrum behavior lasts full duration of routine

4 = Tantrum behavior lasts during most but not all steps of routine

3 = Tantrum behavior lasts for $\frac{1}{2}$ of the routine

2 = Tantrum behavior only occurs for a small part of the routine

1 = No tantrum behavior during any part of the routine

Figure 7.6. Separating baseline from intervention on the PTR-F Behavior Rating Scale.

rule, the PTR-F behavior support plan may need to be in place for the length of time that the challenging behavior occurred and until the family is confident and comfortable implementing the behavior support plan. So, if challenging behavior has been present for 6 months, we recommend keeping PTR-F in place for 6 months as well. At that point in time, if the challenging behavior has been reduced or eliminated and the desirable behavior has increased, teams may want to consider whether the future interests of the child are best served by systematically reducing elements of the PTR-F plan. For example, Lily's challenging behavior has decreased, her desirable behavior has increased, the family feels confident and comfortable, and the family work schedule is about to change, resulting in more hours at work. This change in the family work schedule will likely result in less implementation of the PTR-F plan. In this case, because the family has experienced positive results by implementing the behavior support plan, it would make good sense to begin systematically reducing supports rather than to suddenly and dramatically reduce them. We want to stress the importance of keeping the plan in place and remaining vigilant with the behavior support plan (or with parts of the behavior support plan that continue to be appropriate) until desired changes in the child's behavior occur for a sufficient length of time.

Moreover, teams may want to consider whether elements of the plan could be altered in such a way that the child herself is now implementing components in a self-management fashion. For example, say that the initial reinforce component called for adults to comment positively on the child's behavior when she was actively engaged in a bedtime routine. Eventually, the team may want to consider if teaching the child to self-evaluate and self-reinforce is a viable next step. Like any good intervention with young children, PTR-F encourages teams to eventually think about strategies to enhance children's independent performance. When considering changes in the type and/or reductions in the intensity of PTR-F supports, teams need to keep close tabs on children's challenging behaviors and desirable behaviors. When any variation or change in behavior occurs, no matter how small, we recommend slowing the process, if not reinstating the full plan for a period of time.

 If teams choose to alter elements of the plan to increase child independence and self-management, it might be useful to alter the desirable behavior BRS to track the new behavior(s) that the child is being taught. The team can choose to continue to track the initial desirable behavior, but the use of a new desirable behavior BRS related to the child's independence and self-management will aid in ensuring that the child is receiving the level of support that he or she needs to learn these skills.

In the past, many teams have expanded on the PTR-F process after challenging behavior has been resolved. Specifically, teams have used this careful planning process to guide plans for teaching new skills not related directly to challenging behavior. Understand that the teach strategies in this manual are not just for desirable (and replacement) behaviors, but can be used far more broadly.

What to Do if Progress Is Unsatisfactory

Data on PTR-F suggest that close adherence to the recommended steps in the process will result in satisfactory behavior change in the vast majority of cases. However, given the certainty of some level of uncertainty in the behavioral sciences, we cannot guarantee uniform success with PTR-F. What is possible, however, is to provide a number of tried and true solutions when behavior change is not satisfactory.

In this section, we provide a sequence of steps that teams should follow to improve behavior change when initial tactics have not been successful. We *strongly* suggest that the recommended steps be implemented in the order given. To do otherwise risks the unnecessary expenditure of time and resources.

Step 1: Determine Whether the Behavior Support Plan Tactics Have Been Implemented as Intended

In Chapter 6, we provided recommendations for the collection of fidelity data, which are data on whether the intervention plans are being delivered as intended. In most cases, the use of the PTR-F Fidelity of Strategy Implementation form is enough to ensure that the behavior support plan practices are in place. The use of the PTR-F Fidelity of Strategy Implementation form can also help teams determine whether subtle shifts in behavior support plan procedures have occurred over time or if some adult family members are implementing the behavior support plan with fidelity but others are not. Procedurally, we recommend that teams evaluate implementation fidelity by:

1. Reviewing with all implementers the specific practices that comprise the prevent, teach, and reinforce strategies. Each implementer should be encouraged during a team meeting to describe his or her understanding of each intervention component and when and where it is to be implemented and to demonstrate in a role-playing format with fellow team members how he or she implements each intervention component. The team may conclude at this point that one or more members may need further coaching to develop the skill set needed to implement all intervention components with fidelity.

2. Once the team is certain that all implementers are sufficiently competent to deliver PTR-F, another meeting should be scheduled to examine the current fidelity data collection procedures and to make sure the family is able to implement data collection as often as the team determines is necessary. The goal for this data collection is to assess *each* implementer's behavior for the entire period of time that the interventions are scheduled to occur. In addition to using the established fidelity data systems, we also encourage a designated team member (often the PTR-F facilitator) to make narrative records of implementers' behaviors that may be related to the target child's behaviors but that are not part of the PTR-F plan. For example, if the family is to ignore the challenging behavior, the PTR-F facilitator may note that although the members of the family do not talk to the child, they do provide eye contact while the challenging behavior occurs. The PTR-F facilitator would then specifically coach the family about limiting eye contact while the challenging behavior is occurring, and the team may choose to include limiting eye contact in the behavior support plan. Many teams may find that this entire process can be aided substantially by video recordings. Teams may conclude that PTR-F is indeed being implemented as intended. If so, then we recommend proceeding to step 2. If any fidelity concerns appear, no matter how small, we recommend resolving these prior to moving to the next step. In all foreseeable cases, the lack of fidelity could be resolved by additional coaching or by altering the behavior support plan if there are components or strategies that family members object to or are uncomfortable implementing.

Step 2: Determine Whether the Supposed Reinforcers Are Motivating the Child

Young children change their minds—a lot! They particularly change their minds about what will motivate them to change their behavior when the clear contingency is in place to first engage in the behavior, then get access to the person, material, toy, or event. In many cases, determining reinforcers is quite straightforward. However, when initial plans have gone awry, we recommend the use of a paired-comparison strategy (described next) to maximize the likelihood that the selected reinforcers will, in fact, be motivating to the child (Fisher, Piazza, Bowman, & Amari, 1996). Procedurally, the team should carefully reappraise reinforcers, following these steps:

1. Interview all care providers to determine their judgment as to what things the child most enjoys.

2. Follow up this interview with informal observations (1–2 days) to see if the child seeks out the suggested items or others as well.

3. Meet as a team to create a list of 8–10 (maximum) potential reinforcers (the original selected reinforcers may or may not make this list, depending on findings).

4. Over the course of 2 days, present the child with all possible pairs from the potential reinforcer list. When the child makes a selection, mark down the item selected. Once all possible pairs have been presented, the team will have created a hierarchy of preferred items, from the item most often selected to the item least often selected. We recommend choosing only the top one or two items to use in the context of PTR-F. Assuming that the top one or two items were not originally used in the PTR-F plan, we suggest that the team give the new reinforce intervention procedures a trial of 5–10 sessions and/or days depending on the frequency of the routine before determining that it is necessary to move to step 3.

5. The other side of the reinforce coin is also worth a second look. Not only is it essential to have a powerful reinforcer available for new behaviors, but it is equally important to ensure that the child is not being inadvertently reinforced for continued challenging behavior. The most common examples we see are instances where the intensity or salience of reinforcement has been reduced as planned, but children are still receiving some level of continued feedback for challenging behavior. For example, the parent may no longer engage a child in conversation when challenging behavior occurs (removing attention where the function of challenging behavior is thought to be attention), but he still looks at and frowns at the child. Teams may well want to devote a day or two of observation to ensure that subtle but still important consequences do not follow challenging behavior.

 Do not forget everything you know about reinforcement! For example, be sure to ensure that the team continues to provide reinforcement at the planned rate and in the planned amount. Often, and particularly as the child demonstrates success, reinforcement can be unintentionally faded, which can increase the child's challenging behavior or reduce the child's desirable behavior.

Step 3: Recheck the Function(s) of Challenging Behavior

On rare occasions, teams will find that the original function determined for the behavior was in error. When teams have determined that powerful reinforcers are in place and that the behavior support plan is generally implemented with fidelity, it is time to reexamine the original hypothesis regarding the function of challenging behavior. Keeping in mind that the original hypothesis may be incorrect, teams are encouraged to use the PTR-F assessment forms in Chapter 4. New functions may or may not emerge. Where new functions are determined, teams should proceed with redeveloping a new behavior support plan as previously outlined.

As acknowledged in Chapter 1, circumstances may exist in which the influences underlying a child's challenging behaviors are too difficult for a family-focused team to adequately assess or too intransigent for a home-based intervention. Although we believe that these circumstances are quite rare, it is nevertheless apparent that they exist.

When they do, it is appropriate and necessary to enlist outside expertise. Sometimes, simply having an experienced consultant assist with the functional behavioral assessment and behavior support plan design will be sufficient, and other times, a comprehensive multidisciplinary approach is needed. Regardless, we urge your team to pursue whatever measures are necessary for finding and implementing procedures that will achieve a successful resolution.

NEXT STEPS AFTER PTR-F IS COMPLETE

There are many different paths that families may travel after completing a successful PTR-F journey. Some families may want to work on another challenging behavior. Other families may find themselves ready to tackle different aspects of their long-range vision for their child. The PTR-F facilitator can help in these and many other scenarios by:

1. Emphasizing to the family that the child's change in behavior was due to *their* skill and persistence.

2. Reviewing with the family what strategies worked best for their child and how these strategies might be used in the future with other concerns.

3. Mapping community resources with the family to ensure that they and their child have access to all the services available to achieve their vision.

4. Encouraging and supporting families to share the specifics of their success with others in the child's life (e.g., teachers, childcare providers, grandparents).

5. Setting up a monthly check-in system with families to monitor continued progress and to further encourage use of the practices learned for new situations and challenges.

The case examples at the end of this chapter detail next steps for Timmy and Lucy after the implementation of PTR-F and show the progress both children have made, presenting fully completed BRS forms. Timmy and Lucy are just two of many success stories of how PTR-F can resolve a child's challenging behavior, support his or her healthy development and acquisition of new skills, and make life better for the entire family.

OVERALL SUMMARY AND PLAN IMPLEMENTATION GUIDE

PTR-F is a model of positive assessment and intervention designed to help young children with serious challenging behaviors to learn adaptive social skills and reduce their challenging behaviors. The objective is to help guide these young children toward an improved, healthy trajectory of social–emotional development so that they will be able to succeed in their overall development and enjoyment of friendships and in all phases of their upcoming journey at home, kindergarten, elementary school, and beyond.

We are confident that PTR-F can be an effective approach for you and the families you work with; however, its effectiveness will depend on your team's ability to follow the process faithfully in a step-by-step manner. To help with this process, we offer the PTR-F Plan Implementation Guide (see Figure 7.7). In conjunction with the other forms provided in PTR-F, this guide is intended to help teams organize their information in one document and provides a summary of the steps and requirements described in this manual. The guide follows the self-evaluation checklists at the end of Chapters 3–5, so it is not necessary for teams to use both. The PTR-F Plan Implementation Guide is just one more helpful tool for achieving success in using PTR-F with the families you serve.

FORM
14

PTR-F Plan Implementation Guide

Initiating the Process

Child's name: _____ Age: _____ Date of plan: _____

Location/routine (e.g., home, bedtime routine):

_____

Team members (list all team members):

_____

What are the long-term goals that have been identified as a vision for the child and family?

_____

What is the specific challenging behavior that has been identified?

_____

What is the operational definition of the challenging behavior?

_____

Have the anchors been carefully defined and written down?   ❐ Yes   ❐ No

When will data be collected? (observation period/routine):

_____

Who will collect data? (identify a primary data collector):

_____

Where will the Behavior Rating Scale (BRS) be kept?

_____

PTR-F Assessment

Did the team complete the three PTR-F assessment checklists (i.e., prevent, teach, reinforce)?   ❐ Yes   ❐ No

Who completed the checklists?

_____

Were the completed checklists reviewed by the team and summarized in the PTR-F Assessment   ❐ Yes   ❐ No
Summary Table?

Were hypotheses developed to summarize the team's understanding of the function of the child's   ❐ Yes   ❐ No
challenging behavior and the ways in which the behavior is influenced by the environment?

What is/are the hypothesis statement(s)?

_____

_____

What is the specific desirable behavior that has been identified?

_____

What is the operational definition of the desirable behavior?

_____

(continued)

Figure 7.7.   PTR-F Plan Implementation Guide.

Figure 7.7. *(continued)*

FORM 14   **PTR-F Plan Implementation Guide** *(continued)*

Have the anchors been carefully defined and written down?	☐ Yes ☐ No
Have the desirable behavior anchors been transferred to the BRS so that data collection can occur for the desirable behavior?	☐ Yes ☐ No

PTR-F Intervention

Did the team review the descriptions of intervention strategies (found in the Intervention Guide at the end of the manual)?	☐ Yes ☐ No
Did the team decide on intervention strategies to implement, and did they complete the PTR-F Behavior Support Plan Summary?	☐ Yes ☐ No

Coaching

Did the team complete the PTR-F Fidelity of Strategy Implementation form?   ☐ Yes   ☐ No

Who collects fidelity data using the PTR-F Fidelity of Strategy Implementation form?

_____

How often are fidelity data collected?

_____

Do/Did all coaching sessions involve: 1) a review of progress, 2) a review of the behavior support plan, 3) observation, 4) reflection, 5) feedback, and 6) planning?	☐ Yes ☐ No
Does/Did the PTR-F facilitator complete the PTR-F Coach Planning and Reflection Log during and/or after each coaching session?	☐ Yes ☐ No
If the family implements all strategies and can use the strategies in support of the child, has coaching support moved to maintenance support?	☐ Yes ☐ No

How often (e.g., monthly) and in what form (e.g., in-person meetings, e-mail exchanges, phone conversations, video calls) do maintenance sessions occur?

_____

Using Data and Next Steps

How often are the data reviewed once intervention strategies have been implemented?

_____

Who reviews the data?

_____

What decisions are made based on the data?

_____

If the team has successfully completed PTR-F with the identified challenging behavior, what are the next steps that the team will take (e.g., map community resources to ensure access to services available to achieve the family vision, setting up check-in system, consider other concerns)?

_____

_____

APPENDIX
Case Examples

TEAM MEETING: TIMMY

Using Data and Next Steps

Kaci arrived for what might be the final meeting with Timmy's family. Jodie and Phil reported continued progress and quickly reviewed the Behavior Rating Scale (BRS) and fidelity data. Timmy was continuing to participate in the bedtime routine and successfully falling asleep on his own without any tantrums or other challenging behaviors.

Kaci asked Jodie and Phil to reflect on their implementation, including what worked well and what was a struggle. Jodie commented that it was so helpful having Kaci be at the home to work with them on developing strategies that they could easily put in place, and she thanked Kaci for helping them identify what was problematic and change their parenting practices in order to have a positive impact on Timmy's behavior. She shared that she was not sure if they would have been successful in such a short time if Kaci had not been there to help them. Jodie and Phil were extremely grateful for Kaci's patience, reassurance, and persistence in putting the plan in place.

Jodie and Phil both shared that implementing the plan for weeks was a struggle at first, especially when they had to move so slowly with getting to their ultimate goal. It was initially awkward, and they did not really think they would make much progress because they were not that confident in being able to implement the strategies consistently. They also struggled with changing their whole routine at bedtime, including having each of them put the boys to bed separately, but ultimately they realized that focusing on and teaching an appropriate bedtime routine was essential.

Kaci revisited the Prevent-Teach-Reinforce for Families (PTR-F) Goal Sheet for a brief review and to determine whether there were any next steps to plan. Diapering and bathing were initially identified as problematic routines, but Jodie and Phil reported that they were able to implement strategies from the behavior support plan with diapering and bathing, which made those routines go more smoothly as well. Overall, most of the daily routines were consistently smooth and calm. Life was manageable and progressing in a positive direction. Jodie and Phil felt prepared to handle any other concerns that might come up with Timmy and/or Dakota. They now knew preventative strategies that could possibly be useful in the future.

Kaci reviewed the overall BRS data with Jodie and Phil, pointing out how things were at the beginning of this process and how the data showed a steady increase in desirable behaviors and a fairly rapid decrease in tantrums. Jodie commented that it was nice to see the overall progress because the beginning seemed excruciating at times. She liked seeing "proof" that what they were doing was actually working. (Figures 7.1a and 7.2a show Timmy's complete BRS data.)

Jodie and Phil also commented that Timmy's language has been improving and that he is getting easier to understand. Although they have not worked on Timmy's language skills directly, they feel that being more responsive to Timmy has not only improved his ability to communicate more clearly and understandably, but also has led to an increase in how much he is able to say and talk about. Timmy was still difficult to understand at times, but he was also more willing to repeat what he said for others.

To review and reflect, Kaci reminded Jodie and Phil of the PTR-F process and that challenging behavior serves a purpose or function and is often the result of a communication issue. When they first met, Timmy was communicating that he did not want to go to bed and preferred to be with Mom and Dad. The goal was to determine what skills might be missing and then develop a plan for how to teach those missing skills to meet the communication

FORM 2 — PTR-F Behavior Rating Scale

Child: **Timmy**   Rater: **Mom and Dad**   Routine: **Bedtime**   Month: **July**

Date/time: **7/6/15 - first coaching session**

Date	Desirable behavior: Stay in his room (noise ok) until asleep	Challenging behavior: Tantrums – number of minutes
6/26/15	5 ✓	
6/27/15	5 ✓	
6/28/15	5 ✓	
6/29/15	5 ✓	
6/30/15	5 ✓	
7/1/15	5 ✓	
7/2/15	no data	no data
7/3/15	5 ✓	1 ✓
7/4/15	5 ✓	1 ✓
7/5/15	2 ✓	4 ✓
7/6/15	3 ✓	2 ✓
7/7/15	2 ✓	2 ✓
7/8/15	3 ✓	1 ✓
7/9/15	3 ✓	1 ✓
7/10/15	3 ✓	2 ✓
7/11/15	4 ✓	1 ✓
7/12/15	4 ✓	1 ✓
7/13/15	4 ✓	1 ✓
7/14/15	4 ✓	1 ✓
7/15/15	4 ✓	1 ✓

Notes: 7/2/15 - no data   7/3/15 - start plan   7/3/15 - increase wait time to 2 min.

Desirable behavior: Stay in his room (noise ok) until asleep

5 = 30 minutes or until asleep
4 = 10–20 minutes
3 = up to 10 minutes
2 = 1–3 minutes
1 = 1 minute or less

Challenging behavior: Tantrums – number of minutes

5 = 30 minutes or more
4 = 20–30 minutes
3 = 10–20 minutes
2 = 5–10 minutes
1 = less than 5 minutes

Figure 7.1a. Timmy's complete PTR-F Behavior Rating Scale—Page 1.

FORM 2 — PTR-F Behavior Rating Scale

Child: Timmy   Rater: Mom and Dad   Routine: Bedtime   Month: July/August

Date/time: 7/20/15 - Increase wait time to 5 min.

	7/16/15	7/17/15	7/18/15	7/19/15	7/20/15	7/21/15	7/22/15	7/23/15	7/24/15	7/25/15	7/26/15	7/27/15	7/28/15	7/29/15	7/30/15	7/31/15	8/1/15	8/2/15	8/3/15	8/4/15
Desirable behavior – Stay in his room (noise ok) until asleep	4	4	4	4	4	4	4	4	4	4	4	4	4	4	4	4	4	5	4	5
Challenging behavior – Tantrums	1	1	1	1	1	1	1	1	1	1	1	1	1	1	1	1	1	1	1	1

Desirable behavior: Stay in his room (noise ok) until asleep

5 = 30 minutes or until asleep
4 = 10-20 minutes
3 = up to 10 minutes
2 = 1-3 minutes
1 = 1 minute or less

Challenging behavior: Tantrums - number of minutes

5 = 30 minutes or more
4 = 20-30 minutes
3 = 10-20 minutes
2 = 5-10 minutes
1 = less than 5 minutes

Figure 7.2a. Timmy's complete PTR-F Behavior Rating Scale—Page 2.

need. Finally, reinforcing appropriate or desirable behaviors can increase the occurrence of those appropriate behaviors. Jodie reflected that providing positive feedback to Timmy has made an incredible impact in improving Timmy's behaviors overall, including problematic routines not specifically identified in their goals.

Jodie and Phil greatly appreciated Kaci's guidance, expertise, and patience while working with them to develop and implement a behavior support plan for Timmy. They felt confident that they would be able to handle any concerns that may present themselves in the near future.

TEAM MEETING: LUCY

Using Data and Next Steps

Roberta arrived to discuss Lucy's overall progress and next steps. Lucy's progress had been a little unsteady at first, but after the first few coaching sessions, Gabby was implementing the behavior support plan strategies with fidelity and supporting Lucy's desirable behavior of following and actively participating in the daily routines. Gabby was now able to view Lucy's challenging behaviors as functional and understood that the behavior was Lucy's most efficient way to communicate. She now had a clear structure for how to teach Lucy to be more independent and participate in family activities. Although Lucy could still be physically aggressive from time to time, it was pretty rare now, and Gabby knew how to respond to the aggression without reinforcing it. In fact, it was clear across all situations that providing Lucy with positive feedback when she is being appropriate is the most effective way to interact with Lucy. Gabby reflected that this has helped Lucy in all her relationships with other family members. It was difficult with some of Lucy's uncles at first, because they would laugh at Lucy's aggressive behaviors, but when they were able to see Lucy's improvements in other areas, they laughed at Lucy less and less. Providing positive feedback has improved all of Lucy's relationships with family and friends.

Another positive outcome of the PTR-F process has been that Lucy's verbal language has improved dramatically. At the beginning of this process, Lucy's verbalizations were mostly unintelligible, and she only said a few words that Gabby and Mrs. Williams could understand. Now, Lucy can say several words that almost everyone can understand, and she continues to make progress in this area. This has also helped Lucy's relationships because more people can communicate with her, and Lucy seems motivated to speak more often and more clearly.

Roberta and Gabby looked through the BRS forms, reflecting on the PTR-F process. They reviewed all the weeks of data, looking at the time that was devoted to creating and implementing the behavior support plan. The behavior support plan was successful in reducing Lucy's physically aggressive behaviors and increasing her ability to actively participate in the daily routines. Gabby commented that although the process seemed hard at the time, Lucy had come a long way and life was now more predictable for everyone. Gabby was thankful for Roberta's help, and Roberta reiterated that Gabby did all of the work with Lucy. Even though life with Lucy was not necessarily easy all the time, Gabby felt confident that Lucy's behaviors were manageable and would continue to improve. (Figures 7.3a and 7.4a show Lucy's complete BRS data.)

FORM 2 PTR-F Behavior Rating Scale

Child: Lucy Rater: Mom Routine: Throughout the day Month: August

Date/time: 8/3/15 - started intervention

Behavior	7/29/15	7/30/15	7/31/15	8/1/15	8/2/15	8/3/15	8/4/15	8/5/15	8/6/15	8/7/15	8/8/15	8/9/15	8/10/15	8/11/15	8/12/15	8/13/15	8/14/15	8/15/15	8/16/15	8/17/15
Desirable behavior: Follow morning routine calmly and cooperatively	5	5	5	5	5		1	1	1	1	1	2	1	2	2	2	2	1	2	2
Challenging behavior: Physically aggressive behavior	5	4	4	4	4		5	5	4	3	4	3	3	2	2	3	2	1	2	2

Desirable behavior: Morning routine - calm and cooperative

5 = 1 or 2 steps calm, cooperative, independent
4 = Only 1 or 2 steps partially prompted
3 = Most steps partially prompted
2 = Only 1 or 2 steps fully prompted
1 = Most steps fully prompted

Challenging behavior: Aggressive behaviors

5 = 8 or more
4 = 6–7 times
3 = 3–5 times
2 = 1–2 times
1 = 0

Figure 7.3a. Lucy's complete PTR-F Behavior Rating Scale—Page 1.

FORM 2 — PTR-F Behavior Rating Scale

Child: Lucy

Rater: Mom

Routine: Throughout the day

Month: August/September

Date/time: _____

	8/16/15	8/17/15	8/18/15	8/19/15	8/20/15	8/21/15	8/22/15	8/23/15	8/24/15	8/25/15	8/26/15	8/27/15	8/28/15	8/29/15	8/30/15	9/1/15	9/2/15	9/3/15	9/4/15	9/5/15
Desirable behavior Morning routine - calm and cooperative	2	2	3	2	3	3	3	4	4	4	4	4	4	5	4	4	5	5	5	5
Challenging behavior Aggressive behaviors	2	2	1	2	1	1	2	1	1	1	1	1	2	1	1	1	1	1	1	1

Desirable behavior: Morning routine - calm and cooperative

5 = 1 or 2 steps calm, cooperative, independent

4 = Only 1 or 2 steps partially prompted

3 = Most steps partially prompted

2 = Only 1 or 2 steps fully prompted

1 = Most steps fully prompted

Challenging behavior: Aggressive behaviors

5 = 8 or more

4 = 6-7 times

3 = 3-5 times

2 = 1-2 times

1 = 0

Figure 7.4a.   Lucy's complete PTR-F Behavior Rating Scale—Page 2.

References

Albin, R.W., Lucyshyn, J.M., Horner, R.H., & Flannery, K.B. (1996). Contextual fit for behavior support plans. In L.K. Koegel, R.L. Koegel, & G. Dunlap (Eds.), *Positive behavioral support: Including people with difficult behavior in the community* (pp. 81–98). Baltimore, MD: Paul H. Brookes Publishing Co.

Arndorfer, R.E., Miltenberger, R.G., Woster, S.H., Rortvedt, A.K., & Gaffaney, T. (1994). Home-based descriptive and experimental analysis of problem behaviors in children. *Topics in Early Childhood Special Education, 14,* 64–87.

Bailey, K.M. (2013). *An evaluation of the family-centered Prevent-Teach-Reinforce model with families of young children with developmental disabilities* (Unpublished master's thesis). University of South Florida, Tampa, FL.

Bambara, L., & Kern, L. (Eds.). (2005). *Individualized supports for students with problem behaviors: Designing positive behavior plans.* New York, NY: Guilford.

Banda, D.R., & Grimmett, E. (2008). Enhancing social and transition behaviors of persons with autism through activity schedules: A review. *Education and Training in Developmental Disabilities, 43,* 324–333.

Branson, D., & Demchak, M. (2011). Toddler teachers' use of teaching pyramid practices. *Topics in Early Childhood Special Education, 30,* 196–208.

Brown, F., Anderson, J.L., & DePry, R.L. (Eds.). (2015). *Individual positive behavior supports: A standards-based guide to practices in school and community settings.* Baltimore, MD: Paul H. Brookes Publishing Co.

Brown, W.H., McEvoy, M.A., & Bishop, J.N. (1991). Incidental teaching of social behavior: A naturalistic approach for promoting young children's peer interactions. *TEACHING Exceptional Children, 24,* 35–38.

Brown, W.H., & Odom, S.L. (1995). Naturalistic peer interventions for promoting preschool children's social interactions. *Preventing School Failure, 39,* 38–43.

Carr, E.G., Dunlap, G., Horner, R.H., Koegel, R.L., Turnbull, A.P., Sailor, W., Anderson, J., Albin, R.W., Koegel, L.K., & Fox, L. (2002). Positive behavior support. Evolution of an applied science. *Journal of Positive Behavior Interventions, 4,* 4–16.

Carr, E.G., & Durand, V.M. (1985). Reducing behavior problems through functional communication training. *Journal of Applied Behavior Analysis, 18,* 111–126.

Carr, E.G., Levin, L., McConnachie, G., Carlson, J.I., Kemp, D.C., & Smith, C.E. (1994). *Communication-based intervention for problem behavior: A user's guide for producing positive change.* Baltimore, MD: Paul H. Brookes Publishing Co.

Clarke, S., Dunlap, G., Foster-Johnson, L., Childs, K.E., Wilson, D., White, R., & Vera, A. (1995). Improving the conduct of students with behavioral disorders by incorporating student interests into curricular activities. *Behavioral Disorders, 20,* 221–237.

Connell, M.C., Carta, J.J., Lutz, S., & Randall, C. (1993). Building independence during in-class transitions: Teaching in-class transition skills to preschoolers with developmental delays through choral-response-based self-assessment and contingent praise. *Education and Treatment of Children, 16,* 160–174.

Conroy, M.A., Sutherland, K.S., Vo, A.K., Carr, S., & Ogston, P.L. (2014). Early childhood teachers' use of effective instructional practices and the collateral effects on young children's behavior. *Journal of Positive Behavior Interventions, 16,* 81–92.

Cooper, J.O., Heron, T.E., & Heward, W.L. (1987). *Applied behavior analysis.* Upper Saddle River, NJ: Merrill.

Cooper, J.O., Heron, T.E., & Heward, W.L. (2007). *Applied behavior analysis* (2nd ed.). Upper Saddle River, NJ: Pearson.

Dettmer, S., Simpson, R.L., Myles, B.S., & Ganz, J.B. (2000). The use of visual supports to facilitate transitions of students with autism. *Focus on Autism and Other Developmental Disabilities, 15,* 163–169.

Division for Early Childhood. (2014). *DEC recommended practices.* Retrieved from http://www.dec-sped.org/recommendedpractices

Dooley, P., Wilczenski, F.L., & Torem, C. (2001). Using an activity schedule to smooth school transitions. *Journal of Positive Behavior Interventions, 3,* 57–61.

Duda, M.A., Clarke, S., Fox, L., & Dunlap, G. (2008). Implementation of positive behavior support with a sibling set in a home environment. *Journal of Early Intervention, 30,* 213–236.

Duda, M.A., Dunlap, G., Fox, L., Lentini, R., & Clarke, S. (2004). An experimental evaluation of positive behavior support in a community preschool program. *Topics in Early Childhood Special Education, 24,* 143–155.

Dunlap, G. (2006). The applied behavior analytic heritage of PBS: A dynamic model of action-oriented research. *Journal of Positive Behavior Interventions, 8,* 58–60.

Dunlap, G., Carr, E.G., Horner, R.H., Zarcone, J., & Schwartz, I. (2008). Positive behavior support and applied behavior analysis: A familial alliance. *Behavior Modification, 32,* 682–698.

Dunlap, G., dePerczel, M., Clarke, S., Wilson, D., Wright, S., White, R., & Gomez, A. (1994). Choice making to promote adaptive behavior for students with emotional and behavioral challenges. *Journal of Applied Behavior Analysis, 27,* 505–518.

Dunlap, G., Ester, T., Langhans, S., & Fox, L. (2006). Functional communication training with toddlers in home environments. *Journal of Early Intervention, 28,* 81–96.

Dunlap, G., & Fox, L. (1999). A demonstration of behavioral support for young children with autism. *Journal of Positive Behavior Interventions, 1,* 77–87.

Dunlap, G., & Fox, L. (2011). Function-based interventions for children with challenging behavior. *Journal of Early Intervention, 33,* 333–343.

Dunlap, G., Iovannone, R., Kincaid, D., Wilson, K., Christiansen, K., Strain, P., & English, C. (2010). *Prevent-Teach-Reinforce: The school-based model of individualized positive behavior support.* Baltimore, MD: Paul H. Brookes Publishing Co.

Dunlap, G., & Kern, L. (1996). Modifying instructional activities to promote desirable behavior: A conceptual and practical framework. *School Psychology Quarterly, 11,* 297–312.

Dunlap, G., Kern-Dunlap, L., Clarke, S., & Robbins, F.R. (1991). Functional assessment, curriculum revision, and severe behavior problems. *Journal of Applied Behavior Analysis, 24,* 387–397.

Dunlap, G., Kincaid, D., Horner, R.H., Knoster, T., & Bradshaw, C. (2014). A comment on the term "positive behavior support." *Journal of Positive Behavior Interventions, 16,* 133–136.

Dunlap, G., & Koegel, R.L. (1980). Motivating autistic children through stimulus variation. *Journal of Applied Behavior Analysis, 13,* 619–627.

Dunlap, G., Lee, J., Joseph, J.D., & Strain, P. (2015). A model for increasing the fidelity and effectiveness of interventions for challenging behaviors: Prevent-Teach-Reinforce for Young Children. *Infants and Young Children, 28,* 3–17.

Dunlap, G., Lee, J.K., Strain, P., & Joseph, J. (2016, March). *Prevent-Teach-Reinforce for Young Children: Results from a 4-year randomized controlled trial.* Paper presented at the 13th International Conference on Positive Behavior Support, San Francisco, CA.

Dunlap, G., Newton, J.S., Fox, L., Benito, N., & Vaughn, B. (2001). Family involvement in functional assessment and positive behavior support. *Focus on Autism and Other Developmental Disabilities, 16,* 215–221.

Dunlap, G., Wilson, K., Strain, P., & Lee, J.K. (2013). *Prevent-Teach-Reinforce for Young Children: The early childhood model of individualized positive behavior support.* Baltimore, MD: Paul H. Brookes Publishing Co.

Dunlap, L.K., Dunlap, G., Koegel, L.K., & Koegel, R.L. (1991). Using self-monitoring to increase students' success and independence. *TEACHING Exceptional Children, 23,* 17–22.

Durand, V.M. (1990). *Severe behavior problems: A functional communication training approach.* New York, NY: Guilford Press.

Durand, V.M. (2001). Future directions for children and adolescents with mental retardation. *Behavior Therapy, 32,* 633–650.

Durand, V.M. (2011). *Optimistic parenting: Hope and help for you and your challenging child.* Baltimore, MD: Paul H. Brookes Publishing Co.

Durand, V.M., Hieneman, M., Clarke, S., Wang, M., & Rinaldi, M.L. (2012). Positive family intervention for severe challenging behavior. I: A multisite randomized clinical trial. *Journal of Positive Behavior Interventions, 15,* 133–143.

Durand, V.M., & Moskowitz, L. (2015). Functional communication training: Thirty years of treating challenging behavior. *Topics in Early Childhood Special Education, 35,* 116–126.

Epley, P., Summers, J.A., & Turnbull, A. (2010). Characteristics and trends in family-centered conceptualizations. *Journal of Family Social Work, 13,* 269–285.

Ervin, R.A., Kern, L., Clarke, S., DuPaul, G.J., Dunlap, G., & Friman, P.C. (2000). Evaluating assessment based intervention strategies for students with ADHD and comorbid disorders within the natural classroom context. *Behavioral Disorders, 25,* 344–358.

Fettig, A., & Barton, E.E. (2014). Parent implementation of function-based intervention to reduce children's challenging behavior: A literature review. *Topics in Early Childhood Special Education, 34,* 49–61.

Fettig, A., & Ostrosky, M.M. (2011). Collaborating with parents in reducing children's challenging behaviors: Linking functional assessment to intervention. *Child Development Research, 2011*, 1–10.

Fettig, A., Schultz, T.R., & Sreckovic, M.A. (2015). Effects of coaching on the implementation of functional assessment-based parent intervention in reducing challenging behaviors. *Journal of Positive Behavior Interventions, 17*, 170–180.

Fisher, W.W., Piazza, C.C., Bowman, L.G., & Amari, A. (1996). Integrating caregiver report with systematic choice assessment to enhance reinforce identification. *American Journal of Mental Retardation, 101*, 15–25.

Fixsen, D.L., Blase, K.A., Naoom, S.F., & Wallace, F. (2009). Core implementation components. *Research on Social Work Practice, 19*, 531–540.

Fleisher, L.S., Ballard-Krishnan, S.A., & Benito, N. (2015). Positive behavior supports and quality of life. In F. Brown, J.L. Anderson, & R.L. DePry (Eds.), *Individual positive behavior supports: A standards-based guide to practices in school and community settings* (pp. 485–511). Baltimore, MD: Paul H. Brookes Publishing Co.

Forehand, R., & Long, N. (2011). *Parenting the strong-willed child: The clinically proven five-week program for parents of two- to six-year-olds, third edition.* New York, NY: McGraw-Hill.

Foster-Johnson, L., Ferro, J., & Dunlap, G. (1994). Preferred curricular activities and reduced problem behaviors in students with intellectual disabilities. *Journal of Applied Behavior Analysis, 27*, 493–504.

Fox, L., Dunlap, G., Hemmeter, M.L., Joseph, G.E., & Strain, P.S. (2003). The teaching pyramid: A model for supporting social competence and preventing challenging behavior in young children. *Young Children, 58*, 48–52.

Fox, L., & Hemmeter, M.L. (2014, November). *Implementing positive behavioral intervention and support: The evidence-base of the Pyramid Model for supporting social emotional competence in infants and young children.* Retrieved from http://challengingbehavior.fmhi.usf.edu/

Fox, L., Hemmeter, M.L., Snyder, P., Binder, D.P., & Clarke, S. (2011). Coaching early childhood special educators to implement a comprehensive model for promoting young children's social competence. *Topics in Early Childhood Special Education, 31*, 178–192.

Fox, L., Vaughn, B.J., Dunlap, G., & Bucy, M. (1997). Parent-professional partnership in behavioral support: A qualitative analysis of one family's experience. *Journal of the Association for Persons with Severe Handicaps, 22*, 198–207.

Frea, W.D., & Hepburn, S.L. (1999). Teaching parents of children with autism to perform functional assessments to plan interventions for extremely disruptive behaviors. *Journal of Positive Behavior Interventions, 1*, 112–116.

Grey, I., Healy, O., Leader, G., & Hayes, D. (2009). Using a Time Timer™ to increase appropriate waiting behavior in a child with developmental disabilities. *Research in Developmental Disabilities, 30*, 359–366.

Halle, J., Bambara, L.M., & Reichle, J. (2005). Teaching alternative skills. In L. Bambara & L. Kern (Eds.), *Individualized supports for students with problem behaviors* (pp. 237–274). New York, NY: Guilford Press.

Harding, J.W., Wacker, D.P., Berg, W.K., Cooper, L., Asmus, J., Mlela, K., & Muller, J. (1999). An analysis of choice making in the assessment of young children with severe behavior problems. *Journal of Applied Behavior Analysis, 32*, 63–82.

Hastings, R.P., & Brown, T. (2002). Behavior problems of children with autism, parental self-efficacy, and mental health. *American Journal on Mental Retardation, 107*, 222–232.

Hieneman, M., Childs, K., & Sergay, J. (2006). *Parenting with positive behavior support: A practical guide to resolving your child's difficult behavior.* Baltimore, MD: Paul H. Brookes Publishing Co.

Iovannone, R., Greenbaum, P.E., Wang, W., Kincaid, D., Dunlap, G., & Strain, P. (2009). Randomized control trial of the Prevent-Teach-Reinforce (PTR) tertiary intervention for students with problem behavior. *Journal of Emotional and Behavioral Disorders, 17*, 213–225.

Iwata, B.A., DeLeon, I.G., & Roscoe, E.M. (2013). Reliability and validity of the functional analysis screening tool. *Journal of Applied Behavior Analysis, 46*, 271–284.

Iwata, B., Dorsey, M., Slifer, K., Bauman, K., & Richman, G. (1994). Toward a functional analysis of self-injury. *Journal of Applied Behavior Analysis, 27*, 197–209. (Reprinted from *Analysis and Intervention in Developmental Disabilities, 2*, 3–20, 1982.)

Johnson, L.A., & Monn, E. (2015). Bridging behavioral assessment and behavioral intervention: Finding your inner behavior analyst. *Young Exceptional Children, 18*, 19–35.

Johnston, S.S., & Reichle, J. (1993). Designing and implementing interventions to decrease challenging behavior. *Language, Speech, and Hearing Services in Schools, 24*, 225–235.

Jones, T.L., & Prinz, R.J. (2005). Potential roles of parental self-efficacy in parent and child adjustment: A review. *Clinical Psychology Review, 25*, 341–363.

Kaiser, B., & Rasminsky, J.S. (2003). *Challenging behavior in young children: Understanding, preventing, and responding effectively.* Boston, MA: Allyn and Bacon.

Kazdin, A. (2009). *The Kazdin method for parenting the defiant child.* New York, NY: Mariner Press.

Kazdin, A.E. (2012). *Behavior modification in applied settings.* Long Grove, IL: Waveland Press.

Keen, D. (2007). Parents, families, and partnerships: Issues and considerations. *International Journal of Disability, Development and Education, 54,* 339–349.

Kern, L. (2005). Responding to problem behavior. In L. Bambara & L. Kern (Eds.), *Individualized supports for students with problem behaviors* (pp. 275–302). New York, NY: Guilford Press.

Kern, L., & Clemens, N.H. (2007). Antecedent strategies to promote appropriate classroom behavior. *Psychology in Schools, 44,* 65–75.

Kern, L., & Dunlap, G. (1999). Assessment-based interventions for children with emotional and behavioral disorders. In A.C. Repp & R.H. Horner (Eds.), *Functional analysis of problem behavior: From effective assessment to effective support* (pp. 197–218). Belmont, CA: Wadsworth Publishing.

Kern, L., Sokol, N.G., & Dunlap, G. (2006). Assessment of antecedent influences on challenging behavior. In J.K. Luiselli (Ed.), *Antecedent assessment and intervention: Supporting children and adults with developmental disabilities in community settings* (pp. 53–71). Baltimore, MD: Paul H. Brookes Publishing Co.

Kern, L., Vorndran, C.M., Hilt, A., Ringdahl, J.E., Adelman, B.E., & Dunlap, G. (1998). Choice as an intervention to improve behavior: A review of the literature. *Journal of Behavioral Education, 8,* 151–169.

Kincaid, D., Dunlap, G., Kern, L., Lane, K.L., Bambara, L., Brown, F., . . . Knoster, T. (2016). Positive behavior support: A proposal for updating and refining the definition. *Journal of Positive Behavior Interventions, 18,* 69–73.

Kincaid, D., Knab, J., & Clark, H. (2005). Person-centered planning. In G. Sugai & R. Horner (Eds.), *Encyclopedia of behavior modification and cognitive behavior therapy: Educational applications* (pp. 1412–1415). Thousand Oaks, CA: Sage Publishing.

Koegel, L.K., Koegel, R.L., Boettcher, M.A., Harrower, J., & Openden, D. (2006). Combining functional assessment and self-management procedures to rapidly reduce disruptive behaviors. In R.L. Koegel & L.K. Koegel (Eds.), *Pivotal response treatments for autism: Communication, social, and academic development* (pp. 245–258). Baltimore, MD: Paul H. Brookes Publishing Co.

Koegel, R.L., & Koegel, L.K. (2012). *The PRT pocket guide: Pivotal response treatment for autism spectrum disorders.* Baltimore, MD: Paul H. Brookes Publishing Co.

Kohler, F.W., & Strain, P.S. (1999). Maximizing peer-mediated resources within integrated preschool classrooms. *Topics in Early Childhood Special Education, 19,* 92–102.

Kohlhoff, J., & Morgan, S. (2014). Parent-child interaction therapy for toddlers: A pilot study. *Child & Family Behavior Therapy, 36,* 121–139.

Kontos, S. (1999). Preschool teachers' talk, roles, and activity settings during free play. *Early Childhood Research Quarterly, 14,* 363–382.

Kuoch, H., & Mirenda, P. (2003). Social story interventions for young children with autism spectrum disorders. *Focus on Autism and other Developmental Disabilities, 18,* 219–227.

Landy, S. (2002). *Pathways to competence: Encouraging healthy social and emotional development in young children.* Baltimore, MD: Paul H. Brookes Publishing Co.

Latham, G.I. (2000). *The power of positive parenting.* Salt Lake City, UT: Northwest Publishing.

Lequia, J., Machalicek, W., & Rispoli, M.J. (2012). Effects of activity schedules on challenging behavior exhibited in children with autism spectrum disorders: A systematic review. *Research in Autism Spectrum Disorders, 6*(1), 480–492.

Lorimer, P.A., Simpson, R.L., Myles, B.S., & Ganz, J.B. (2002). The use of social stories as a preventative behavioral intervention in a home setting with a child with autism. *Journal of Positive Behavior Interventions, 4,* 53–60.

Lucyshyn, J.M., Albin, R.W., Horner, R., Mann, J., Mann, J., & Wadsworth, G. (2007). Family implementation of positive behavior support with a child with autism: A longitudinal, single case experimental and descriptive replication and extension. *Journal of Positive Behavior Interventions, 9,* 131–150.

Lucyshyn, J., Dunlap, G., & Albin, R.W. (Eds.). (2002). *Families and positive behavior support: Addressing problem behaviors in family contexts.* Baltimore, MD: Paul H. Brookes Publishing Co.

Luiselli, J.K. (Ed.). (2006). *Antecedent assessment and intervention: Supporting children and adults with developmental disabilities in community settings.* Baltimore, MD: Paul H. Brookes Publishing Co.

McCormick, K.M., Jolivette, K., & Ridgley, R. (2003). Choice making as an intervention strategy for young children. *Young Exceptional Children, 6,* 3–10.

Miltenberger, R.G. (2008). *Behavior modification: Principles and procedures.* Belmont, CA: Thomson Wadsworth.

Nunnelley, J.C. (2002). *Powerful, positive, and practical practices: Behavior guidance strategies.* Little Rock, AR: Southern Early Childhood Association.

O'Brien, J., & O'Brien, C.L. (2002). *Implementing person-centered planning: Voices of experience.* Toronto, Ontario, Canada: Inclusion Press.

O'Neill, R.E., Horner, R.H., Albin, R.W., Storey, K., Sprague, J.R., & Newton, J.S. (1997). *Functional assessment of problem behavior: A practical assessment guide.* Pacific Grove, CA: Brooks/Cole.

Poston, D., Turnbull, A., Park, J., Mannan, H., Marquis, J., & Wang, M. (2003). Family quality of life: A qualitative inquiry. *Mental Retardation, 41,* 313–328.

Quill, K. (1997). Instructional considerations for young children with autism: The rationale for visually cued instruction. *Journal of Autism and Developmental Disorders, 27,* 697–714.

Reeve, C.E., & Carr, E.G. (2000). Prevention of severe behavior problems in children with developmental disorders. *Journal of Positive Behavior Interventions, 2,* 144–160.

Repp, A.C., & Horner, R.H. (Eds.). (1999). *Functional analysis of problem behavior: From effective assessment to effective support.* Belmont, CA: Wadsworth Publishing.

Rush, D.D., & Shelden, M.L. (2008). Coaching: Quick reference guide. *Briefcase, 1,* 1–2.

Sailor, W., Dunlap, G., Sugai, G., & Horner, R. (Eds.). (2009). *Handbook of positive behavior support.* New York, NY: Springer.

Sainato, D.M., Strain, P.S., Lefebvre, D., & Repp, N. (1990). Effects of self-evaluation on the independent work skills of preschool children with disabilities. *Exceptional Children, 56,* 540–549.

Sandall, S., Hemmeter, M.L., Smith, B., & McLean, M. (2005). *DEC recommended practices: A comprehensive guide for practical application in early intervention/early childhood special education.* Missoula, MT: CEC, DEC.

Sandall, S.R., & Schwartz, I.S. (2002). *Building blocks for teaching preschoolers with special needs.* Baltimore, MD: Paul H. Brookes Publishing Co.

Schmit, J., Alpers, S., Raschke, D., & Ryndak, D. (2000). Effects of using a photographic cueing package during routine school transitions with a child who has autism. *Mental Retardation, 38,* 131–137.

Schneider, N., & Goldstein, H. (2010). Using social stories and visual schedules to improve socially appropriate behaviors in children with autism. *Journal of Positive Behavior Interventions, 12,* 149–160.

Schreibman, L., Dawson, G., Stahmer, A.C., Landa, R., Rogers, S.J., McGee, G.G., . . . Iess, S. (2015). Naturalistic developmental behavioral interventions: Empirically validated treatments for autism spectrum disorder. *Journal of Autism and Developmental Disorders, 45,* 2411–2428.

Sears, K.M., Blair, K.-S., Iovannone, R., & Crosland, K. (2013). Using the Prevent-Teach-Reinforce model with families of young children with ASD. *Journal of Autism and Developmental Disorders, 43,* 1005–1016.

Singer, G.H.S., & Wang, M. (2009). The intellectual roots of positive behavior support and their implications for its development. In W. Sailor, G. Dunlap, G. Sugai, & R.H. Horner (Eds.), *Handbook of positive behavior support* (pp. 17–46). New York, NY: Springer.

Smith, B., & Fox, L. (2003). *Systems of service delivery: A synthesis of evidence relevant to young children at risk or who have challenging behaviors.* Tampa, FL: University of South Florida, Center for Evidence-based Practice: Young Children with Challenging Behavior. Retrieved October 4, 2015, from http://challengingbehavior.fmhi.usf.edu/explore/publications_docs/systems_of_service.pdf

Snyder, P.A., Crowe, C.D., Miller, M.D., Hemmeter, M.L., & Fox, L. (2011, April). *Evaluating implementation of evidence-based practices in preschool: Psychometric evidence of the Teaching Pyramid Observation Tool.* Paper presented at the American Educational Research Association, New Orleans, LA.

Strain, P.S. (2001). Empirically-based social skill intervention. *Behavioral Disorders, 27,* 30–36.

Strain, P.S. (2002). *Positive parenting practices (trainers manual).* Tualatin, OR: Teacher's Toolbox.

Strain, P.S., & Danko, C.D. (1995). Caregivers' encouragement of positive interaction between preschoolers with autism and their siblings. *Journal of Emotional and Behavioral Disorders, 3,* 2–12.

Strain, P.S., & Kohler, F.W. (1998). Peer-mediated social intervention for young children with autism. *Seminars in Speech and Language, 19,* 391–405.

Strain, P.S., & Schwartz, I. (2001). Applied behavior analysis and social skills intervention for young children with autism. *Focus on Autism and Other Developmental Disorders, 8,* 12–24.

Strain, P.S., Wilson, K., & Dunlap, G. (2011). Prevent-Teach-Reinforce: Addressing problem behaviors of students with autism in general education classrooms. *Behavioral Disorders, 36,* 160–171.

Sugai, G., & Horner, R.H. (2006). A promising approach for expanding and sustaining school-wide positive behavior support. *School Psychology Review, 35,* 245–259.

Touchette, P.E., MacDonald, R.F., & Langer, S.N. (1985). A scatter plot for identifying stimulus control of problem behavior. *Journal of Applied Behavior Analysis, 18,* 343–351.

Turnbull, A.P., & Ruef, M. (1996). Family perspectives on problem behavior. *Mental Retardation, 34,* 280–293.

Turnbull, A.P., & Turnbull, H.R. (2001). *Families, professionals, and exceptionality: Collaborating for empowerment*. Upper Saddle River, NJ: Prentice Hall.

Umbreit, J., Ferro, J., Liaupsin, C., & Lane, K.L. (2007). *Functional behavioral assessment and function-based intervention: An effective, practical approach*. Upper Saddle River, NJ: Pearson.

Vaughn, B.J., & Fox, L.K. (2015). Cultural and contextual fit: Juan's family as active team members. In F. Brown, J.L. Anderson, & R.L. DePry (Eds.), *Individual Positive Behavior Supports: A standards-based guide to practices in school and community settings* (pp. 433–446). Baltimore, MD: Paul H. Brookes Publishing Co.

Volkert, V.M., Lerman, D.C., Trosclair, N., Addison, L., & Kodak, T. (2008). An exploratory analysis of task-interspersal procedures while teaching object labels to children with autism. *Journal of Applied Behavior Analysis, 41*, 335–350.

Waldron-Soler, K.M., Martella, R.C., Marchand-Martella, N.E., & Ebey, T.L. (2000). Effects of choice of stimuli as reinforcement for task responding in preschoolers with and without developmental disabilities. *Journal of Applied Behavior Analysis, 33*, 93–96.

Webster-Stratton, C. (1992). *The incredible years: A troubleshooting guide for parents*. London, United Kingdom: Umbrella Press.

Winterling, V., Dunlap, G., & O'Neill, R.E. (1987). The influence of task variation on the aberrant behavior of autistic students. *Education and Treatment of Children, 10*, 105–119.

Zanolli, K.M., Saudargas, R.A., & Twardosz, S. (1997). The development of toddlers' responses to affectionate teacher behavior. *Early Childhood Research Quarterly, 12*, 99–116.

Intervention Guide

A. PREVENT INTERVENTIONS

Introduction

The following descriptions are of common, evidence-based interventions that can be used as strategies for the prevent component of Prevent-Teach-Reinforce for Families (PTR-F). For PTR-F behavior support plans, at least one prevent intervention must be selected; however, many behavior support plans include more than one prevent intervention. Prevent interventions are strategies that involve antecedent manipulations. The general idea is that prevent interventions should make the challenging behavior less likely to occur, and the effects are usually seen in a short period of time.

Provide Choices

Strategy: Provide opportunities to choose between two or more options.

Description of Strategy: This strategy involves providing the child with an opportunity to make choices among activities, the order of activities, materials, snacks, play partners, or many other possibilities in which there may be more than one alternative. This strategy involves identifying when, where, how, and how often choices will be provided to the child to reduce challenging behaviors. Teams need to create a plan that includes all of these components.

Rationale for Using Strategy: When provided as a prevent strategy, choice making can be effective because 1) it allows the child to select an option that is preferred (and when children are engaged with preferred activities or stimuli, they tend to exhibit fewer challenging behaviors) and 2) it allows the child to have some control over what happens. As adults, we seek to organize our environment by making choices throughout the day in a variety of ways and in a variety of situations. Providing choices for children teaches them how to manage or have some control in their environment. A great deal of research has shown that choice making can reduce the occurrence of challenging behaviors if the choices are relevant to the context in which challenging behaviors tend to occur. Providing choices prevents challenging behavior by allowing children to express a preference and to engage with that preferred option. This is a valuable process and problem-solving skill, and in some situations, the act of "control" in and of itself is reinforcing and can thereby reduce challenging behaviors.

Considerations for Using Strategy

Consider using this strategy when the PTR-F assessment indicates that

▲ Challenging behavior occurs when the child is asked to do something that the child finds disagreeable.

▲ Challenging behavior occurs when the child is given a direction.

▲ Challenging behavior occurs when the child transitions from a preferred activity (e.g., play) to a nonpreferred activity (e.g., bedtime).

▲ A child says "no" to everything.

▲ A child regularly refuses to do what is asked of him or her.

Steps for Implementation

1. Determine when choices will be offered. This should usually be shortly before the time that challenging behaviors are anticipated to occur (as identified by the PTR-F assessment). Choices may be offered many times per day or only before especially difficult routines. It depends on the child and the frequency of challenging behaviors.

2. Determine what choice options will be made available. All options should be reasonable from the perspective of the family and the child, and it is understood that the child's choice must be honored.

3. Determine how the choices will be presented. Often choices are best offered with both verbal and visual cues. A choice "menu" in the form of a pictorial array may need to be prepared.

4. When choice-making opportunities are presented, the child's choice should be honored immediately.

Strategy Ideas: Listed below are some sample ideas that can be used as choices; there are many more. This is intended to illustrate some options of how and when to integrate choices. Teams are encouraged to be creative with choices and to ensure these choices fit the function of the behavior and within family routines and activities.

Mealtimes

▲ Choose where to sit

▲ Choose between two different placemats or cups with preferred characters or colors

▲ Choose drink, snack item

Riding in car

▲ Choose toy to take

▲ Choose song to listen to

▲ Choose blanket or pillow to have in car seat

Bath

▲ Choose bath toys

▲ Choose washcloth or sponge

▲ Choose towel

Transition

▲ Choose toy to bring

▲ Choose transition movement (e.g., hop on one foot)

Important Considerations

▲ Choices should be offered immediately before an activity that has been associated with challenging behavior.

▲ Choices should be made among two or three possible selections.

▲ The child's selection should be honored immediately. Delayed selections do not tend to be effective with young children.

▲ Choices may need to be presented in a variety of ways (e.g., pictures, talking devices, objects) to ensure children with all abilities can make meaningful choices. Many young children require visual cues in order to make accurate choices.

▲ Some children may not know how to make choices and will need some careful instruction before the procedure can be effective.

    ▲ Offered choices should be stated positively, should be acceptable and desirable to the child, and must be honored by the adults. If something is not an option, is not acceptable, or is not available, do not offer it as a choice.

Supporting Evidence

Dunlap, G., dePerczel, M., Clarke, S., Wilson, D., Wright, S., White, R., & Gomez, A. (1994). Choice making to promote adaptive behavior for students with emotional and behavioral challenges. *Journal of Applied Behavior Analysis, 27*, 505–518.

Dunlap, G., & Kern, L. (1996). Modifying instructional activities to promote desirable behavior: A conceptual and practical framework. *School Psychology Quarterly, 11*, 297–312.

Harding, J.W., Wacker, D.P., Berg, W.K., Cooper, L., Asmus, J., Mlela, K., & Muller, J. (1999). An analysis of choice making in the assessment of young children with severe behavior problems. *Journal of Applied Behavior Analysis, 32*, 63–82.

Kern, L., Vorndran, C.M., Hilt, A., Ringdahl, J.E., Adelman, B.E., & Dunlap, G. (1998). Choice as an intervention to improve behavior: A review of the literature. *Journal of Behavioral Education, 8*, 151–169.

McCormick, K.M., Jolivette, K., & Ridgley, R. (2003). Choice making as an intervention strategy for young children. *Young Exceptional Children, 6*, 3–10.

Waldron-Soler, K.M., Martella, R.C., Marchand-Martella, N.E., & Ebey, T.L. (2000). Effects of choice of stimuli as reinforcement for task responding in preschoolers with and without developmental disabilities. *Journal of Applied Behavior Analysis, 33*, 93–96.

Intersperse Difficult or Nonpreferred Tasks with Easy or Preferred Tasks

Strategy: Intersperse difficult or nonpreferred tasks with easy or preferred tasks.

Description of Strategy: This strategy involves reducing challenging behaviors that are associated with difficult or unpleasant activities by mixing in (interspersing) "tasks" that are easy for the child or that the child clearly enjoys. Task interspersal makes the overall context of the activity more pleasant and more successful for the child and thereby serves to reduce challenging behaviors.

Rationale for Using Strategy: When tasks are difficult, we tend to avoid them, or do not put much effort into the tasks. If something is hard for us to do and then we fail at it, we will likely not want to do it anymore. Providing multiple opportunities for children to be successful and to be able to demonstrate appropriate skills while "sprinkling" in harder or more difficult tasks provides children with opportunities to persist with activities or tasks that are difficult or not preferred. Interspersing difficult tasks with easy tasks prevents challenging behavior by allowing more opportunities for children to be successful, and the use of this strategy creates an environment where learning is fun and enjoyable. Children who do not respond well to failure, have difficulty learning new skills, take a long time to learn new skills, or have limited skills and/or interests may benefit from interspersing difficult or nonpreferred tasks with easy or preferred tasks. For example, children may use problem behavior to avoid tasks that are difficult for them or that they do not want to do. Some children have limited interests and choose to play with the same toys all the time or only engage in a few activities. This strategy may help children be successful in engaging in a variety of activities and expanding on their skills and interests.

Considerations for Using Strategy

Consider using this strategy when the PTR-F assessment indicates that challenging behavior occurs when

▲ The child is avoiding or refusing a particular task or activity

▲ The child is corrected or told that something he or she did is wrong

▲ The child is being taught something new (e.g., a new task or activity is introduced)

▲ A preferred activity ends or when transitioning to a nonpreferred activity

Steps for Implementation

1. Identify activity or routine in which challenging behavior occurs and in which the challenging behavior appears to be related to the difficulty or the unpleasant nature of the activity. This should occur during the PTR-F assessment process.

2. Identify activities (or "tasks") that the child seems to enjoy and that he or she can do fluently. These tasks will be interspersed among the difficult expectations or tasks, so they should also be compatible with the overall context. Sometimes, the task can be as simple as "Give me 5!"

3. During the difficult activity or routine, sprinkle in the easy, preferred activities with a dense enough ratio (i.e., a high, or at least equal, number of easy and preferred tasks when compared to the number of difficult tasks) so that challenging behavior is reduced or eliminated.

Strategy Ideas: Listed below are ideas for interspersing difficult or nonpreferred tasks with easier and more pleasant tasks; of course, there are many more options. This list is intended to illustrate some options of how and when to integrate this strategy; how your team chooses to implement this strategy will depend on the task itself and the skills the child already possesses. Teams are encouraged to be creative and to ensure these choices fit the function of the behavior and fit within a family's routines and activities.

Bedtime routine

▲   If a child often demonstrates challenging behavior when prompted to put on his or her pajamas, the family can change the order of the routine so that this nonpreferred task is interspersed with preferred ones. If the child only resists putting on his or her pajamas (and the other tasks are, therefore, easy and preferred), the family could structure the bedtime routine in the following order: brush teeth, go to the bathroom, put on pajamas, and read a bedtime story.

Mealtime

▲   If the child does not like to eat a particular nonpreferred food (e.g., meat), the family could prompt the child to take a few bites of a preferred food (e.g., potato), then prompt him or her to take one bite of meat, and then prompt the child to eat a bite of potato or take a sip of juice (a preferred drink).

Free play

▲   To expand a child's play skills, set up a simple turn-taking sequence (e.g., your turn, brother's turn). First, allow the child a few minutes to play a preferred activity independently. Then, practice the nonpreferred turn-taking sequence by prompting turn taking between the child and brother. After the turn-taking sequence, allow the child to play the preferred activity independently again. Frequently repeat this sequence when possible. The amount of time spent practicing the turn-taking sequence should be based on the child's ability to be successful with turn taking. Many children might start by completing one sequence that can be lengthened with more exchanges as he or she more successfully completes the turn-taking sequence over time.

Special Considerations

Consider the following when interspersing nonpreferred or difficult tasks with preferred or easy tasks for children who may have differing needs or when special circumstances are present.

▲   Tasks may need to be broken up into smaller steps, and the steps may need to be taught and practiced more often (provide multiple opportunities for instruction) when a child has cognitive delays or has difficulty learning new tasks.

▲ The amount of time spent on nonpreferred activities should be relatively short compared to the amount of time spent on preferred activities. These activities need to be arranged so that children can be successful engaging in nonpreferred activities, and children may be able to handle only a few seconds initially.

Implementation Considerations

When implementing these strategies, ensure the following:

▲ Requirements for difficult tasks should be attainable for the particular child; the child must be successful.

▲ Ensure that when you intersperse nonpreferred with preferred tasks, these are planned in advance and any required materials are prepared and available.

▲ The expectations for the nonpreferred tasks need to be clear and well defined.

▲ Preferred or easy tasks should be positively reinforced on a consistent basis.

Supporting Evidence

Dunlap, G., & Koegel, R.L. (1980). Motivating autistic children through stimulus variation. *Journal of Applied Behavior Analysis, 13,* 619–627.

Koegel, R.L., & Koegel, L.K. (2012). *The PRT pocket guide: Pivotal response treatment for autism spectrum disorders.* Baltimore, MD: Paul H. Brookes Publishing Co.

Schreibman, L., Dawson, G., Stahmer, A.C., Landa, R., Rogers, S.J., McGee, G.G., . . . Halladay, A. (2015). Naturalistic developmental behavioral interventions: Empirically validated treatments for autism spectrum disorder. *Journal of Autism and Developmental Disorders, 45,* 2411–2428.

Volkert, V.M., Lerman, D.C., Trosclair, N., Addison, L., & Kodak, T. (2008). An exploratory analysis of task-interspersal procedures while teaching object labels to children with autism. *Journal of Applied Behavior Analysis, 41,* 335–350.

Winterling, V., Dunlap, G., & O'Neill, R.E. (1987). The influence of task variation on the aberrant behavior of autistic students. *Education and Treatment of Children, 10,* 105–119.

Embed Preferences into Activities

Strategy: Embed child preferences into routines and activities.

Description of Strategy: This strategy involves incorporating a child's likes and preferences into activities to prevent challenging behaviors. Preferences can be incorporated into any aspect of a child's day and can include what is incorporated into activities, who participates, where activities occur, how activities are presented, or when activities occur.

Rationale for Using Strategy: Most people personalize their home environments with pictures of loved ones, scented candles, special mementos, favorite music, or other decorations. Some people personalize their environments with multiple items, whereas others do little personalization. Some people will incorporate fun or preferred activities into regular household routines or activities (i.e., chores) to make completing those tasks more tolerable. This could include listening to music while doing the dishes, dancing while vacuuming, or listening to an electronic book during a long drive. For children who struggle with particular activities, incorporating or embedding their personal preferences into activities can increase their interest and engagement in the activities and improve their knowledge in a variety of ways. When children are engaged in and enjoy activities, it is highly unlikely that they will exhibit any challenging behavior. One way to prevent challenging behavior is to incorporate preferences into activities to gain a child's interest and keep a child actively engaged in a variety of activities. Using preferences and things a child likes helps motivate the child to do a variety of activities, and the activities become naturally reinforcing for the child. This strategy can be effective for a child who may have limited interests, has a strong interest in a few things, avoids particular activities or does not participate in activities for long, or does not like being told what to do.

Considerations for Using Strategy

Consider using this strategy when the PTR-F assessment indicates the following:

▲ Challenging behavior occurs when the child is asked or told to do a nonpreferred activity.

▲ Challenging behavior occurs during a particular activity.

▲ Challenging behavior occurs when transitioning to or beginning a particular activity.

▲ Challenging behavior occurs when an activity is not an option.

▲ Challenging behavior occurs at a certain time of the day.

▲ Challenging behavior occurs when a parent is attending to someone else.

▲ A child refuses to participate in activities or routines.

Steps for Implementation

1. Identify the activity or routine in which challenging behavior occurs and in which the challenging behavior appears to be related to the difficulty or the unpleasant nature of the activity. This identification should occur during the PTR-F assessment process.

2. Identify child's preferences, such as types of animals (e.g., dinosaurs, horses), vehicles (e.g., trucks, spaceships), or TV characters or personalities.

3. Determine how preferences can be incorporated into difficult activities or routines. This may require some creativity but can usually be accomplished with materials, pictures, or photographs.

Strategy Ideas: There are innumerable ways that a child's preferences can be embedded into activities. How your team chooses to implement this strategy will depend on the types of preferences the child has, how the preferences are embedded into activities, and when preferences are used. Teams are encouraged to be creative and to ensure these choices fit the function of the behavior and fit within daily routines and activities.

Getting ready for school (morning routine)

▲ Sarina always sleeps with her bunny stuffed animal "bun-bun," and getting ready for school is a struggle. Sarina's mom allows her to bring "bun-bun" during the process of getting ready for school, and then "bun-bun" is left at the door when it is time to leave.

▲ Payton does not like getting ready for school, but he likes to pretend he is a superhero, so his mom asks him which superhero he is in the morning and calls him by the superhero name throughout the morning routine. Payton's mom also buys clothing featuring superheroes because getting dressed is a difficult part of getting ready in the morning.

Mealtime/snack time

▲ Jamal does not like to sit and eat at the table, but he likes to pour his own milk to drink, so his mom provides a small container with a small amount of milk at the table.

▲ Cecilia loves being near her mom as much as possible, so her mom sits next to her during meals and snacks.

Brushing teeth

▲ Gemma does not like to brush her teeth but loves anything "princess." Gemma's mom sings princess songs during toothbrushing and buys princess toothbrushes.

▲ Ida does not like to brush her teeth, but loves her big brother because he is always being silly with her. Ida's big brother brushes his teeth in the bathroom with Ida, making faces in the mirror and making games out of brushing different sections of teeth.

Special Considerations

The following are some considerations when embedding preferences into activities for children who may have differing needs or when special circumstances are present.

▲ For children with limited interests, identifying preferences that can be embedded into activities may be difficult. It may be necessary to conduct a preference assessment. However, in our experience, it is always possible to find something that inspires a child's interest and pleasure.

▲ When preferences have been identified, make sure they do not interfere with any parental or household rules, values, or preferences.

Implementation Considerations

When implementing these strategies, make sure that

▲ Whoever is implementing the strategy is agreeable to including the child's preferences into the activity, and that the strategy supports the child in becoming more independent for the identified routine or activity.

▲ It is clear what preferences will be included, how those preferences will be included, and when those preferences will be included. The plan should include explicit details about including the child's preferences into routines or activities.

Supporting Evidence

Clarke, S., Dunlap, G., Foster-Johnson, L., Childs, K.E., Wilson, D., White, R., & Vera, A. (1995). Improving the conduct of students with behavioral disorders by incorporating student interests into curricular activities. *Behavioral Disorders, 20,* 221–237.

Dunlap, G., & Kern, L. (1996). Modifying instructional activities to promote desirable behavior: A conceptual and practical framework. *School Psychology Quarterly, 11,* 297–312.

Dunlap, G., Kern-Dunlap, L., Clarke, S., & Robbins, F.R. (1991). Functional assessment, curriculum revision, and severe behavior problems. *Journal of Applied Behavior Analysis, 24,* 387–397.

Foster-Johnson, L., Ferro, J., & Dunlap, G. (1994). Preferred curricular activities and reduced problem behaviors in students with intellectual disabilities. *Journal of Applied Behavior Analysis, 27,* 493–504.

Enhancing Predictability with Schedules

Strategy: Use schedules and other cues to enable children to understand and follow activity sequences. This strategy may be particularly useful with transitions.

Description of Strategy: This strategy involves purposefully planning a routine to prepare a child for his or her day (prior review of schedules and routines) or a transition (visual timers, break signal). This strategy is preventive, and required materials should be prepared and readily available. If a visual schedule is used, a preparation routine would include reviewing the schedule with the child prior to a change or transition and prior to beginning the activity on the schedule. If a timer is used for transition warnings, the team must also plan for having the timer available and accessible and make sure it is where the child can see it.

Rationale for Using Strategy: When we are not prepared for our day or not prepared for transitions, many challenging behaviors can arise. Think about a time when you may have lost your own schedule, electronic or handwritten, and think about how that made you feel. When we do not know our own schedule or cannot review it, we get anxious and stressed. A child, regardless of developmental levels, also needs to know the daily schedule, the routine within the activity, and when a transition is coming. Often, when a child begins to resist a transition, we then get a schedule to review. This strategy involves reviewing a schedule to prepare a child for the day, or changes in the day, to prevent challenging behaviors from occurring. When children are prepared for their day and know the routines within their schedule, they can be more successful in all activities and routines.

Considerations for Using Strategy

Consider using this strategy when the PTR-F assessment indicates that

▲ Challenging behavior occurs when following the daily routine.

▲ Challenging behavior occurs around transitions.

▲ Challenging behavior occurs at specific times of the day.

▲ Challenging behavior occurs when the child is given a direction.

▲ Challenging behavior occurs when transitioning to a nonpreferred activity.

▲ Challenging behavior occurs when a preferred activity ends.

▲ Challenging behavior occurs at the beginning or end of an activity.

▲ Challenging behavior occurs when there is a change in the schedule.

Steps for Implementation

1. Identify activities and routines during which the child has challenging behaviors and in which it is possible that the child is unsure of the sequence or timing of activities. This information should be derived from the functional behavioral assessment process.

2. Determine the types of schedules that will be necessary to help the child understand the sequence of upcoming events and where favored activities will be occurring.

3. Develop or obtain materials needed.

4. Implement procedures to help child understand the schedules at times during the day when challenging behaviors have been observed to occur.

Strategy Ideas: Listed below are ideas that can be used to prepare a child for his or her day, changes in schedule, and transitions. Preparing a child for the daily routine, schedule changes, and transitions requires action prior to the events occurring.

Prepare for bedtime

▲ When it is time to begin the bedtime routine, a visual sequence can be used for the steps of the routine. The first picture might show story time, with an indication of how many books will be read to the child. The next picture might show a goodnight kiss and hug, followed by a picture of turning on the nightlight. The final pictures in the sequence might show the parent turning off the overhead light and leaving the bedroom.

Prepare for getting in car to do errands in the community

▲ The parent might use a series of pictures to illustrate where the child and parent will go after getting in the car. For example, the pictures might include an illustration of the child choosing what toy to bring in the car. A photo of the grocery store, a photo of the gas station, a photo of the park, and a photo of home could be used. The parent can review the schedule prior to getting in the car and then after every activity is completed by indicating an errand is finished and identifying what is coming next. The visual schedule should be designed so that the photos can be arranged in sequence and removed when completed.

Special Considerations

When a child has differing needs or special circumstances are present, here are some points to consider when preparing the child for his or her daily schedule and routines, changes in the schedule or routines, and transitions.

▲   When a child has cognitive delays or has difficulty with change, the steps of the transition may need to be broken up into very small steps, for example: "Time to eat. Find your chair. Get in chair. What cup do you want?" Preparation for this transition would involve reviewing each step.

▲   Daily schedules may need to be mobile and portable, especially if the child has difficulty transitioning. The schedule should be designed so that the family member can bring the schedule to the child or take the schedule into various activity settings.

Implementation Considerations

When implementing these strategies, ensure that

▲   Time is planned to review schedule prior to activities, routines, transitions, or changes.

▲   Visual schedules and routines are prepared and accessible.

Supporting Evidence

Banda, D.R., & Grimmett, E. (2008). Enhancing social and transition behaviors of persons with autism through activity schedules: A review. *Education and Training in Developmental Disabilities, 43,* 324–333.

Dettmer, S., Simpson, R.L., Myles, B.S., & Ganz, J.B. (2000). The use of visual supports to facilitate transitions of students with autism. *Focus on Autism and Other Developmental Disabilities, 15,* 163–169.

Dooley, P., Wilczenski, F.L., & Torem, C. (2001). Using an activity schedule to smooth school transitions. *Journal of Positive Behavior Interventions, 3,* 57–61.

Lequia, J., Machalicek, W., & Rispoli, M.J. (2012). Effects of activity schedules on challenging behavior exhibited in children with autism spectrum disorders: A systematic review. *Research in Autism Spectrum Disorders, 6,* 480–492.

Use Timers and Other Visual or Auditory Supports for Added Information or Structure

Description of Strategy: This strategy involves the use of timers, visual cues, or other auditory cues to help the child understand the expectations of an activity, direction, or routine.

Rationale for Using Strategy: Adults will typically verbalize what is expected from the child within a routine or activity. However, a young child might not listen to the direction, have difficulty understanding the direction, or need more support to follow the direction. For example, a parent might say, "In a few minutes, it's bedtime. Hurry up and finish your book," with the expectation that the child has heard the warning and will be able to comply with the direction of "Okay, time for bed." If the child has not heard or understood the direction, the child's reaction might be to resist or protest when the parent insists that it is bedtime. The use of timers, additional auditory cues, or visuals can give the child additional information about what to expect. For example, a timer might be set to indicate to a child how long the child has in the current activity before transitioning to another activity. Similarly, a parent might play a song to indicate how long an activity will last (e.g., "We are going to brush your teeth. When I finish singing 'Twinkle, Twinkle,' we will be all done"). Another example is the use of a visual cue such as a stop sign on the refrigerator or pantry to give the child additional information about the direction that "Snack time is over. You can't open the pantry door."

Considerations for Using Strategy

Consider using this strategy when the PTR-F assessment indicates that

▲ Challenging behavior occurs when following the daily routine.

▲ Challenging behavior occurs around transitions.

▲ Challenging behavior occurs when the child is given a direction.

▲ Challenging behavior occurs when transitioning to a nonpreferred activity.

▲ Challenging behavior occurs when a preferred activity ends.

▲ Challenging behavior occurs at the beginning or end of an activity.

Steps for Implementation

1. Identify activities and routines during which the child has challenging behaviors and for which it is possible that the child is unsure of the expectations or directions of the activities. This information should be derived from the functional behavioral assessment process.

2. Determine the types of visuals, timers, or other cues that will be helpful for ensuring the child understands the directions and expectations of the activity or routine.

3. Develop or obtain materials needed (e.g., get a timer, make the stop sign, decide on the song).

4. Implement the strategy paired with a verbal direction to help the child follow the routine or expectations.

Strategy Ideas: Some ideas that can be used to assist the child in understanding the directions or expectations of common routines and activities include the following:

Use of stop sign

▲ Stop signs might be used to indicate when materials are not to be used, when the child might not enter a room, or when access to items is not allowed.

▲ Place the stop sign while verbally indicating that access is not allowed.

▲ Point to stop sign when the child approaches and verbally state that access is not allowed (e.g., "See, it says stop. We can't open the door.").

▲ Follow the prohibition with a choice for the child ("We can't go outside, but we can play with toys or look at books.").

Use of timer

▲ Determine what kind of timer will be used (e.g., kitchen timer, large child's sand timer, visual timer, timer app on a tablet, cell phone timer).

▲ Set the timer to indicate the duration of an activity that might be difficult for the child. For example, a timer could indicate how long to sit at the table or how long bath time might last. State to the child that you are setting the timer and that the child will do the activity until the timer is finished (e.g., the buzzer goes off or the music ends).

▲ Another option might be to use the timer to indicate when an activity will have to end. For example, set the timer for how long the child can continue to be on the computer or how long the child might play before a transition. Set the timer while verbally telling the child how many minutes and what is coming up next. Provide a warning to the child when the time is almost done (e.g., "5 more minutes," "2 more minutes").

Auditory cues

▲ Identify the auditory cue that you want to use (e.g., song, bell).

▲ Determine how the cue will be activated and when it will be used prior to providing direction or instruction to the child.

▲ Use a verbal direction in addition to the auditory cue to explain to the child what to expect. For example, you might say, "When you hear the clean-up song, it will be time to pick up toys and get ready for bedtime" or "When the bell rings, it will be time to get up and get dressed for school."

Implementation Considerations

When implementing these strategies, make sure that

▲ You have the materials readily available for strategy use

▲ When using timers, you are consistent in the time intervals and warnings and you honor the time given to the child.

Supporting Evidence

Fettig, A., & Ostrosky, M.M. (2011). Collaborating with parents in reducing children's challenging behaviors: Linking functional assessment to intervention. *Child Development Research, 2011,* 1–10.

Grey, I., Healy, O., Leader, G., & Hayes, D. (2009). Using a Time Timer™ to increase appropriate waiting behavior in a child with developmental disabilities. *Research in Developmental Disabilities, 30,* 359–336.

Lequia, J., Machalicek, W., & Rispoli, M.J. (2012). Effects of activity schedules on challenging behavior exhibited in children with autism spectrum disorders: A systematic review. *Research in Autism Spectrum Disorders, 6,* 480–492.

Alter Physical Arrangement of the Environment or Activity Area

Strategy: Alter the physical arrangement of the environment or activity area.

Description of Strategy: This strategy involves changing or moving elements of the environment and/or activity area in order to prevent challenging behaviors. This can include, for example, changing, reorganizing, or removing a play area in the home; changing the seating arrangement during a mealtime; altering elements within a play room or area or room of the home; removing or restricting particular items from an area or room; making items more accessible for the child; increasing the amount of materials available; and keeping certain pets separate from the child.

Rationale for Using Strategy: Changing aspects of our physical environment can affect our behavior and prevent us from doing certain things. Creating an environment so children can be successful can prevent challenging behaviors. Altering the physical arrangement of the home, a particular room, or a particular space within a room can prevent challenging behavior by changing the environment in a way that promotes the appropriate behavior. When environments are altered or created in ways that make expectations clear, it reduces the number of directions, commands, and demands that adults have to give to children. A reduction in commands and demands can reduce power struggles, increase children's independence in daily routines, and increase opportunities for families to make positive comments about children's appropriate behavior.

Considerations for Using Strategy

Consider using this strategy when the PTR-F assessment indicates that challenging behaviors occur

▲ In a particular area of a room or in a particular room more than in other spaces

▲ In the presence of particular materials, toys, objects, pets, etc.

▲ During a particular activity

▲ As part of power struggles

▲ When a child is told "no" or given a direction

▲ When a lot of adult direction or prompting around daily routines and transitions is required

Steps for Implementation

1. Identify activities and routines in the home that are associated with a child's challenging behaviors (from the PTR-F assessment). Determine whether there are physical elements in the home setting associated with those activities that might be contributing to the challenging behaviors.

2. If there are physical arrangements that can be modified to facilitate desired behavior change, proceed to make the modifications.

Strategy Ideas: Many possibilities exist for adjusting the physical arrangement of the home. How your team chooses to implement this strategy will depend on the home space and what resources the family has available. Teams are encouraged to be creative and to ensure these choices fit the function of the behavior and fit within the family's preferences and daily routines and activities.

Mealtime

▲ If challenging behaviors occur due to sibling interactions when the child and his or her sibling sit beside each other during mealtime, the family can set rules around who sits where during mealtime. The rules can be made so that the child does not sit by this sibling.

Playtime

▲ If the child frequently demonstrates challenging behavior while playing with a particular toy, the toy can be removed from the play area until the family and PTR-F facilitator are able to teach the child skills that he or she can use to play with the toy without demonstrating challenging behavior.

Leaving home

▲ If the child requires a lot of prompting to leave the home in the morning, the family can set up the environment so that the items the child needs and activities the child should complete are in an order that guides the child through successful task completion. For example, if the child has to complete a sequence of tasks (put on shoes, put on coat, put on backpack, grab lunchbox), the family can set the child's shoes, coat, backpack, and lunchbox on the floor in order so that the arrangement naturally prompts him or her through the sequence.

Special Considerations

The following are some points to consider when altering the physical home arrangement for children who may have differing needs or when special circumstances are present:

▲ If the child has any physical impairments or delays in gross motor skills, the physical arrangement of the home setting will need to be considered based on any needs of the child. If the child uses a wheelchair, walker, crutches, or any other device to physically move around, it is crucial to make sure there is enough space for the child to navigate through the home as independently as possible.

▲ If the child has a visual and/or hearing impairment, it may be necessary to make accommodations based on those specific needs.

Implementation Considerations

When implementing this strategy, make sure that

▲ Teams are flexible with their physical home arrangements. What works for one child may not be as effective with a different child.

▲ Teams attempt to arrange the room so that adults are likely to see the child from any part of the room.

Supporting Evidence

Duda, M.A., Clarke, S., Fox, L., & Dunlap, G. (2008). Implementation of positive behavior support with a sibling set in a home environment. *Journal of Early Intervention, 30,* 213–236.

Kohlhoff, J., & Morgan, S. (2014). Parent-child interaction therapy for toddlers: A pilot study. *Child & Family Behavior Therapy, 36,* 121–139.

Sandall, S.R., & Schwartz, I.S. (2002). *Building blocks for teaching preschoolers with special needs.* Baltimore, MD: Paul H. Brookes Publishing Co.

Remove Triggers for Challenging Behaviors

Strategy: Remove triggers for challenging behaviors.

Description of Strategy: This strategy involves removing or avoiding something or someone that serves as an immediate trigger for a child's challenging behavior to prevent the challenging behavior from occurring. If a specific activity, item, request, or person serves as an immediate trigger to challenging behavior, the strategy involves removing it so that it no longer serves as a trigger. This is a common and effective strategy, but it depends on an accurate process of PTR-F assessment to identify the specific trigger. Also, like other prevent strategies, removing a trigger is effective as a short-term procedure and must be accompanied by appropriate teach and reinforce strategies to produce long-term benefits and generalization.

Rationale for Using Strategy: Removing triggers is a well-established procedure that is based on a major principle of learning known as "stimulus control." For our purposes, stimulus control means that behavior (including challenging behavior) is influenced by antecedent (and contextual) events. If we change the antecedent stimuli, we can change the child's behavior. In addition, when we remove triggers, we open up opportunities to help the child learn crucial social and problem-solving skills. Therefore, it is important to remember that the removal of triggers is almost always a temporary measure that can be implemented only when we have enough control to make sure that the trigger does not occur. However, in most cases, it is likely that the trigger will occur in other settings and in the future. For this reason, it is important to be sure that the child has opportunities to learn how to handle the triggers more effectively.

Considerations for Using Strategy

Consider using this strategy when the PTR-F assessment indicates that

▲ Challenging behavior occurs around specific people on a consistent basis.

▲ Challenging behavior occurs when starting or during a particular activity on a consistent basis.

▲ Challenging behavior occurs when a particular activity ends or is signaled to end.

▲ Challenging behavior occurs when a particular word or phrase is said to the child (e.g., told "no," asked to do something).

▲ Challenging behavior occurs when the child transitions to a particular activity or area.

▲ Challenging behavior occurs when the child is given a direction.

Steps for Implementation

1. Identify the triggers for challenging behavior. The triggers should be identified during the PTR-F assessment process (see Chapter 4) and, specifically, by using the prevent assessment checklist and through the discussion during the assessment meeting.

2. Determine whether the trigger can be removed for the child. Sometimes, the trigger (such as a specific activity or the presence of a specific person) can be removed from the child's immediate presence. At other times, however, removal of the trigger could involve too much of an accommodation. If this is the case, then perhaps the impact of the trigger might be ameliorated by using another strategy such as choice making or embedding preferences or interests.

3. Determine exactly when and how the trigger will be removed, and what instruction, activity, item, or person might need to serve as a replacement.

Strategy Ideas: The following are some ideas that can be used as ways to eliminate immediate triggers for challenging behaviors; there are many more. This list is intended to illustrate some options of how and when to integrate this strategy; how your team chooses to implement this strategy will depend on the specific triggers for the child and your ability to eliminate the triggers. Teams are encouraged to be creative and to ensure these choices fit the function of the behavior and within typical routines and activities.

Meals/snacks

▲ If challenging behavior occurs when a particular food item is present, stop offering that particular food item. If it is not a particular nutritional concern, the food item can be reintroduced at a later time after other skills have been taught.

Nap/rest time

▲ If challenging behavior occurs if a child is not allowed to have a particular item during nap or rest time, allow the child to take the item to bed (as long as there are no safety concerns and this is acceptable).

Toileting/diapering

▲ If the challenging behavior occurs when the parent says, "Time for potty" or "Time for diaper change," the phrase, which is the trigger, can be eliminated by using a picture or object to signal this activity. For example, a parent may hand a picture of the bathroom to the child to take with them to the bathroom. This is most effective when the parent hands the child the picture without saying anything. Objects can also be used, such as giving a child the wipes when it is time to change his or her diaper.

184

Prevent-Teach-Reinforce for Families

Special Considerations

Consider the following when eliminating immediate triggers for challenging behavior for children who may have differing needs or when special circumstances are present.

▲ For children with significant needs, triggers may need to be eliminated for a longer time in order to teach more appropriate behaviors.

▲ It is always important to use this strategy in conjunction with an effective teaching strategy to teach alternative behaviors.

Implementation Considerations

When implementing these strategies, make sure that

▲ All adults who interact with the child on a regular basis are agreeable to eliminating the specific triggers that the team identifies for a defined period of time.

▲ When triggers are eliminated, there is a plan for how to teach appropriate replacement skills.

Supporting Evidence

Dunlap, G., & Kern, L. (1996). Modifying instructional activities to promote desirable behavior: A conceptual and practical framework. *School Psychology Quarterly, 11,* 297–312.

Kern, L., & Dunlap, G. (1999). Assessment-based interventions for children with emotional and behavioral disorders. In A.C. Repp & R.H. Horner (Eds.), *Functional analysis of problem behavior: From effective assessment to effective support* (pp. 197–218). Belmont, CA: Wadsworth Publishing.

Reduce Distractions or Competing Events or Materials

Strategy: Reduce distractions, competing events, or materials to prevent challenging behavior.

Description of Strategy: This strategy involves limiting or getting rid of distractions that may be contributing to challenging behavior. If specific activities, items, people, or events are distracting and contributing to challenging behavior, this strategy involves removing or limiting the distractions. This is a common and effective strategy and depends on an accurate PTR-F assessment process to identify the specific distraction(s). Like other prevent strategies, this may be an effective short-term procedure and must be accompanied by appropriate teach and reinforce strategies to produce long-term benefits and generalization.

Rationale for Using Strategy: Distractions may cause disruptions in our ability to concentrate or persist on a particular task, and limiting or eliminating distractions can improve our ability to complete a task in a timely and/or efficient manner. For children with persistent challenging behavior, distractions may hinder the ability to teach desirable behaviors. Although limiting or removing distractions could serve as a trigger for challenging behavior, it is important to remember that reducing distractions is almost always a temporary strategy. In many cases, the team may consider distractions as a potential functional reinforcer that could be used to strengthen desirable behavior.

Considerations for Using Strategy

Consider using this strategy when the PTR-F assessment indicates that

▲ Challenging behavior occurs during a particular activity on a consistent basis.

▲ Challenging behavior occurs when transitioning to or beginning a particular activity.

▲ Challenging behavior occurs when a particular activity ends.

▲ Challenging behavior occurs when certain people are around.

▲ Challenging behavior occurs at a certain time of the day.

▲ Challenging behavior occurs in the presence of specific items.

Steps for Implementation

1. Identify whether the challenging behavior appears to occur during the presence of a particular activity or item. This identification should occur during the PTR-F assessment process.

2. Identify ways that the distraction can be limited or eliminated.

3. Determine how and when the distraction will be limited or eliminated and develop a specific plan for doing so. Like other prevent strategies, this may require some creativity, but the parent will likely have ideas for what will work best for the child.

Strategy Ideas: The following are some ideas of ways to reduce distractions that contribute to challenging behavior; there are many more. This list is intended to illustrate some options of how and when to integrate this strategy; how your team chooses to implement this strategy will depend on the specific distractions and your ability to limit or eliminate the distractions. Teams are encouraged to be creative and to ensure this strategy fits the function of the challenging behavior and within typical routines and activities.

▲ Norah wakes up and turns on the TV in the morning. Her mom has to provide her with multiple reminders (prompts) to get ready in the morning to go to school, which leads to tantrums, screaming, crying, and/or being late for school. Norah's mom wakes up early to ensure that Norah is not able to wake up and turn on the TV on her own. This strategy is used in combination with the teach strategy of using visual supports to promote independence and providing a list of the steps that Norah needs to complete to be ready for school. Once Norah is completely ready for school, she can watch TV until it is time to leave.

▲ Miles uses a pacifier as a soothing/calming item when he sleeps. He also likes it when he is upset. When Miles has his pacifier and is asked to do anything, he is noncompliant and refuses to follow any instructions. He will cry, scream "NO," throw things, and run away. Miles's mom makes sure he is calm, has him put his pacifier back in his bed, and then presents the instruction.

▲ Video and computer games are a distraction for Eugene, and when he is playing games, he ignores anything anyone says to him. His mom limits the amount of time he is able to play games and limits talking to him or giving instructions while he is playing games.

Special Considerations

Consider the following when reducing distractions for children who may have differing needs or when special circumstances are present.

▲ For children with significant needs, this strategy would likely need to be combined with another prevent strategy in addition to the teach and reinforce strategies.

▲ Instructions may need to be simplified, including limiting the number of words said, the complexity of vocabulary used, and/or how distractions are reduced.

Implementation Considerations

When implementing these strategies, make sure that

▲ It is possible to limit or eliminate the distraction, activity, or item.

▲ When distractions are limited or eliminated, the child has the skills to access the distraction in an appropriate way.

▲ The item or activity serving as a distraction is considered as a functional reinforcer and, if used as such, is only accessible by demonstrating the desirable behavior.

Supporting Evidence

Dunlap, G., & Kern, L. (1996). Modifying instructional activities to promote desirable behavior: A conceptual and practical framework. *School Psychology Quarterly, 11,* 297–312.

Kern, L., & Dunlap, G. (1999). Assessment-based interventions for children with emotional and behavioral disorders. In A.C. Repp & R.H. Horner (Eds.), *Functional analysis of problem behavior: From effective assessment to effective support* (pp. 197–218). Belmont, CA: Wadsworth Publishing.

Modify What Is Explicitly Asked of the Child

Strategy: Modify what is explicitly asked of the child.

Description of Strategy: This strategy involves changing the way that commands and requests are stated to and/or asked of the child. As opposed to providing more general commands in which a child is asked to do something that is not necessarily a choice or telling a child what he or she should not be doing, families using this strategy explicitly tell, or ask in some cases, the child what is expected of him or her through clear commands and/or requests. When commands are general (e.g., "It's time for bed," "Clean up"), children might not know exactly what is expected of them in regard to completing the routine. When children are asked whether they will perform particular tasks (e.g., "Will you please put your dishes in the sink?" "Can you stop yelling at your sister?"), a situation is created that often seems like a choice for children—a choice that can be answered with "no." In addition, when children are told what not to do ("Don't put that in your mouth," "Stop jumping on the couch"), they are not being told what to do in order to obtain reinforcement. By only letting them know what is not permitted or okay, they are provided little support for learning what is allowed and what is okay. Many families use this strategy already, and when it is incorporated into behavior support plans, it is important that the factors described above are considered when developing the plan.

Rationale for Using Strategy: By modifying what is explicitly asked of, or told to, a child, the child will know exactly what is expected of her or him. By telling the child specifically what to do, families are able to determine whether or not the child is doing what he or she is supposed to be doing. The use of this strategy decreases ambiguity around behavior. It can decrease arguments regarding what the child was or was not doing based on parental expectations, and it increases the likelihood that families reinforce a behavior because they know exactly what they are looking for in regard to appropriate behaviors the child can and should be exhibiting.

Considerations for Using Strategy

Consider using this strategy when the PTR-F assessment indicates that challenging behaviors occur

▲ During specific routines in which the child requires a lot of prompting to complete

▲ When adults have to give directions over and over

▲ When many family prompts use phrases telling the child not to do something or to stop doing something

▲ To obtain attention from adults

▲ During arguments that happen between the child and adults regarding whether or not the child was following expectations

Steps for Implementation

1. Determine the specific behaviors that are expected during the routine.

2. Decide how, if the child is not engaging in the expected behaviors, the family will prompt the child to demonstrate the behaviors. Sometimes, brainstorming on how to phrase a particular behavior is helpful. For example, instead of saying, "Stop jumping on the couch," families could say, "Please sit with your bottom on the couch."

3. Use this strategy frequently, and pair it with reinforcement once the child engages in the desired behavior.

Strategy Ideas:

Arrival home

▲ When arriving home, the family can prepare the child for entering by explicitly telling the child what he or she should do when the child gets inside. For example, if a child can follow two-step directives, the family might say, "When we get inside, put your shoes in the closet and put your lunchbox on the kitchen counter."

Playtime

▲ If, during playtime, a child struggles to share with his or her sibling, rather than saying, "Don't take that from your sister," the family could say, "Ask your sister if you can use the toy," or even more specifically, the family could prompt the child by stating, "Say, 'Can I have the car?'"

At the grocery store

▲ If the child demonstrates challenging behavior in the checkout line at the grocery store by grabbing candy and putting it in the shopping cart, the parent can provide explicit prompts around what the child should do while in the checkout line, such as "Keep your hands in the cart," "Hold onto the cart," or "Help mom put the groceries on the belt" (an incompatible behavior to putting candy in the cart).

Important Considerations

▲ Some children will require prompts that lead to successive approximations of a skill. For example, rather than saying, "Put all of the toys away where they belong," families might start by saying, "Put the cars in the car bin" or "Put all of the blocks in the blocks box."

▲ Children who are learning to perform multiple-step directions will have to be provided one direction at a time.

Supporting Evidence

Strain, P.S. (2002). *Positive parenting practices (trainers manual)*. Tualatin, OR: Teacher's Toolbox.

Change How Instructions Are Delivered

Strategy: Change how instructions are delivered.

Description of Strategy: This strategy involves making changes to how parents give their child instructions for things to do throughout the day during typical routines and activities. Although this strategy may seem similar to other prevent strategies (e.g., remove triggers, modify what is explicitly asked, embed preferences into activities), this strategy involves a variety of ways an instruction or demand can be presented to the child in order to prevent challenging behavior from occurring. This can include, for example, differences in tone of voice, presenting requests versus demands, voice inflection, and using nonverbal cues and can be an effective preventative strategy.

Rationale for Using Strategy: The way people talk to us can make a big difference in the way that we interpret or perceive what they are saying. If we regularly interact with someone who always yells when he or she wants something done, we may try to avoid that person, talk about the person in a negative way, turn around and roll our eyes, or engage in other types of "challenging" behavior. On the other hand, if someone asks us to do something with a pleasant tone of voice, smiles at us, and uses "please," we may be more likely to comply, or follow through, with that person's request. In other words, it comes down to the type of relationship that two individuals have with each other, and the more positive the interactions overall, the higher the likelihood that a person will do what the other person wants. When interacting with young children, this may not be how a parent regularly communicates with his or her child, but again, it can be a useful strategy for preventing challenging behavior.

Considerations for Using Strategy

Consider using this strategy when the PTR-F assessment indicates that

▲ Challenging behavior occurs when the child is asked or told to do a nonpreferred activity.

▲ Challenging behavior occurs during a particular activity.

▲ Challenging behavior occurs when transitioning to or beginning a particular activity.

▲ Challenging behavior occurs when an activity is not an option.

▲ Challenging behavior occurs at a certain time of the day.

▲ Challenging behavior occurs when a parent is attending to someone else.

▲ The child refuses to participate in activities or routines or often says "no" when given an instruction.

Steps for Implementation

1. Identify the activity or routine in which challenging behavior occurs and in which the challenging behavior appears to be related to the difficulty or the unpleasant nature of the activity. This identification should occur during the PTR-F assessment process.

2. Identify different ways that instructions can be given (e.g., using different types of voices or character voices, changing the tone of voice, presenting instructions as a request versus a demand).

3. Determine how and when the new instructions will be delivered, and identify exactly what will be said. This may require some creativity, but a parent will know what will work best for his or her child.

Strategy Ideas: There are innumerable ways that instructions can be delivered. How your team chooses to implement this strategy will depend on what instructions are problematic, how the instructions can be delivered differently, and how often challenging behavior occurs. Teams are encouraged to be creative and to ensure these changes fit the function of the behavior and within daily routines and activities.

Mealtime/snack time

▲ Taylor mostly eats a select group of foods and is resistant to try new food items. To encourage Taylor to try new foods, Taylor's mom pretends to feed the bite to Taylor's favorite baby doll and then asks Taylor, "Do you want a bite?"

▲ Jeremiah likes to move around a lot in his chair while at the table (e.g., rocking the chair back from the table, standing up on the chair, swinging his legs from side to side and hitting his brother). Jeremiah's mom has a picture of him sitting properly at the table and shows Jeremiah the picture to remind him of sitting safely.

Bath time

▲ Jacob does not like to take a bath. Mom tells Jacob it is time to take a bath and asks him if he wants a little bit of bubbles or a lot of bubbles.

▲ Amelia loves the bath and does not want to get out. Dad says they are going to take turns cleaning up the bath toys and when the toys are put away, it will be time to dry off and get dressed.

Washing hands

▲ Jasvir likes to play in the water instead of washing her hands. Her mom makes up a silly song about the steps to wash her hands and sings it while completing the instructions in the song.

Getting dressed

▲ Zoe struggles with getting dressed every morning. As Zoe puts on each clothing item, mom says she is going to tickle her, and when the clothing item is on, she tickles that part of her body (Zoe loves getting tickled). Once Zoe is fully dressed, mom gives Zoe tickles all over her body.

Special Considerations

The following are some points to consider when changing how instructions are delivered for children who may have differing needs or when special circumstances are present:

▲ For children with limited language and communication skills, using visual supports to promote understanding may be beneficial as a preventative and teaching strategy.

▲ Instructions may need to be simplified, including limiting the number of words said, the complexity of vocabulary used, and/or how many times an instruction is given.

Implementation Considerations

When implementing these strategies, make sure that

▲ Whoever is implementing the strategy is agreeable to changing how he or she will give instructions.

▲ The different ways in which instructions will be delivered are clear, and examples are written into the plan. It is not acceptable to just tell someone to change how he or she provides instructions to his or her child. Details and examples should be specified.

Supporting Evidence

Dunlap, G., & Kern, L. (1996). Modifying instructional activities to promote desirable behavior: A conceptual and practical framework. *School Psychology Quarterly, 11,* 297–312.

Harding, J.W., Wacker, D.P., Berg, W.K., Cooper, L., Asmus, J., Mlela, K., & Muller, J. (1999). An analysis of choice making in the assessment of young children with severe behavior problems. *Journal of Applied Behavior Analysis, 32,* 63–82.

Provide a Warning to Inform the Child of Follow-Up Activities

Strategy: Provide a warning to inform the child of follow-up activities.

Description of Strategy: This strategy is useful when a child's behavior is maintained by escape or if it is displayed in an attempt to escape particular nonpreferred activities that often cannot be escaped. During a nonpreferred routine or activity, families can let children know that the activity is about to end and/or how long the routine or activity will continue until it is over. Then, once the task, activity, or routine has been completed satisfactorily, the routine ends and reinforcement is administered (often in the form of negative reinforcement, or the removal of the nonpreferred, aversive routine or activity).

Rationale for Using Strategy: By providing a child with a warning that the nonpreferred activity or routine is about to end, it reduces the child's uncertainty regarding the length of time that he or she will have to remain engaged in the routine (Johnston & Reichle, 1993). Thus, any behaviors that are associated with the child's uncertainty may be reduced when he or she is told how long he or she will have to continue in the nonpreferred routine or activity.

Considerations for Using Strategy

Consider using this strategy when the PTR-F assessment indicates that challenging behaviors occur

▲ During a nonpreferred activity

▲ During an extended or lengthy activity

▲ To escape from an activity

▲ To avoid completing particular extended tasks, activities, or routines

Steps for Implementation

1. Determine how long the task, routine, and/or activity will be. For example, will the child be required to engage in a task for a certain amount of time? Will the child be required to complete a predetermined number of steps of the routine? Will the child be required to perform particular tasks associated with the routine? The team should know what is expected of the child, and these expectations should be explicitly stated to the child before the task, routine, and/or activity begins. Also, these expectations should initially be within the child's repertoire of skills, and they should be able to be completed by the child without demonstrating challenging behavior.

2. Determine what the warning will be based on the child's individual needs and also on the task, routine, and/or activity.

3. Use the warning signal during the routine just prior to the child's demonstration of challenging behavior. Or, in other words, deliver the warning when the child has almost completed the number of tasks or participated in the routine for the number of minutes that he or she is capable of without demonstrating challenging behavior.

4. End the task, routine, and/or activity.

Strategy Ideas:

Bedtime routine

▲ If the child demonstrates challenging behavior to avoid brushing his or her teeth during the bedtime routine, and if the family has determined that the child should brush his or her teeth for 30 seconds (the amount of time the family knows that the child can brush his or her teeth without demonstrating challenging behavior), the family can provide a warning at 25 seconds of teeth brushing by saying, "We're almost done, just 5 more seconds." Then, once 30 seconds have passed, teeth brushing can be terminated.

Play routine

▲ If a child has difficulty sharing, the family might use a timer to signify how long each child, or each person if an adult is playing with the child, gets to play with a particular toy during a sharing exchange. When the other person or child is playing with the toy, the family member facilitating the sharing can point to the timer while providing a verbal warning (e.g., "It's almost your turn! Just 5 more seconds and then you get to play with the truck!") when the child is about to get to play with the toy again.

Cleanup

▲ If the child often demonstrates challenging behavior to escape cleanup, the family can provide a warning to indicate that the cleanup is almost over. For example, the family might know that the child can successfully put 10 figurines in the doll house. Once the child has put eight figurines away, before challenging behavior is exhibited, the family can say, "Two more dolls in the doll house and then we're all done with cleanup!"

Important Considerations

▲ Do not terminate the task, routine, or activity if the child is demonstrating challenging behavior. If the child demonstrates challenging behavior, the duration of the routine, the tasks required of the child during the activity, and so forth should be reconsidered so that expectations of the child are made simpler to increase the likelihood of the child's success. Again, expectations can be gradually increased for the child; however, the team will want to set the child up for success (i.e., for completing expectations without challenging behavior) when initially using this strategy.

▲ Some children may require more than just verbal warnings, so the child's individualized needs should be assessed when determining what the best warning will be for the child.

▲ The warning should be provided prior to the demonstration of challenging behavior. If the child continues to demonstrate challenging behavior, the expectations should be reconsidered and demands reduced to ensure the child's success.

▲ Warnings should include the amount of time that is left or the number of tasks remaining in the routine, and they should be given close to the end of the routine. Warnings should start out with simple and small requirements (e.g., "Ten more seconds," "One more block," "After you put on your shirt, we're done") that can be gradually increased in duration and/or difficulty as the child becomes more successful with the tasks, activity, or routine.

▲ Children will have to be taught a desirable behavior to replace challenging behavior during the routine. Expectations should become increasingly more demanding as the child continues to have more success with the routine. Initially expecting that a child should demonstrate no challenging behavior during the routine or that he or she should use desirable behavior at optimal levels might be requiring too much of the child to start.

▲ Some routines may need to be initially shortened and then extended in duration over time.

Supporting Evidence

Carr, E., & Durand, V.M. (1985). Reducing behavior problems through functional communication train-
    ing. *Journal of Applied Behavior Analysis, 18,* 111–126.
Johnston, S.S., & Reichle, J. (1993). Designing and implementing interventions to decrease challenging
    behavior. *Language, Speech, and Hearing Services in Schools, 24,* 225–235.

Use Scripted Social Stories to Describe Problematic Situations and Potential Solutions

Strategy: Use scripted social stories to describe problematic situations and potential solutions.

Description of Strategy: This strategy involves providing the child with a social script for what might occur during a routine or activity and what is expected of the child. It is used to prepare the child for the activity or routine.

Rationale for Using Strategy: All people encounter activities or situations where they might be unsure of what is expected or might not know what is coming next. For many people, the uncertainty about events or expectations causes anxiety or stress. Adults might cope with these kind of situations by expressing their confusion, asking someone for direction or information, stating their distress, or engaging in a self-regulation strategy. A child might not have the capacity to cope with the uncertainty or might not have the social or communication skills to ask for assistance. A social script provides the child with guidance about what to expect and how to behave within a particular activity, setting, or routine.

Considerations for Using Strategy

Consider using this strategy when the PTR-F assessment indicates that

▲ Challenging behavior occurs during specific activities or routines.

▲ Challenging behavior occurs in specific settings.

Steps for Implementation

1. Identify activities and routines during which the child has challenging behaviors and in which it is possible that the child does not understand or has difficulty complying with the expectations of the setting or activity. This information should be derived from the functional behavioral assessment process.

2. Develop the social script of what is expected in the activity or routine. This should be written in a story format and from the child's perspective, and the story should incorporate the child's feelings and view.

3. In writing the social script, include the events and expectations that are likely to occur as well as any variations that might happen. For example, a social script about eating out might include the following statements: "Sometimes we might sit down and wait for someone to take our order and bring our food, and sometimes we order at the counter. After we order, we have to wait for our food."

4. The social script tells the "story" of what will happen through descriptions of the events, who is in the setting, what people might do and why they are doing it (e.g., "When people are inside, they walk"), and perspective sentences that describe the thoughts and feelings of the person (e.g., "It is hard to wait for my food"). The story should also include sentences that provide directions to the child about how to behave that are stated in a positive manner. The directive sentences can begin with "I can try . . ." or "I will . . ." or a similar phrase that is focused on what the child can do in the situation.

For example, rather than write, "I won't cry when I have to wait," one might write, "I will try to look at my book and wait patiently for my food."

5.   The story should be illustrated with visuals that explain the major components of the activity. Illustrating the book with photographs from the child's routine and environment is recommended, although some children might understand illustrations that are drawings or graphics.

6.   Once the script is written (try to be brief so that the child will attend to the story) and visuals are gathered, the information should be placed in a book format.

7.   Prior to engaging in the activity or routine, the social script is read to the child several times as preparation for the activity or routine. Immediately preceding the activity or routine, the script should be read to the child. The family should use the script to prompt the child through the steps of the routine if needed.

Strategy Ideas: The following are some ideas for using scripted stories to prepare a child for a routine or activity that is difficult.

Prepare for grocery shopping

▲   A story can help the child understand the major components of the activity (e.g., getting in the shopping cart, selecting groceries, paying for groceries, putting groceries in the cart). The story might help the child understand waiting in line to pay and options for what to do (e.g., "When we wait, I can look at my book or play with my toy"), what the expectations for the routine are ("I must sit in the cart. Sitting is safe. I must sit in the cart until we are finished and I get in my car seat to go home"), and when the child might receive a treat (e.g., "When the groceries are in the car and I am sitting in my car seat, I will get a snack").

Prepare for bedtime

▲   The scripted story could help the child understand and follow a bedtime routine. The story could include getting ready for bed by putting on pajamas; what activity will occur prior to bed, such as reading a story; what happens once the parent says "goodnight" and leaves the room; and when the child can get up (e.g., "I must stay in my bed until mommy and daddy come to me and say, 'It's time to get up'").

Prepare for playtime with a peer

▲   A scripted story can help a child prepare for playtime with a peer by describing what the play choices might be, how to ask for a turn or offer a play idea to a peer, and what to do if frustrated during play (e.g., "When my friends play with my favorite toys, I want to tell them not to touch them. I have to let my friend have a turn. After my friend's turn, I can play with the toy again").

Special Considerations

The following are some considerations for using a social story when preparing a child for daily schedules and routines, changes in the schedule or routines, and transitions.

▲   When a child has cognitive delays, the story should be brief, and the expectations of the child should match the child's level of understanding and ability to follow directions.

▲   The story must be short enough that it can be read immediately prior to the routine or activity.

▲   This strategy is most successful with children who are able to listen to a story and are interested in looking at photographs or books.

Implementation Considerations

When implementing this strategy, make sure that

▲ You plan time to review the social story prior to activities, routines, transitions, or changes.

▲ Visual schedules and routines are prepared and accessible.

Supporting Evidence

Kuoch, H., & Mirenda, P. (2003). Social story interventions for young children with autism spectrum disorders. *Focus on Autism and other Developmental Disabilities, 18,* 219–227.

Lorimer, P.A., Simpson, R.L., Myles, B.S., & Ganz, J.B. (2002). The use of social stories as a preventative behavioral intervention in a home setting with a child with autism. *Journal of Positive Behavior Interventions, 4,* 53–60.

Schneider, N., & Goldstein, H. (2010). Using social stories and visual schedules to improve socially appropriate behaviors in children with autism. *Journal of Positive Behavior Interventions, 12,* 149–160.

B.   TEACH INTERVENTIONS

Introduction

The following descriptions are of common, evidence-based interventions that can be used as strategies for the teach component of PTR-F. For PTR-F behavior support plans, at least one teach intervention must be selected. Teach interventions are strategies that involve instruction and building new skills for the child. As such, it is expected that the results of teach strategies will be of ongoing benefit for the child. A few things should be noted about teach interventions. First, teaching occurs best in the absence of challenging behaviors. Teach strategies are not responses to challenging behaviors. Rather, they should serve to reduce the need for the child to engage in challenging behaviors because they increase the child's ability to manage his or her environment without having to rely on challenging behaviors. Second, most teach strategies are most effective if they are implemented in the natural context in which the child's new behaviors are to be demonstrated. That is, the instruction should occur in the context of ongoing activities and routines. Finally, a critical part of effective instruction is practice. Therefore, it is important to plan for as many opportunities for instruction (and practice) to occur throughout the day as possible.

Teach Appropriate Ways to Communicate

Strategy: Teach appropriate ways to communicate. This strategy is also known as functional communication training (FCT).

Description of Strategy: This is the most commonly used and generally the most effective of all the teach strategies in PTR-F. This strategy is supported by a great deal of research, and it can help children in the short term as well as the long term. FCT can be extremely effective if it is implemented carefully and consistently.

FCT involves 1) identifying the function or purpose of a child's challenging behavior and 2) teaching the child a more appropriate, communicative behavior that serves the same purpose or function. The idea behind FCT is to get the child to use the appropriate form of communication instead of the challenging behavior. For this to happen, the appropriate form of communication must be at least as effective for the child as the challenging behavior in terms of getting what the child wants. For example, if a child has been observed to hit other children in order to get access to a desired toy, the child can be taught to use a more desirable communicative method to ask the other children for a turn with the toy.

The method of communication that is selected must be one that the child can already use or that can be taught easily. It must also be a communication method that will be noticed by anybody who will be expected to respond. The communicative method can be speech, pictures, gestures, sign language, technology-aided communication output, or a combination of these methods. Remember that the goal of FCT is not necessarily to teach a child a new method of communication. Instead, the goal of FCT is to teach the child to use a more appropriate method of communication as a replacement for challenging behavior.

Rationale for Using Strategy: When children engage in challenging behavior instead of using appropriate communication skills, it is usually because children do not know how to communicate in a way that is as efficient and effective as using the challenging behavior. Therefore, children need to be directly taught how to use a more appropriate method of communication. The challenging behavior works quickly and, in many cases easily, to obtain wants and needs. So, to reduce and eventually eliminate the challenging behavior, children need to learn that appropriate communication also works and, in fact, that it works better. A vital part of this teaching strategy is to allow the child opportunities to either get what he or she wants or to avoid something that he or she does not want (particularly when FCT begins) when the child uses appropriate communicative behavior. If a child's communication is not honored (listened to) the way that the challenging behavior is, the child will stop making the effort to communicate.

Considerations for Using Strategy

Consider using this strategy when the PTR-F assessment indicates that challenging behaviors occur

▲ When the child is avoiding and/or refusing a particular task or activity

▲ During a particular activity

▲ During a transition to a nonpreferred activity

▲ When a preferred activity ends

▲ When interacting with other children

  FCT should be considered when the PTR-F assessment has identified a clear function for the challenging behavior and when the team can identify an appropriate communicative behavior that can serve as a replacement for the challenging behavior.

Steps for Implementation

1. Identify the function of the challenging behavior. This should occur in the PTR-F assessment process. What is the child trying to communicate? Remember that the function is usually "to get something" (such as attention or a toy) or "to get rid of something" (such as a difficult request, too many demands, or a required transition).

2. Identify a desirable way for the child to communicate the same message as the challenging behavior, but in a more appropriate manner. Choose a new communicative behavior that the child can already do or one that would be simple and quick for the child to learn. Make sure the replacement communicative behavior is one that will be conspicuous enough to be noticed when the child uses it.

3. Identify situations that typically result in the child's using challenging behavior to communicate. These situations will be the contexts in which instruction will take place. Arrange for these situations to occur many times per day because the child will only learn through many good opportunities to practice. Be sure to have any materials ready that you may need.

4. Do your best to anticipate when the challenging behavior might occur, and then prompt the child to use the new communicative behavior as a replacement for the challenging behavior. When the child uses the new communicative behavior, be sure to honor the child's request.

5. Create and plan for multiple opportunities to practice this new communicative behavior throughout the day, and be sure that every time the child uses it that it "works" for the child.

6. If the replacement communicative behavior is to be used with a peer, it is important for an adult to facilitate these interactions and communications until the child can perform the behavior independently on a regular basis. It is also important for the adult to ensure that the peer responds to the child's new communicative behavior in a positive way and that it "works" for the child when interacting with peers as well.

7. As the child learns to use the replacement communicative behavior instead of challenging behavior, gradually remove the amount of adult assistance (prompting) so that the child uses the behavior on his or her own. Be careful not to remove the assistance too rapidly.

Strategy Ideas:

Outside play between child (Zoe) and siblings (Penelope and Ryan) at the park

▲ Zoe's PTR-F assessment revealed that challenging behavior often occurred while she was playing at her neighborhood park with her siblings Penelope and Ryan. Zoe would typically run up to the slide and push her brother and sister out of the way, sometimes hitting them, so she could slide down the slide. The function was clearly to gain access to the slide. The team decided to teach Zoe to say, "My turn." Because her mother was implementing a behavior support plan for Zoe, she was willing to take Zoe and her siblings to the park on a regular basis to ensure many practice opportunities. Part of the planning was to prepare Penelope and Ryan to cooperate. When Zoe was learning her new communicative behavior, as she approached the slide, her mother would tell Zoe, "If you want to slide, say 'My turn.'" If necessary, Zoe's mother was ready to use more than one prompt. When Zoe said, "My turn," she was allowed to slide. She was praised for saying "My turn" and encouraged to continue playing. Zoe's mother stayed close to the playground, and particularly the slide, to continue to facilitate appropriate communication and to ensure that Zoe's interactions were positive and successful. Over time, as Zoe became successful with the use of "My turn," she was gradually taught other ways to communicate her wants and also how to be respectful of other children's play activities.

Transitioning off the iPad

▲ A family's child engages in tantrum behavior when asked to turn off the tablet (iPad). If during the PTR-F assessment, it is determined that the challenging behavior (i.e., tantrum) is exhibited to delay or escape the transition away from the preferred activity (i.e., the iPad), the child can be taught to request "3 more minutes" when told to turn off the iPad. When the child requests "3 more minutes" as a replacement for engaging in a tantrum behavior, the family will then honor the child's request and provide him or her with 3 more minutes of playtime with the iPad.

Washing hands after going to the bathroom

▲ If a child who uses sign language to communicate hits and kicks adults when required to wash his or her hands after going to the bathroom, the child can be taught to use sign language to say "All done" when he or she wants to be finished with handwashing. When it is apparent that the child is about to start hitting or kicking (perhaps precursor behaviors are noted), the family can prompt the child to sign "All done" by modeling it, saying "All done," and using hand-over-hand prompting to sign "All done." Once the child has signed "All done" (either on his or her own or with prompts), he or she should be permitted to leave the sink. This prompting strategy should be used each time the child is required to wash his or her hands (a routine that should occur many times per day for practice) until the child can successfully sign "All done" independently.

Special Considerations

▲ When a child has limited or restricted verbal skills, it is important to find a method of communication that is easy for the child.

▲ When a child has physical limitations, it is important to find a method of communication that is feasible and practical for the child.

▲ When a child has cognitive delays or has difficulty learning new skills, the child may need many opportunities to practice the skill before progress is demonstrated.

Implementation Considerations

When implementing these strategies, make sure that:

▲ The communication method chosen is simple and easy for the child to use.

▲ The child is only required to say what is necessary to communicate the message. When first teaching this skill, do not require appropriate grammar, full sentences, or pleasantries (e.g., please, thank you). Allow the child the easiest way to communicate the message when first teaching communication skills.

▲ The new communicative behavior works for the child every time (the child gets what he or she wants or avoids something he or she does not want).

▲ If materials are needed (e.g., pictures, devices), they are always available and accessible to the child, and everyone knows how to appropriately respond.

▲ If using sign language or gestures, everyone who interacts with the child (peers and adults) knows what the sign language or gesture looks like for the child and how to respond to it.

▲ Multiple opportunities are created for the child to practice the new communication, and times are planned for when the child will work on that skill.

Supporting Evidence

Carr, E.G., & Durand, V.M. (1985). Reducing behavior problems through functional communication training. *Journal of Applied Behavior Analysis, 18,* 111–126.

Carr, E.G., Levin, L., McConnachie, G., Carlson, J.I., Kemp, D.C., & Smith, C.E. (1994). *Communication-based intervention for problem behavior: A user's guide for producing positive change.* Baltimore, MD: Paul H. Brookes Publishing Co.

Dunlap, G., Ester, T., Langhans, S., & Fox, L. (2006). Functional communication training with toddlers in home environments. *Journal of Early Intervention, 28,* 81–96.

Dunlap, G., & Fox, L. (1999). A demonstration of behavioral support for young children with autism. *Journal of Positive Behavior Interventions, 1,* 77–87.

Durand, V.M. (1990). *Severe behavior problems: A functional communication training approach.* New York, NY: Guilford Press.

Reeve, C.E., & Carr, E.G. (2000). Prevention of severe behavior problems in children with developmental disorders. *Journal of Positive Behavior Interventions, 2,* 144–160.

Teach Social Skills

Strategy: Directly teach skills that help a child interact effectively with peers and adults, including skills such as sharing, taking turns, waiting, identifying emotions, playing cooperatively, following rules, and other social skills.

Description of Strategy: This strategy involves purposefully teaching children skills for interacting effectively and positively with adults and peers. The process of functional behavioral assessment should be useful for identifying the context in which challenging behaviors occur. If the context involves peer or adult interaction, then social skill instruction is usually recommended. The team can determine what specific social skills are to be targeted. These may include sharing, requesting, sustaining an interaction, initiating an interaction, and cooperating with others' requests.

Rationale for Using Strategy: All children must learn to interact with adults and peers in a manner that is cooperative and reciprocal. Social interactions are an important basis for virtually all development, and they are crucial for a child's success throughout childhood, adolescence, and adulthood. They are the essential foundation for the establishment of friendships and all other types of relationships. In addition, social skills are key to the presence or absence of challenging behaviors. Social skills are instrumental for children in getting their needs met, and if a child can meet his or her needs through the use of good social skills, then there may be little need for challenging behaviors.

Steps for Implementation

1. Identify the specific social skill that is targeted for instruction. When identifying the skill, it is important to operationalize the skill precisely. For example, you might state the skill as "will ask the adult or peer to take a turn" versus stating the skill as "will play cooperatively." The more precisely the skill is defined, the easier it is to teach the child to learn the skill.

2. Identify when you might give the child learning opportunities within everyday routines and activities. When teaching a skill, we want to offer as many learning opportunities as possible within natural contexts. Teaching should occur within activities and routines where the child is not likely to have challenging behavior with a goal of helping the child learn the skill and be able to use it within the routine or activity that is often associated with the challenging behavior.

3. Identify how the social skill will be taught. It will be important to use a systematic instructional procedure that ensures the child will be successful in using the skill. For example, you might use a least-to-most prompting approach that involves waiting briefly to see whether the child uses the skill in the presence of the natural cue. If the child does not use the skill, the adult provides a verbal prompt. If the child does not use the skill on the verbal prompt, then the adult might physically assist the child as the final prompt. The child should always be successful, and the goal is that the child will eventually learn to use the skill with no prompting. Other systematic instructional procedures that might be considered are most-to-least prompting (in this strategy, begin with full assistance and then fade prompts) or incidental teaching.

Considerations for Using Strategy

Consider using this strategy when the PTR-F assessment indicates that:

▲ Challenging behavior occurs when sharing is necessary.

▲ Challenging behavior occurs when taking turns.

▲ Challenging behavior occurs when beginning interactions with peers or adults.

▲ Challenging behavior occurs when responding to or answering peers or adults.

▲ Challenging behavior occurs when engaging in interactions.

▲ Challenging behavior occurs when playing with toys and materials with peers or adults.

▲ Child has difficulty establishing and maintaining relationships with peers or adults.

Strategy Ideas: The following are some ideas for teaching social skills and embedding opportunities to practice these skills.

Playtime with other children

▲   Prepare the child for interaction with other children by teaching the skill prior to play-time. For example, you might practice taking turns with a toy by modeling the skill and then prompting the child. Support the child to be ready to practice the skill by reminding the child of the skill to use (e.g., "When Joey wants to play ball, you can take turns") and then be available to guide the interaction and reinforce the child (e.g., "Yay, you did it! You took a turn") for using the skill.

Playtime with a parent

▲   Identify the activity you might want to do with your child that requires social interaction (e.g., reading a story, doing a puzzle, drawing with markers, building with blocks). Set up a brief playtime for you to teach your child using the systematic instructional procedures. Persist with offering opportunities to perform the skill (e.g., my turn, your turn) until your child loses interest in the activity.

Simple chores

▲   Simple chores such as watering plants, putting laundry in the hamper, clearing the table, or feeding a pet can provide a context for teaching a child to take turns, make requests, or cooperate with requests. Identify one or two of these that can occur daily and offer teaching and practice opportunities for learning the targeted social skill.

Special Considerations

The following are some points to consider when teaching social skills, such as sharing, taking turns, entering play, and following another's lead, to children who might have differing needs or when special circumstances are present.

▲   When a child has developmental delays or has difficulty learning new skills, steps may need to be broken up into smaller pieces, and the steps may need to be taught and practiced more often (provide multiple opportunities for instruction).

▲   Consider setting up opportunities to practice the skill that are more likely to be successful. For example, Marcus might be more willing to begin sharing when it involves a marker rather than if it was his favorite truck.

▲   Extra reinforcement may be needed if the child is not initially motivated to use the new skill. For example, when Sophie grabs a toy from a peer, she typically gets the toy. Therefore, to have the child ask for a toy and wait for a response may require extra reinforcement. That could be verbal praise or a high five, as well as tangibles.

▲   Do not attempt to teach the social skill when the child is engaging in challenging behavior. Redirection can be used, but effective instruction occurs when challenging behavior is absent.

Implementation Considerations

When implementing these strategies, make sure that:

▲   Many opportunities are planned for the child to practice the skill. This means that multiple opportunities will need to be created to practice the skill throughout the day.

▲   The child is recognized for using his or her new skill (e.g., "Wow, Sarah shared her blocks with Tim, what a nice friend!").

Supporting Evidence

Brown, W.H., McEvoy, M.A., & Bishop, J.N. (1991). Incidental teaching of social behavior: A naturalistic approach for promoting young children's peer interactions. *TEACHING Exceptional Children, 24,* 35–38.

Brown, W.H., & Odom, S.L. (1995). Naturalistic peer interventions for promoting preschool children's social interactions. *Preventing School Failure, 39,* 38–43.

Kohler, F.W. & Strain, P.S. (1999). Maximizing peer-mediated resources within integrated preschool classrooms. *Topics in Early Childhood Special Education, 19,* 92–102.

Strain, P.S. (2001). Empirically-based social skill intervention. *Behavioral Disorders, 27,* 30–36.

Strain, P.S., & Danko, C.D. (1995). Caregivers' encouragement of positive interaction between preschoolers with autism and their siblings. *Journal of Emotional and Behavioral Disorders, 3,* 2–12.

Strain, P.S., & Kohler, F.W. (1998). Peer-mediated social intervention for young children with autism. *Seminars in Speech and Language, 19,* 391–405.

Strain, P.S., & Schwartz, I. (2001). Applied behavior analysis and social skills intervention for young children with autism. *Focus on Autism and Other Developmental Disorders, 8,* 12–24.

Teach Self-Monitoring

Strategy: Teach children to self-monitor their behavior.

Description of Strategy: Self-monitoring is a strategy that involves teaching the child to observe his or her own behavior. It may also involve having the child record the behavior using a checklist or counter. When using self-monitoring, teach the child to indicate or notice when the behavior occurs, and then have adults provide rewards for changes in the designated behavior as well as for successful self-monitoring. Research has shown that when children observe their own behavior, the behavior tends to improve. The strategy is usually most effective with and most appropriate for young children who are 4 or 5 years of age or older, although some self-monitoring procedures have been used with younger children. The procedures have also been used with children with moderate and severe disabilities; however, using self-monitoring strategies with these children usually requires considerable care and precision.

Rationale for Using Strategy: When adults are expected to monitor and change their own behavior, it is important to be able to identify when the behavior is occurring and document or record what is happening. This strategy is often a part of plans for dieting, weight loss, staying on a budget, and so forth. When children are able to observe their own behavior, talk about it, and record whether the behavior occurs or not, they are showing awareness of their behavior. This awareness can be an important step toward behavior change and self-control. The more self-control a child demonstrates, the greater is the likelihood of maintenance and generalization of the behavior change. Research has shown that self-monitoring can lead to improvements in language, completing tasks, and academic and preacademic performance.

Considerations for Using Strategy

Consider using this strategy when the PTR-F assessment indicates that:

▲ There is a need to increase specific desirable behaviors.

▲ The child is capable of demonstrating awareness of his or her behaviors.

▲ Self-control or self-regulation is an important objective.

Steps for Implementation

The best methods for teaching a child to use self-monitoring will vary depending on the child's level of functioning and the nature of the behavior. Behaviors that are easier to observe will generally be easier to monitor. In general, the recommended steps for teaching a child to use self-monitoring are as follows.

1. Define the target behavior carefully. The target behavior can be almost any behavior that is important for the child and that is clearly observable. The behavior should always be a desirable behavior that you want to increase. For example, self-monitoring has been used to increase behaviors such as wearing glasses, staying in a chair, and using an "indoor voice." It is important to define the behavior in terms that cause no misunderstandings for the parent or the child.

2. Identify effective rewards. For self-monitoring to work, the child will have to receive some kind of effective reward for engaging in accurate self-monitoring and for desired changes in the target behavior. Rewards can be almost anything that the child desires (e.g., praise, stickers, special privileges), but they must be effective for the individual child. Reinforcement will need to occur frequently in the initial stages but can be reduced as the child gains fluency with the procedures and as the behavior demonstrates improvement.

3. Determine the period (or periods) during which the child will use the self-monitoring strategy. This will depend on the target behavior and when the target behavior is expected to occur. For instance, wearing glasses is a target behavior that may be important for the full day, but staying in the child's seat may be important for only 5 or 10 minutes at a time.

4. Determine how the child will observe and monitor the behavior. A first consideration is how the child will indicate whether the behavior occurred or not. At first, this indication may be a response to a parent's question, such as, "Are you wearing your glasses?" or "Are you sitting in your chair?" But then, when the child can respond accurately, the child should record the correct answer with a simple device, such as a yes/no checklist or a counter or sticker chart. This will depend on the child's level and preference.

5. Teach the child to self-monitor and to use the self-monitoring device. At first, instruction will require a good amount of parent involvement. The child will need to be prompted to answer correctly, and it may be important to demonstrate good and poor examples of the target behavior. When the child answers correctly almost all of the time, then it is time to introduce the recording device and teach the child to record his or her answers on the device. The child should be rewarded for doing this successfully.

6. Gradually reduce the amount of parental assistance. The goal is for the child to use the self-monitoring device successfully and independently, so eventually the amount of parental assistance should be faded. However, this should not occur too rapidly. Also, it is important to continue to provide reinforcement for both accurate self-monitoring and for desired improvements in the target behavior.

Special Considerations

The following are some points to consider when teaching self-management skills to children who may have differing needs or when special circumstances are present.

▲ When a child has cognitive delays or has difficulty learning new skills, self-monitoring instruction may need to be broken into smaller steps, practiced more often, and reinforced more frequently.

▲ Teaching periods should be as frequent as possible (and reasonable).

▲ Materials should be customized to the child's level and should incorporate the child's abilities and interests.

▲ Celebrate all efforts the child makes toward success at self-monitoring.

Implementation Considerations

When implementing these strategies, make sure that:

▲ All materials that will be needed are complete and accessible.

▲ There is short, direct teaching time planned.

▲ The child is recognized and rewarded for efforts and progress related to self-monitoring and improvement in the target behavior.

Supporting Evidence

Connell, M.C., Carta, J.J., Lutz, S., & Randall, C. (1993). Building independence during in-class transitions: Teaching in-class transition skills to preschoolers with developmental delays through choral-response-based self-assessment and contingent praise. *Education and Treatment of Children, 16,* 160–174.

Dunlap, L.K., Dunlap, G., Koegel, L.K., & Koegel, R.L. (1991). Using self-monitoring to increase students' success and independence. *TEACHING Exceptional Children, 23,* 17–22.

Koegel, L.K., Koegel, R.L., Boettcher, M.A., Harrower, J., & Openden, D. (2006). Combining functional assessment and self-management procedures to rapidly reduce disruptive behaviors. In R.L. Koegel & L.K. Koegel (Eds.), *Pivotal response treatments for autism: Communication, social and academic development* (pp. 245–258). Baltimore, MD: Paul H. Brookes Publishing Co.

Sainato, D.M., Strain, P.S., Lefebvre, D., & Repp, N. (1990). Effects of self-evaluation on the independent work skills of preschool children with disabilities. *Exceptional Children, 56,* 540–549.

Tolerate Delay of Reinforcement

Strategy: Teach a child to tolerate waiting for reinforcement.

Description of Strategy: This strategy involves purposefully teaching a child how to wait for reinforcement or gratification. Timers and other methods of counting down wait time are often used to assist in teaching a child how to wait for reinforcement. Typically, initial wait times may be rather short and are then gradually extended as the child becomes more successful with waiting.

Teaching a child how to wait and tolerate delay will require knowledge of the child's current ability to wait. For example, a child who exhibits no current ability to wait may need to start with a wait time of less than 1 minute, or even just a few seconds. This strategy needs to be specific to meet the child's current abilities. Refer back to the PTR-F assessment to determine specific wait times with which to begin. If the team thinks they do not have enough information to decide, plan for another observation to gather specific information on the child's ability to wait.

Rationale for Using Strategy: Waiting and tolerating delay are embedded parts of everyone's day; everyone must learn how to tolerate waiting. Although waiting can be difficult for all of us from time to time, some children consistently exhibit challenging behavior when waiting and delayed gratification are necessary. Direct teaching of how to wait can help children increase their ability to participate in activities, make and sustain friendships, follow schedules and routines, and control anger and impulses.

Considerations for Using Strategy

Consider using this strategy when the PTR-F assessment indicates that the challenging behaviors occur when:

▲ The child is told to wait.

▲ The child has difficulty waiting (e.g., for a turn, for requested food at mealtime).

▲ Anger and impulse control are difficult for the child.

▲ A family member is giving attention to others.

Steps for Implementation

Effectively teaching a child to wait involves systematically planning for teaching opportunities, then directly instructing the child on how to wait when he or she can be supported; adults need to be ready and available to assist. There are multiple teaching strategies for waiting; these involve setting the child up for success by beginning instruction with a wait time that is achievable for the child, structuring the wait time to allow a visual countdown of the wait time that remains, positive praise, and immediate access to the preferred activity when the wait time has ended. A teaching process or methodology could look like the following:

1. Discuss with the child that waiting can be difficult, and yet sometimes we need to wait. Use specific situations that relate to the child's experience (e.g., sometimes we need to wait for our turn with the iPad, and that can be hard).

2. Develop a planned visual sequence for waiting. Use a timer or sand timer to display how much wait time is left.

3. Directly teach the child about the timer, helping him or her to wait by showing how the timer works (e.g., it will be your turn when all the sand runs out; it will be your turn when all the red disappears from the timer).

4. Practice waiting and using the timer with the child.

5. Set up specific structured opportunities for the child to practice using the timer and waiting.

6. Be sure to comment and give specific praise when the child is waiting patiently.

7. The duration of the wait time should be gradually extended when the child has learned how to be successful with waiting.

Strategy Ideas:

Taking turns with a sibling

▲ Set up an activity that requires turn taking (e.g., a simple board game). The game should be one that the child is interested in. A visual turn-taking schedule could be created with the child's picture, his or her sibling's picture, and a moveable arrow. Initially the family member could move the arrow so that it points to the child's picture when it is the child's turn, and then move the arrow to the sibling's picture when it is his or her turn. Over time, the child can learn to move the arrow by himself or herself to keep track of whose turn it is.

Art project

▲ Art projects are a great time to practice waiting, particularly if the art activity requires that children take turns with particular items that are required to complete the project (e.g., glue, scissors). Again, the project should be something that the child is interested in doing. The family can have a timer that indicates how long each person can use the glue, scissors, or other item before it is someone else's turn to use it. The timer can be reset each time a new family member is using the item(s). Over time, the child can learn to use the timer as a solution when he or she wants something, and the child can use the timer independently to wait for his or her turn with the item.

Waiting for a family member's attention

▲ If a child demonstrates challenging behavior when his or her adult family member is not paying attention to him or her (e.g., the family member is talking on the phone or talking to a sibling), the family can teach the child to use a timer to wait for the family member's attention. For example, the child can be taught to watch a kitchen timer to know when he or she will get the desired attention. The family can use quickly consumed reinforcers (e.g., small treats such as chocolate chips or gummy bears cut in half) to give to the child when the timer goes off. This can be taught over the course of just a few sessions if the child does not already know the purpose of a timer in obtaining reinforcement after waiting. The amount of time that the child waits can be gradually increased from a few seconds to multiple minutes with practice. Once the child understands the use of the timer, when the child wants the adult's attention, he or she can be taught to set the timer for a predetermined amount of time (one that the family knows the child can tolerate and wait successfully for). When the timer goes off (after the predetermined amount of time), the adult family member can ensure that the child receives attention immediately for waiting.

Special Considerations

▲ When a child has cognitive delays or has difficulty learning new skills, initial wait times may be very short, and more encouragement and praise may be necessary.

▲ Consider setting up opportunities to practice skills that are more likely to be successful with a clear end to the wait time, such as timers and counting down remaining wait time.

▲ The team must be sure to use a countdown method that will fit the child's learning needs when a child has a vision or hearing impairment, processing delays, or other developmental delays.

▲ Extra reinforcement may be needed for a particular child when teaching waiting that is specific to what the child really likes.

▲ Wait times need to be structured so the child can see a clear beginning and end to the delay.

▲ Children should be set up to be successful, and wait times may be short at first.

Implementation Considerations

Ensure the following when implementing this strategy:

▲ Opportunities to teach this skill need to be planned and systematic. Although opportunities to wait may be naturally occurring, this strategy requires planned wait times.

▲ Adults need to be sure they are available to assist the child with wait time when teaching this skill. Plan opportunities when the additional support is available.

▲ Be sure to comment on and praise all attempts to wait patiently, giving greater attention to the child when he or she is waiting.

▲ Children who need to learn this skill and have not yet mastered it need to have many successful opportunities.

Supporting Evidence

Carr, E.G., Levin, L., McConnachie, G., Carlson, J.I., Kemp, D.C., & Smith, C.E. (1994). *Communication-based intervention for problem behavior: A user's guide for producing positive change*. Baltimore, MD: Paul H. Brookes Publishing Co.

Halle, J., Bambara, L.M., & Reichle, J. (2005). Teaching alternative skills. In L. Bambara & L. Kern (Eds.), *Individualized supports for students with problem behaviors* (pp. 237–274). New York, NY: Guilford Press.

Teach Independence with Visual Schedules

Strategy: Directly teach the child to use schedules to increase independence.

Description of Strategy: This teach strategy focuses on teaching the child how to use visuals to follow schedules in either brief episodes (e.g., handwashing routine) or for extended periods (daily schedule). The visual schedule provides guidance for the child who needs support to understand and predict the sequence of events. For example, if the child exhibits challenging behavior during handwashing, the visual schedule might identify each step of the routine, with the child being instructed to move through each step independently. Note that this strategy is similar to the prevent strategy of using visual supports, but this teach strategy involves instruction and a goal of producing independent responding.

Rationale for Using Strategy: Directly teaching children how to follow schedules can help children be more successful throughout their day. Some children will need to be taught how to follow and manage their daily schedule and might also need direct instruction regarding following a routine or sequence. Sometimes, children learn this skill quickly, but other times, visuals, smaller steps, direct instruction, and additional support need to be provided.

Steps for Implementation

Methods for teaching a child self-management skills should vary depending on what skills the child currently has, what the next reasonable steps should be, and the child's individual strengths and learning styles. Most of this information can be gathered from the data already collected (such as the goal sheet and the PTR-F assessment). However, if you feel as a team that you do not know exactly where the child is regarding current skills and strengths, we advise that you spend a bit more time observing and gathering that specific information. This will be necessary in guiding the teaching process. A teaching process or methodology could look like the following:

1. First identify the child's current level of skill and learning style; it is helpful to have some knowledge of the child's interests as well. For example, Liam exhibits challenging behavior consistently during handwashing. Liam will resist the initial direction to wash his hands, refuse to use soap once at the sink, and resist turning off the water after rinsing. However, he will rub his hands together when washing, can turn the water on and off, and is able to dry his hands independently.

2. Identify the skill that will be taught to help the child self-manage. The team decided to teach Liam the routine of handwashing using a visual schedule that had a picture of each step of the routine. It was posted in the bathroom next to the sink.

3. Introduce the strategy to the child, communicate the purpose of the strategy, and describe how it will be used. Continuing with our example, Liam's mother showed him the schedule and reviewed the steps. She told Liam that he should follow the steps to "do it all by yourself."

4. Facilitate the use of the schedule initially, giving instructions related to how to use it. Liam's mother pointed to each picture while giving the verbal prompt of "What's next?" to teach Liam to look at the schedule.

5. Be conscious to fade back support as soon as the child begins to demonstrate the skill. After a week, Liam's mother stopped pointing to the pictures and just said "What's next?" if Liam seemed to get stuck on a step. After 2 weeks, Liam's mother was able to guide him to the bathroom and say, "Don't forget to follow your steps."

6. Reinforce and celebrate each success. After completing the handwashing sequence, Liam's mother gave him praise and a high five for washing his hands.

Considerations for Using Strategy

Consider using this strategy when the PTR-F assessment indicates that:

▲ Challenging behavior occurs when transitioning between activities.

▲ Challenging behavior occurs during daily routines.

▲ Challenging behavior occurs when required to follow direction.

▲ Challenging behavior occurs when following the daily schedule.

▲ Challenging behavior occurs around staying engaged in activities.

▲ Challenging behavior occurs when getting engaged in an activity.

Strategy Ideas: The following are some ideas that illustrate how to teach children to follow schedules, routines, and directions. Keep in mind that these teaching strategies need to be set up to meet the child's current skill level and learning styles and that they should incorporate the child's interests whenever possible.

Eating at the table

▲ Joseph was having behavioral issues during meals that involved repeatedly getting up from the table or taking food off his plate and walking away. Prior to intervention, his father would leave his meal or snack on the table for several hours because it took so long for him to finish. A visual schedule was developed to show the steps of the meal (e.g., sit at table, eat what is on your plate, drink your drink, say "All done," and leave the table). The schedule had removable pictures that were photographs of the steps and an "all done" pocket for the photo once the step was finished. The schedule was decorated with dinosaurs, as they were a preferred interest for Joseph. Initially Joseph was prompted by his father to do each step and to put the photo of each step as it was completed in the "all done" pocket. When Joseph completed all the steps, his father gave him a dinosaur stamp on his hand and praised him for using the pictures.

Tooth brushing

▲ Tooth brushing was a nightmare for Emily and her grandmother. She cried when her grandmother put the toothbrush in her mouth and pulled away. If her grandmother persisted in trying to brush her teeth, she would drop to the floor and cover her mouth with her hands. A visual schedule was developed to assist Emily with doing the tooth brushing steps independently. Her grandmother asked her to help her make the schedule and pose for the photographs of each step. Emily loves having her picture taken and was cooperative. The schedule was placed on a white board, and next to it was a checkbox for each step. Two steps incorporated choice and illustrated the choices. Emily could pick what toothbrush (Little Mermaid or red one) and what toothpaste to use (bubble gum flavored or regular mint paste). To teach Emily to use the schedule, her grandmother reviewed the steps and then told Emily that she had to brush her teeth but that she could do it by herself or have grandmother help her. Her grandmother demonstrated how to mark each step with a marker. The white board was hung in the bathroom near the sink. For the first session, her grandmother prompted each step and reminded Emily to mark the step as done. When Emily finished, she received a big hug and an enthusiastic, "I am so proud of you. You can do this by yourself." After two more sessions, Emily was ready to do the schedule independently and told her grandmother when she started the routine, "I can do it by myself."

Special Considerations

▲ When a child has cognitive delays or has difficulty learning new skills, steps may need to be broken up into smaller pieces, taught and practiced more often, and reinforced more frequently.

▲ Teaching episodes should be short and positive experiences. Building on the child's interests can be important in creating positive experiences.

▲ When a child has a vision or hearing impairment, has processing delays, is primarily a visual learner, or has other developmental delays, materials may need to be made and customized to incorporate the child's abilities and interests.

▲ Celebrate all efforts the child makes toward independence—every step is important.

▲ Remember to fade back assistance when the child is beginning to manage himself or herself. Have a "fade back" plan that involves continued support for the child yet allows for independent mastery of the self-management skill.

Implementation Considerations

When implementing these strategies, make sure that:

▲ All materials that will be needed are complete and accessible.

▲ There is short, direct teaching time planned for teaching the new self-management skill.

▲ The child is recognized for efforts and progress related to the new self-management skill.

Supporting Evidence

Duda, M.A., Dunlap, G., Fox, L., Lentini, R., & Clarke, S. (2004). An experimental evaluation of positive behavior support in a community preschool program. *Topics in Early Childhood Special Education, 24,* 143–155.

Quill, K. (1997). Instructional considerations for young children with autism: The rationale for visually cued instruction. *Journal of Autism and Developmental Disorders, 27,* 697–714.

Sandall, S.R., & Schwartz, I.S. (2002). *Building blocks for teaching preschoolers with special needs.* Baltimore, MD: Paul H. Brookes Publishing Co.

Schmit, J., Alpers, S., Raschke, D., & Ryndak, D. (2000). Effects of using a photographic cueing package during routine school transitions with a child who has autism. *Mental Retardation, 38,* 131–137.

Teach Active Participation

Strategy: Directly teach the child to actively participate in the specified routine or activity.

Description of Strategy: Active participation involves direct instruction about how to get the child to engage in the specified routine or activity more independently. Rather than just "going through the motions," this strategy is intended to create specific steps for what is supposed to be done and/or accomplished during the specified routine or activity. For some children, this requires direct instruction over multiple days or weeks. For other children, it may just require repeating a brief verbal description of the steps of the routine or activity several times. In a school or classroom setting, we would consider active participation being "engaged" in the specified activity.

Rationale for Using Strategy: Actively participating in daily routines and activities requires a level of independence in accomplishing these tasks. For adults, these routines become so fluent that we do not even think about the steps, such as the steps required for washing our hair. This is why they are "routine" or automatic, and we want children to build this level of fluency with daily routines, especially when the routine itself, or getting the child to actively participate in the routine, is challenging. For some children, this may require breaking down the routine into more manageable steps and directly teaching them how to actively participate in each one of the steps. For children who may require more intensive support, visual supports or visual schedules can be beneficial for strengthening the children's understanding of the expectations for the routine, and we recommend teaching independence with visual schedules for certain situations.

Considerations for Using Strategy

Consider using this strategy when the PTR-F assessment indicates that:

▲ There is a need to increase specific desirable behaviors in a specified routine or activity.

▲ Challenging behavior occurs during a specified routine or activity.

▲ Challenging behavior occurs to avoid or escape a specified routine or activity.

▲ Increasing active participation (engagement) in routines or activities is desired by the parent.

Steps for Implementation

Teaching active participation will vary depending on the routine or activity, the child's level of functioning for each of the specific steps of the routine or activity, and the nature of the behavior. Routines are a collection or series of specific steps that typically occur in a predictable order. Routines with a smaller number of steps will likely be accomplished in a shorter amount of time than routines with multiple and/or complex steps. In general, the recommended steps for teaching active participation are as follows:

1. Identify the target routine or activity for instruction. If there are multiple routines, it is helpful to follow this process for each of the routines. It may be more manageable to start with one routine, and as the child becomes more independent in a single routine, add another routine, and so on.

2. Identify the specific steps for the routine. Think about how you would teach someone to wash his or her hands or make a sandwich. List out every single step for accomplishing the task.

3. Identify how you want the child to participate in each step of the routine. What is the child going to be doing for each step? Write out an operational definition (observable and measurable) of what the child will be doing for each step so that it is clear whether or not the behavior is occurring.

4. Identify which steps the child can and cannot do independently. It is important to pinpoint whether there are specific steps that the child may not be able to do on his or her own, and those individual steps will need more direct instruction than steps that the child can already do independently.

5. Determine how you will teach the individual steps that the child needs direct instruction in. This instruction may happen separately from the specified routine, or it may happen during the specified routine. Are there materials that are needed? Make sure all details are developed for teaching these individual steps.

6. It is crucial to determine how you will effectively monitor progress in learning the steps of the routine. Some children may acquire some of the steps more quickly than others. Creating ways to detect small improvements will help in documenting progress.

7. Reinforce as much of the desirable behaviors (active participation) as possible, especially in the early teaching stages. The effort required in even trying or attempting a step should be reinforced initially until the child demonstrates the ability to accomplish the step independently most of the time.

Special Considerations

▲ When a child has cognitive delays or has difficulty learning new skills, active participation may need to be broken into even smaller steps, practiced more often, and reinforced more frequently.

▲ Teaching periods should be as frequent as possible (and reasonable).

▲ Materials should be customized to the child's level and should incorporate the child's abilities and interests.

▲ Celebrate all efforts the child makes toward success at active participation.

▲ The child's effort should be celebrated based on the complexity of the step and the child's abilities. If a child is actively participating in small increments of a step, those should be celebrated and reinforced in order to increase the likelihood that the child will continue to put effort into completing the individual steps.

Implementation Considerations

When implementing these strategies, make sure that:

▲ Any materials that will be needed are complete and accessible.

▲ There is short, direct teaching time planned.

▲ The child is recognized and rewarded for efforts and progress related to active participation and improvement in the specified routine/activity.

C. REINFORCE STRATEGY

Introduction

This section of the Intervention Guide provides instructions about reinforcing desirable behaviors and removing reinforcement for challenging behaviors. The crucial part of the reinforce intervention strategy is to identify a functional reinforcer(s) for the child and then use the identified reinforcer to strengthen the desirable behavior so that it occurs more often than challenging behavior. For all PTR-F behavior support plans, the reinforce strategy includes three components, which will be explained in more detail.

There are a few things that need to be emphasized about the use of the reinforce strategy. First, we often use the term "reward" to mean the same thing as "positive reinforcer," and rewards (or positive reinforcers) are the consequences that produce the effect known as positive reinforcement. We will use the term "reward" to mean the same thing as "positive reinforcer," or just "reinforcer." In addition, reinforcers are also referred to as "maintaining consequences" for both challenging and desirable behavior. Second, the definition of positive reinforcement means that the act of following a behavior with a reinforcer results in an increase in the behavior. The definition is based on its effect on behavior. So, sometimes what we think of as a reward (or reinforcer) might not actually be a reward for that particular child and that particular behavior. For example, sometimes attention serves as a reward, but sometimes it does not. It depends on the child, the behavior, and the circumstance. Sometimes an item that served as a reinforcer on one day (like a graham cracker) will not serve as a reinforcer on the next day. A general and important rule is to make sure that what is being used as a reinforcer actually works to increase the behavior. If it does not, you should find a more effective item (or activity) to use as a reinforcer.

It is preferable for reinforcers to be as natural as possible. Praise is natural. Smiles and high fives are natural. If these are effective as reinforcers, that is great. However, sometimes something extra is needed, such as stickers, bits of snack items, or a special activity. The basic idea is that a reinforcer needs to work, even if it might seem a little artificial or like it is going "overboard." If the behavior is important to change, a more powerful reinforcer may be needed for a while, at least until the behavior begins to positively change. Then, when the change is well established, the amount of reinforcers can (and should!) gradually be reduced and even changed. The behavior should become a natural part of what the child does, and the consequences should also become natural.

Third, we want to emphasize that reinforcers should always be a major part of the home environment. As discussed in Chapter 5, it is important to use a high ratio of positive to negative interactions. We strongly recommend a ratio of five positives to one negative, and this is for all children, including (and especially) a child with challenging behaviors.

Reinforce Strategy

Title: Reinforce strategy for reinforcing desirable behavior and removing reinforcement for challenging behavior

Description of Strategy: This reinforce strategy involves a three-step process:

1. Identify a functional reinforcer(s).

2. Provide reinforcer for desirable behavior.

3. Remove reinforcement for challenging behavior.

It is extremely important for the PTR-F facilitator to help the family create a clear and concise plan for how desirable behaviors will be reinforced and how reinforcement for challenging behavior will be eliminated or reduced. In PTR-F, the desirable behavior is almost always a socially appropriate behavior, which might (and is likely to) include communication, but the desirable behavior can be almost anything that the family decides is an important target and need not be a behavior that is functionally related to the child's challenging behavior.

Rationale for Using Strategy: It is important to identify a functional reinforcer(s) to be able to strengthen desirable behaviors. The identified reinforcer then serves to increase the frequency of desirable behaviors, and the use of positive reinforcement is the most direct and efficient approach. The reason that a challenging behavior occurs is because it "works" for the child in the sense that it produces a reinforcing consequence. If the challenging behavior no longer works to produce the consequence, then the behavior should decrease. This is a well-known and well-established principle of behavior. In practice, however, it can sometimes be tricky to implement, especially if the maintaining consequence is difficult to control, such as when the maintaining consequence is attention from others. Ultimately, if a child can access positive reinforcement more efficiently by engaging in desirable behaviors rather than challenging behaviors, the child is more likely to demonstrate the desirable behavior more often, thereby accessing more positive reinforcement.

Steps for Implementation

1. Identify a functional reinforcer(s). The PTR-F facilitator should help the family identify a functional reinforcer or a list of reinforcers that can be used as a part of the PTR-F behavior support plan. For some children, it will be easy to identify multiple functional reinforcers; for others, it may be more challenging and may require a preference assessment. For some children, attention or positive interactions with a parent are the most powerful and effective reinforcers, which makes it simple and easy to reinforce desirable behaviors, but problematic for removing reinforcement for challenging behaviors. Reinforcers may be extremely effective at one time and completely ineffective at another time. It is important to continue to monitor the effectiveness of a reinforcer on a consistent basis,

but ultimately, an identified reinforcer should be effective a majority of the time. Other common reinforcers include screen time (e.g., computer, tablet, games/apps on smart phone, video games), activities with a parent (e.g., reading, rough-housing, going to the park and playing together), physical affection (e.g., hugs, squeezes, tickles, sitting on parent's lap, cuddling/snuggling), treats or edibles (e.g., ice cream, candy, chips, pop-corn), access to specific activities (e.g., blowing bubbles, playing in the water, playing a board game, coloring with special markers), or being able to go somewhere (e.g., pet store to look at the animals, a friend's or relative's house, a library to borrow new books). Once a functional reinforcer(s) is identified, it is important for that reinforcer to only be available for the desirable behavior. If it is not possible for a reinforcer to be withheld or restricted, an alternative and/or backup reinforcer(s) should be identified.

2. Provide reinforcer for desirable behavior. Determine exactly how the reinforcer(s) will be provided when the child engages in the desirable behavior. This might require planning to determine who will be available to deliver the reinforcer and how it will be delivered. It is essential that the reinforcer is provided immediately following the desirable behav-ior or as immediately as possible, especially in the early stages of implementation. As a reminder, we recommend providing as many natural reinforcers as possible (e.g., praise), but reinforcers need to be more powerful and tangible (e.g., special snacks, access to a specific toy) at first.

3. Remove reinforcement for challenging behavior. The first step is to identify the maintain-ing consequences (reinforcers) for the challenging behavior. This is accomplished during the PTR-F assessment process using the reinforce checklist. Second, determine how the maintaining consequences for the challenging behavior can be removed or discontinued. This can be relatively straightforward if the reinforcer is under the direct control of the parent (e.g., parent attention, providing access to TV), but it can also be complicated (e.g., attention from a sibling, sibling giving up a toy). In cases where there might be complications, it is important to determine how to arrange things so that the challenging behavior no longer "works" to obtain the maintaining consequences. When others are involved (e.g., siblings, other family members), there might be a need for the parent to intervene and enlist cooperation from the other person to not respond to the challeng-ing behavior. The final step is to make sure that the maintaining consequence (reinforcer) is accessible to the child by engaging in the desirable behavior. The point is that when a child can access the desired reinforcer when he or she is not engaging in challenging behavior, then the motivation to engage in challenging behavior is reduced.

Important Considerations

▲ A common consideration when using this strategy is that the behavior may get worse before it gets better. This is logical because, in a sense, the behavior may be viewed as "trying harder" to obtain the reinforcer that has been the expected consequence. There-fore, parents are often advised to be prepared for an initial burst of higher intensity challenging behavior. However, this temporary escalation need not occur if the behavior support plan includes effective prevent strategies and a clear way for the child to use desirable behavior to access the same reinforcer. With these additional strategies in place, the temporary burst usually does not take place.

▲ For the reasons described above, because this strategy involves removing reinforcers that had previously been available, it is especially important that the child have access to ample reinforcers for desirable behavior.

▲ To be effective, it is necessary to know exactly what item or event has been the reinforcer (reward) for the challenging behavior. Remember that the maintaining consequence could be that the child receives something when challenging behavior occurs (such as attention, physical contact, or a toy), or it could be that the child avoids or gets rid of something (such as a demand, a transition, or the presence of a disliked classmate). In other words, this strategy is especially dependent on a good PTR-F assessment.

Supporting Evidence

Cooper, J.O., Heron, T.E., & Heward, W.L. (1987). *Applied behavior analysis.* Upper Saddle River, NJ: Merrill.

Kaiser, B., & Rasminsky, J.S. (2003). *Challenging behavior in young children: Understanding, preventing, and responding effectively.* Boston, MA: Allyn & Bacon.

Kern, L. (2005). Responding to problem behavior. In L. Bambara & L. Kern (Eds.), *Individualized supports for students with problem behaviors* (pp. 275–302). New York, NY: Guilford Press.

Landy, S. (2002). *Pathways to competence. Encouraging healthy social and emotional development in young children.* Baltimore, MD: Paul H. Brookes Publishing Co.

Nunnelley, J.C. (2002). *Powerful, positive, and practical practices: Behavior guidance strategies.* Little Rock, AR: Southern Early Childhood Association.

D.   EMERGENCY INTERVENTION PLAN

For children who are engaging in behaviors that may be dangerous or harmful to themselves or others, there is guidance about creating an emergency intervention plan. Although an emergency plan is outside the scope of a PTR-F behavior support plan, it is important to consider the need to develop a plan for how to address an emergency situation.

Emergency Intervention Plan

Description of Strategy: This strategy is included only for those rare circumstances in which a child is known to have a history of behavior that is so violent that it presents real danger to the child or others. The strategy consists of clear plans for ensuring the safety of everyone and for calming the situation to the point that regular routines can resume.

An emergency intervention plan is outside the scope of the PTR-F approach, and it should not be considered to be part of a behavior change effort. However, in the rare situations in which dramatically out-of-control behavior might be anticipated, it is important for the family to be fully prepared. The preparation should involve plans for ensuring safety and for deescalating the behavior.

For further information about positive strategies for addressing explosive behavior and avoiding the use of restraint and seclusion, we refer teams to an Issue Brief produced by the Technical Assistance Center on Social-Emotional Interventions titled "Preventing the Use of Restraint and Seclusion with Young Children: The Role of Effective, Positive Practices," by Dunlap, Ostryn, and Fox (2011). The Issue Brief is available online at http://challengingbehavior .fmhi.usf.edu/do/resources/documents/brief_preventing.pdf.

Index

Figures are indicated by *f* and tables are indicated by *t*.